LESS THAN FOREVER

LESS THAN FOREVER

*The Rise and Decline
of Union Solidarity
in Western Pennsylvania, 1914–1948*

Carl I. Meyerhuber, Jr.

Selinsgrove: Susquehanna University Press
London and Toronto: Associated University Presses

© 1987 by Associated University Presses, Inc.

Associated University Presses
440 Forsgate Drive
Cranbury, NJ 08512

Associated University Presses
25 Sicilian Avenue
London WC1A 2QH, England

Associated University Presses
2133 Royal Windsor Drive
Unit 1
Mississauga, Ontario
Canada L5J 1K5

The paper used in this publication meets the requirements
of the American National Standard for Permanence of Paper
for Printed Library Materials Z39.48-1984.

Library of Congress Cataloging-in-Publication Data

Meyerhuber, Carl I., 1940–
    Less than forever.

    Bibliography: p.
    Includes index.
    1. Trade-unions—Pennsylvania—History—20th
century.   I. Title.
HD6517.P4M49   1987   331.88'09748   86-62504
ISBN 0-941664-27-9 (alk. paper)

PRINTED IN THE UNITED STATES OF AMERICA

For Lisa

Contents

Preface

MORE THAN SIXTY YEARS HAVE PASSED SINCE WILLIAM Z. FOSTER PUBLISHED his book on the great steel strike of 1919. It was that book, and more specifically, a captioned photograph of the battered body of Fannie Sellins, which aroused my interest in the struggle of industrial labor. Sellins's death occurred but a few miles from my home. In my attempts to unearth the facts surrounding her demise, I discovered that the region north of Pittsburgh harbored a vast and largely untold story of American labor history. A few years later, I took up residence in Apollo, a small town in the Kiskiminetas Valley, which had been the scene of bitter coal and steel strikes. Although I was a stranger and not even a native Pennsylvanian, my interest in the region's labor history evoked an enthusiastic and generous response. Colleagues at the New Kensington campus of Penn State and friends at the Russellton Miners' Clinic supplied the names of and introductions to workers who had been involved in the district's labor wars. Doors were opened, and interviews granted. Slowly, this study of regional labor history began to take shape.

Hopefully, this work will fill a void in the industrial history of Pennsylvania. For although industrial unrest in western Pennsylvania is often mentioned in the literature of labor history, it has rarely been the subject of serious, intensive inquiry. *1877: Year of Violence,* by Robert Bruce, and *The Homestead Strike of 1892,* written by journalist Arthur Burgoyne, focus upon industrial labor in western Pennsylvania during the late nineteenth century. Studies by John Fitch and Margaret Byington, which were part of the well-known Pittsburgh Survey, focus upon conditions in the mill towns in the early twentieth century. More recently, Peter Shergold's *Working-Class Life* compares the standard of living enjoyed by Pittsburgh steelworkers and their counterparts in Birmingham, England. The works of Foster and David Brody deal with attempts to unionize steelworkers in the nonunion era, but neither focuses specifically upon western Pennsylvania. *Them and Us,* by James Matles and James Higgins, is a study of the United Electrical Workers, but like Brody's *Steelworkers in America,* is a national rather than regional study. No work comparable to Harold Aurand's study of the anthracite region exists for the bituminous miner and industry of western Pennsylvania.

In historical literature and popular folklore, Pittsburgh has been por-
trayed as a "workingman's town." The city and its industrial environs
have enjoyed the reputation as both a birthplace and a bastion of Big
Labor. In *A History of Pennsylvania*, Philip Klein and Ari Hoogenboom
discuss the career of industrial labor in terms of a struggle against
corporate power. They attribute the ultimate success of organized labor
to the Great Depression, to the unions it spawned, and to the political
reforms it generated. The commonwealth's repudiation of the industrial
police system, passage of the Little Wagner Act, and the election of a
union official to the lieutenant governorship of Pennsylvania appeared
to end the era of corporate domination. Big Labor had, according to
Klein and Hoogenboom, come of age. The alliance of labor with the
Democratic Lawrence machine in Pittsburgh seemed to create a permanent power base for the industrial worker in western Pennsylvania.

Local legend completes labor's story in the region. After decades of
struggle, honest, courageous workers subdued the steel magnates and
coal barons. Decent wages and working conditions were secured. Unfortunately, so the story goes, workers succumbed to their own greed, sloth,
and the machinations of labor bosses. The unbridled power of labor,
unreasonable contract demands, and the loss of worker productivity
drove business and industry from the region. In sum, the economic
malaise of western Pennsylvania is more often than not attributed to an
all-powerful but irresponsible labor movement.

The central premise advanced in this study is that the alleged power of
Big Labor in the region was an illusion. The industrial solidarity
achieved during the New Deal was little more than an aberration, and
labor unity endured for less than half a decade. Industrial labor had not
simply been the victim of corporate and official repression. Organizational rivalry and sectarian bickering had divided western Pennsylvania
labor for decades, and not even the Depression crisis healed labor's
internal wounds. The legislative achievements of labor were real
enough, but beyond the bargaining table and picket line, labor's authority in the community evaporated rapidly. The ink on CIO contracts
had barely dried before new power struggles and a controversy over
Communism erupted. None of this enhanced labor's moral authority.
The departure of John L. Lewis from the CIO presidency in 1940
robbed industrial labor of its vital core—the UMWA. Labor's impotence
is perhaps best illustrated by its failure to play a significant role in the
Pittsburgh Renaissance. According to historian Roy Lubove, the decisions that directed the revitalization of Pittsburgh after World War II
were made by a corporate and professional elite. In the decades that
followed, labor did little to address the problem of the region's eroding
industrial economy. Indeed, it seemed that organized labor was unwill-

ing or unable to deal with problems that could not be solved by means other than traditional industrial warfare.

The industrial union is the principal vehicle employed in this study to examine the evolution of the labor movement west of the Alleghenies. Industrial unionism was not at issue in the Railroad Strike of 1877, the Homestead Strike of 1892, or at McKees Rocks in 1909. The United Mine Workers of America introduced industrial unionism to the region, and the experiences of the union miner remain at the core of this work. Outside soft coal, the first strike by an industrial union occurred in 1914 at Westinghouse's plants in the Turtle Creek Valley, and not in the steel mill towns in 1919 as is so commonly believed. At Westinghouse not only was corporate and state power arrayed against industrial unionists, but they were hampered by ethnic differences, radicalism, personal ambition and union rivalries as well. In 1919 and during the decade that followed, racism undermined the efforts of coal miners and steelworkers to organize, and in large measure destroyed the moral authority of their unions.

Peter Shergold suggests that during the early twentieth century, the blue-collar community of Pittsburgh was divided into two labor markets, separated by immense differences of skill, income, ethnicity, and opportunity. The labor market of western Pennsylvania was probably even more complex than that, for blacks constituted a distinct labor market, as did the murky, ill-defined pool of strikebreakers. The industrial-union movement that emerged during the Depression, however, seemed to ameliorate those conditions in the labor market, but that was clearly not the case. The central labor union, an institution that might have been used to reconcile the divergent interests of industrial workers at the grass roots, was never nurtured. It was instead assigned to the periphery of the labor movement, where it languished. By the eve of World War II, the thin veneer of labor solidarity had worn thin. Egalitarianism gave way to business unionism, red-baiting, and the personal ambitions of union bureaucrats. Workers reverted to their old squabbling ways, and their unions exhibited behaviors not very unlike those associated with the old crafts. Power through unity had once again proven to be ephemeral.

This study is clearly not a definitive work on industrial conflict in western Pennsylvania. The sheer magnitude and diversity of the region's industrial working class renders the writing of a comprehensive history an unlikely probability. However, this study encompasses four major groups of industrial workers including those in aluminum, coal, electrical equipment, and steel. The ensuing discussion of their experiences will perhaps sustain my goal of writing a history that is representative rather than encyclopedic. I also recognize the preeminence of Pittsburgh in western Pennsylvania; nevertheless, it was my intention that

Pittsburgh not dominate this work, for so much of western Pennsylvania's conflict occurred far from urban environments. From Snow Shoe to Rossiter, Iselin to Yatesboro, Avella to Bentleyville, the drama of industrial conflict was played out by workers living in distinctly rural communities. But that rural quality was not confined to remote coal patches. Mill towns such as Apollo, Vandergrift, and Natrona were industrial enclaves carved out of rolling hill country inhabited by conservative farmers. Few of these mill-town workers ever left their small-town world, and even fewer looked to Pittsburgh for leadership or inspiration.

This study is not part of the "new labor history," for it employs traditional sources and methodology rather than quantification. At times, especially in the absence of written sources, this study relies heavily upon evidence supplied by oral interviews. Readers are forewarned that the historical sources used to write this book are of neither consistent nor uniform quality. The Aluminum Workers Papers are among the most complete labor manuscript collections in the nation. Records for the United Mineworkers District 5, which encompassed virtually all of western Pennsylvania, do not exist for the years prior to 1933. Nevertheless, sufficient sources do exist to support a discussion of major themes in labor history as they apply to the industrial scene in western Pennsylvania.

Although the rise and decline of industrial unionism occupies the core of this work, four subordinate but related topics are also subject to inquiry. First, this study attempts to assess the importance of ideology and the degree to which the region's workers advocated and adhered to the doctrines of Communism, Socialism, and participatory union democracy. Second, it seeks to evaluate the importance workers assigned to union organization and structure. Third, it explores labor's sources of authority in the community. Fourth, the study examines industrial labor's pursuit of power and how it was used, both internally and externally.

This work is above all, a study of local and regional rank-and-file movements and the communities that produced them. The author seeks to redress the worker and community anonymity that pervades the all-too-meager body of existing historical literature. Local leadership, including that supplied by women and ethnic and racial minorities, is stressed. Radicalism is evaluated in terms of its local origins, expression, successes, and failures. Industrial communities are examined generally, and as case studies, in which local differences and similarities are discussed. This work also seeks to capture the flavor of an industrial era in which the coming of industrial unions was a burning issue in every western Pennsylvania village, city, and town. Students of Pennsylvania history should find it to be a useful introduction to a regional conflict that was no less dramatic than the Whiskey Rebellion.

Acknowledgments

I AM INDEBTED TO COLLEAGUES AND FRIENDS WHO OFFERED INDISPENSABLE aid, advice, and encouragement that expedited the completion of this study. Dan and Anita Fine, Bob Szymczak, Joe Perrino, Jean Kerr, and Kep Rau supplied the contacts and introductions that made most of the oral interviews used in this book possible. Harold Aurand, John Frantz, Gerry Eggert, and Bob Carnahan shared their knowledge of Pennsylvania history as well as insights into industrial working-class behavior with me. Bob Arbuckle approved my request for sabbatical leave and arranged for other substantive support as well. Al Miller and his library staff were tenacious in their pursuit of all-too-often elusive and obscure research materials. Karen Fassinger was equally forbearing while typing the manuscript copy.

Labor archivists, librarians, and representatives of local historical societies also supplied critical assistance. Jack Owens provided access to the Alle-Kiski Historical Society collections. Frank Zabrosky guided me through the Industrial Society collections at Hillman Library, University of Pittsburgh. Ron Filippelli was equally helpful at the Pennsylvania State University labor archives. The staffs at the Pennsylvania State Museum and Historical Commission Archives, Harrisburg, the U.S. Labor Department Library, Catholic University of America, and Lilly Library, University of Indiana, also facilitated my use of manuscripts and documents.

Since traditional archival sources for western Pennsylvania labor history are sparse, oral interviews play an important role in this study. I deeply appreciate the confidence, trust, and many other kindnesses shown by the men and women who shared their work and union experiences with me.

I owe debts of another sort to my wife. Although I am unable to find words sufficient to express my appreciation, she knows why this book is dedicated to her.

LESS THAN
FOREVER

1

Industrial Unionism in the Turtle Creek Valley: The Westinghouse Strikes of 1914 and 1916

INDUSTRIAL UNIONS FIRST APPEARED AT WESTINGHOUSE AND NOT, AS IS commonly supposed, in the steel industry. In 1914 and again in 1916, Westinghouse workers forged "new unions" that abandoned the old crafts for industrial solidarity. They embraced an egalitarian ideology that bade welcome to all: the skilled, unskilled, foreign born, and women. The industrial unions demanded negotiated wage rates and job security. They also pursued "worker control of the workplace"[1] by demanding an end to piecework, premium pay, bonus systems, and Taylorite efficiency schemes. These demands did not find a sympathetic ear at Westinghouse, a corporation second only to United States Steel in its devotion to the open shop.

Socialist Fred Merrick, editor of *Justice*, a local labor newspaper, observed and faithfully reported the organization of the Allegheny County Industrial Union. Merrick also served as consultant to and publicist for the Westinghouse strikers, much as he had done during the National Tube strike in 1912. According to Merrick, the creation of a union and the subsequent strike at Westinghouse was not due to the efforts of professional labor organizers. On Saturday, 17 January 1914, angry workers called a mass meeting at Turner Hall in East Pittsburgh. They had been driven to fury by a 17 percent wage cut and innovations in company production methods that subjected all shop workers to increasing regimentation. Michael J. Barrett called for the establishment of an industrial union and was elected presiding officer of the incipient labor organization.[2]

Open-air rallies and meetings were held throughout the Turtle Creek valley during the week of 20 January. An executive committee composed of ten workers was chosen to draft a charter and establish policy. Women and immigrant workers were recognized as an integral part of the new organization. Their representatives were particularly active as recruiters, and non-English-speaking workers were regularly addressed in their native tongue. The participation of women and immigrants reflected the leadership's commitment to building an organization based upon all Westinghouse departments without regard to craft, nationality, sex, or age.

On 24 January Merrick boasted that the Westinghouse workers of the Turtle Creek valley were in a state of open revolt against their employer. He treated the union's "resolution of principles" as nothing less than a proletarian manifesto, giving it top billing in *Justice*:

> We, the shopmen of the Westinghouse Electric and Manufacturing Company, in mass meeting assembled, hereby set forth to the working class of Pittsburgh, and the world, our grievances against the company which has been built from a small industry to a wealthy, greedy, giant corporation, without sympathy or consideration for the men and women whose toil and suffering have made possible the great plants now owned by a small group of capitalists.
>
> In the early days a spirit of fraternity was assumed toward the wage earners employed by this company, but as it has grown in wealth and power it has continuously devised new and more ingenious systems of exploitation by which the workers are separated from an increasing proportion of their production with a correspondingly increased profit to the owners who do not add anything to the value of the plant but take from the producers all they make over and above the wages allowed us for a miserable existence.
>
> These successive steps of tyranny as exemplified by the inauguration of the slave driving piece, premium, bonus and Taylor efficiency systems, have been accepted by us in the past in a spirit of submission because we felt each step would be the last the company would adopt.
>
> We find, however, that this submissive attitude has encouraged the company to a new outrage which is absolutely intolerable and to which we emphatically refuse to submit.
>
> Pittsburgh has become a by-word among the workers of America, as a synonym of slavery and of all the working hells in this district, Westinghouse is recognized as the chief penitentiary.
>
> This company, in spite of the living conditions under which we are forced to exist and rear our families, has cut our wages sixteen and two-thirds per cent at a time when the owners of this company propose to continue to live in luxury and idleness. We refuse to inflict further privation and suffering upon our children to furnish unlimited wealth to our non-producing employers.
>
> We commend the spirit of revolt shown by the clerks and stand ready to cooperate with them in the organization of a union throughout the Westinghouse plants which should make no distinction as to craft, age, nationality or sex to the end that we may compel as a matter of right the wages, hours, and conditions which we have too long expected as a matter of generosity for the corporation whose only

interest is in coining of profits rather than the welfare of its indispensible employees.

We recognize the hopelessness of organizing a union excepting as there shall be room for every productive worker with an equal vote and voice. To the organization of such a union we pledge our moral and financial support, our undying loyalty, our lives and our sacred honor.

In doing this we are improving the working class conditions for every wage earner in Pittsburgh, and we call upon all wage slaves in the steel mills, coal mines, and the factories of the Pittsburgh district as well as other plants of the Westinghouse companies to raise the flag of industrial revolt and organize a union of working men and women who shall no longer submit to the greed, brutality and heartlessness for which Pittsburgh millionaires have become internationally famous.

We send forth to the world this truthful statement of the conditions under which we toil and the declaration that we shall proceed to the organization of a great, all inclusive union in the firm assurance of the justice of our cause and of the unfaltering loyalty of all wage earners where common interests demand fearless solidarity and bold action at this important moment.[3]

The rebellious Westinghouse workers had good reason to make industrial solidarity the chief principle of the ACIU. Most had witnessed the brutal suppression of the 1909 strike at the Pressed Steel Car Company in nearby McKees Rocks. The disunity of American and foreign-born workers had proven fatal in that conflict. McKees Rocks had been a labor uprising rather than a well-organized strike with coherent long-range goals. Not even the belated arrival and intervention of the Industrial Workers of the World had made the establishment of a permanent industrial union a priority there.[4] The founders of the ACIU understood that the strength of their adversary demanded the presentation of clearly defined objectives and unity of purpose.

E. M. Herr, president of Westinghouse Electric and Manufacturing Company, received the news of the 5 June walkout calmly. Company spies planted in the union camp had kept him well informed of events. Union activists had been fired, and Herr steadfastly refused to recognize or negotiate with the ACIU. Herr rebuffed union petitions on 4 June, knowing full well that a strike was coming at three Westinghouse plants.

Herr expressed satisfaction with his "splendid force of employees," and announced that he would accord them "all courtesy and consideration." Westinghouse would listen, but would not negotiate, for wages and production methods were company prerogatives. Herr concluded his public statement with assurances that he had no intention of turning his company over "to the mercies of outside agitators." The timing of Herr's antiradical statement is of interest, for that very afternoon the *Pittsburgh*

Press announced that William Troutmann of the Detroit IWW was in town and supporting the strikers.[5]

Pittsburgh's newspapers were mildly apprehensive about the arrival of the IWW in the Turtle Creek valley. That organization was vaguely associated with the riots and loss of life during the McKees Rocks strike. Indecisive press coverage probably reflected a general ignorance of the IWW, its goals, methods, internal schisms, and numerical strength. The IWW was destined, in spite of reports to the contrary, to remain on the fringes of the Westinghouse strike. The organization had split into two warring factions: the original militant body, organized in Chicago in 1905, and the "peaceful" Detroit branch, founded by Daniel DeLeon a few years later. The latter reflected the views of the archschismatic DeLeon, who had abandoned the parent Chicago body to violent "bums, anarchists, force destroyers and slum proletarians" like Bill Haywood. An organization controlled by the imperious DeLeon was not likely to have many members. William Troutmann, whose name had been linked with the McKees Rocks strike, jumped to the Detroit branch in 1913 while condemning the "folly of direct action." Troutmann was on hand for the Westinghouse strike, but the organization that he represented existed largely on paper. It was clearly incapable of directing a strike against Westinghouse. The Chicago branch was not much stronger. Joseph Ettor, who became famous during the Lawrence, Massachusetts, textile strike in 1912, worked among steelworkers on Pittsburgh's South Side in 1910 and allegedly organized an IWW local there. The Chicago body conducted a meeting of 2,000 steelworkers at Pittsburgh's old city hall in 1910 and sponsored an Ettor-Giovannetti rally at Kennywood Park in August 1912. Bill Haywood, Elizabeth Gurley Flynn, and Fred Merrick shared the speakers' platform, but such rallies did not necessarily yield a significant membership.[6]

Organizers for the Chicago IWW discovered that the "community in and around Pittsburgh was among the most conservative districts" in the nation. The city was the home of the "Steel Trust." Its industrial spy system made "the Russian police seem like amateurs." The Pennsylvania constabulary, or "cossacks," was an efficient force of trained murderers. However, it was, according to the IWW, the "conservative temper of Proletarian Pittsburgh" that made the region's industrial workers so difficult to recruit. Four generations of American labor radicals, including the IWW, the Socialists, and the Communists would discover that official and corporate repression were not necessarily the most formidable obstacle that they faced. The reluctance of the western Pennsylvania worker to embrace radical causes, in spite of obvious economic, political, and social degradation, frustrated all but the CIO. The sources of working-class conservatism in the region remain elusive. Yet that conservatism was as pervasive as the industrial discontent that permeated the region. Labor radicals had great difficulty in dealing with that contradiction. At times they supplemented revolutionary rhetoric with discussions of higher wages, the value of "shop control," and the Taylorization of the work place. But more often than not, those discussions implied reform rather than destruction of the industrial system, a position that the AFL had taken for years. In 1913 the IWW admitted that it had virtually no standing except with some of the foreigners in the Pittsburgh district. However, "seething discontent, more or less irrational in its manifestations [had] hardened into a cool determination to organize industrially. The crust of conservatism [was] breaking up. Under increasing economic pressure, the English speaking proletarian [was] getting his petty prejudice squeezed out of him."[7]

During the twentieth century's second decade, industrial Pittsburgh was in fact racked by industrial unrest, but it is doubtful that the IWW was responsible for very much of it. Usually, "Wobbly" organizers rushed into communities where industrial conflicts had already begun. In so doing, the IWW seemed to be an opportunist rather than the author of such strikes. In McKees Rocks, Turtle Creek, Pittsburgh, New Castle, and even in Grove City, IWW organizers moved in and attempted to make "irrational spontaneous" strikes their own. Probably their single greatest success was among the cigar makers of Pittsburgh's Hill District. The IWW was apparently able to overcome dissension among "Jewish and Gentile" stogie makers in order to direct a bitter strike that endured for more than four months. At strike's end, the IWW claimed that Local 101 had 2,000 members employed in the cigar industry. But the IWW enjoyed no such success in aluminum, glass, or steel, and few if any Wobblies successfully penetrated the coalfields. Defector William Troutmann charged that a "scavenger crew" from Chicago had frittered away twenty-two IWW locals that had once functioned in the Pittsburgh district. Those locals no doubt existed on paper, but the strength of their memberships is virtually impossible to determine. Nevertheless, Troutmann blamed their demise on the "corrupt, pernicious, underhanded work" of organizers Joseph Ettor and Harry Goff, as well as the "parasitic lawyer" Clarence Darrow.[8]

Neither Chicago nor Detroit sought credit for the Westinghouse strike in 1914. Troutmann was in East Pittsburgh during the early stages of the strike, but there is no evidence that he was invited to East Pittsburgh by the strikers. It is probable that he joined the conflict on his own, much as he had in McKees Rocks. Furthermore, it appears that his leadership was confined to oratory. His chief contribution in that regard was to warn the strikers against the use of violence. That sentiment may be attributed to his belief that the Allegheny County Industrial Union was a wayward

child of the "Chicago bummery." According to Troutmann, the "bummery" had nursed its "comic creature" to an "infantile state" only to be
rejected finally by its "disobedient child." Troutmann believed that
Michael Barrett had attempted to betray the ACIU to the Chicago IWW.
The result was a precipitous decline in membership on the eve of the
strike. Too many leaders working at cross-purposes, and the inflammatory presence of the Chicagoans among them, made the ACIU vulnerable to the work of "Agents Provocateurs" employed by management.
Troutmann viewed the ACIU as little more than "a crude expression of
working class solidarity," but admitted that the organization had planted
the "seeds of industrial unionism" in the Turtle Creek valley. Despite its
brush with the "bummery," the ACIU might outgrow "its crude and
clumsy forms" and become the nucleus for "a strong democratic industrial union."[9]

Troutmann's optimism regarding the future of the ACIU was misplaced, but his candid commentary regarding its origins is revealing. In
his opinion, the emergence of an industrial-union movement in the
Turtle Creek valley flowed not from the work of the IWW but from
worker anger. Neither Detroit nor Chicago actually controlled the militant Westinghouse workers. The speedup, bonus system, Taylorism, and
the firing of shop committee spokesmen had aroused the workmen. The
"bummery" might stir the fires of discontent, and the Detroit men might
advise nonviolence, but neither branch directed events. The decision of
Westinghouse to import evangelist Billy Sunday to preach the lesson of
"Servants, obey your masters" only inflamed opinion in its shops. Rank-
and-file spontaneity, and not the machinations of radicals, moved men
and events in the Westinghouse shops.[10]

Spokesmen for the Chicago IWW were even less charitable toward the
fledgling ACIU. They characterized the organization as a "freak industrial union" dominated by all manner of politicians, Socialists, and such
unprincipled opportunists as Troutmann. The Chicago branch freely
predicted that Turtle Creek's "new born babe" would not survive its first
act—a strike called solely to keep the union together. The great mass of
Westinghouse workers did not support the strike and walked out only to
avoid being condemned as scabs. The Chicagoans argued that the ACIU
membership had fallen to fewer than 400 due to "miserable leadership"
supplied by the likes of the traitorous Troutmann and local street demagogue Fred Merrick. A strike could not save the ACIU from the consequences wrought by a self-serving leadership. Chicago had no doubt
that the labor solidarity manifested in the Turtle Creek district was the
direct result of IWW literature and propaganda disseminated by its
"floating members" during a two-year period. But the strike was not of

their making. Like Detroit, Chicago denied any direct connection to the walkout. The rival organizations agreed upon one other point: The conflict had thrown Fred Merrick, an unprincipled opportunist, into the limelight. Merrick, they agreed, was a danger to all.[11]

Fred Merrick continued to make news long after the IWW had ceased to be the subject of serious conversation in Pittsburgh. As late as 1918, federal authorities continued to insist that a large and dangerous IWW contingent existed in the city. Twice they swept down on its "headquarters." The raids netted a field secretary, antidraft literature, charters, red flags, and minutes. The year 1914 may have been the high-water mark of the IWW in western Pennsylvania, if indeed it ever had one. The organization did not direct a single industrial strike after that year, and IWW "activity" in the region may well be attributed to romanticism or nostalgia. Indeed, the issue of greatest interest regarding the IWW in western Pennsylvania may be its inability to establish itself as a force in the region—but Merrick lingered on. He, and not William Z. Foster, probably deserves the title of Pittsburgh's most durable, if unsuccessful, labor radical. Merrick was forever in evidence and was condemned by the Right and Left alike. Merrick's ideas were given top billing on the front page of the *Iron City Trades Journal* in January 1910. At that time, he spoke of "class struggle" and "democratic collectivism," and called working-class Pittsburgh to the Socialist banner. He urged workers to employ their power at the ballot box in order to affect change. Four years later, the *Iron City Trades Journal* reported that the Socialist party of Allegheny County had denounced Merrick and his newspaper. Merrick's work was "filthy, indecent, scandalous and untrustworthy," and brought odium and disrepute upon the Socialist party. Fred Merrick, and *Justice,* did not speak for Socialists in the Pittsburgh district.[12]

The career of Pittsburgh's radical-for-all-seasons spanned more than a decade and a half. During that period, he was identified with the Socialist party, the IWW, anarchism, and Communism. Merrick managed, sooner or later, to offend virtually every faction in the labor movement. Conservative craft unionists wrote him off as an extremist. It was reported that he was thrown out of a meeting by conservative Westinghouse workers in 1914. The Detroit IWW condemned *Justice* as an "anarchist sheet." When Merrick's paper foundered, he was accused of exploiting his friendship with some Westinghouse workers in order to obtain a contract to publish their newspaper. In 1912 Merrick had nothing but high praise for the IWW. He shared speakers' platforms with its luminaries and was quoted in *Solidarity.* Two years later *Solidarity* repudiated the "famous Merrick" as a "ranting notoriety seeker." The IWW described *Justice* as a "self-styled revolutionary sheet" that thrived upon sensationalism and the exploitation of the principles of the IWW. Merrick was merely a "revolutionary demagogue" dispensing "antiquated tommy-rot" to the working class.[13]

If Merrick's ideological commitments and political connections are not easily defined, it is nevertheless apparent that he and other local Socialists provided the radical leadership in the Westinghouse strike. A divided IWW, though often cited by the press, the state police, and federal labor authorities, was in no position to lead in the Turtle Creek valley. Merrick was easily the most visible figure in the radical community, but he was probably not at its head. Bridget Kenny, a Socialist and former Westinghouse employee, emerged as the leader of outdoor strike actions. Kenny alleged that she had been discharged because of her activities in the ACIU. If that was the case, Westinghouse succeeded only in reinforcing the convictions of an implacable enemy. Tireless, courageous, and charismatic, Kenny was everywhere—exhorting strikers, recruiting, and leading parades. Other militant women joined Kenny in leadership roles: Alice Findley served as secretary of the Strike Relief Committee; Hazel Kennedy was secretary of the ACIU; and Hazel O'Brien alternated with Kenny as a speaker and parade director.[14]

If the execution of on-street strike tactics fell to militant women, the identities of those who conceived and implemented the grand strategy for the strike remain uncertain. Federal mediator Charles Mills believed that "socialists and I.W.W. interests" directed the strike. Sensing growing dissatisfaction among the "better elements" connected with the walkout, Mills predicted that the emergence of a conservative leader would quickly end the domination by the radicals. Mills never identified specific strike leaders—radical or otherwise—nor did he enumerate specific sources of worker discontent with the strategy or conduct of the strike. When Mills met with the strikers, he dealt with committees, not with individuals. He was, nonetheless, impressed with the organizational cohesiveness, discipline, and peaceful demeanor exhibited by the strikers pursuant to a well-defined strategy.[15]

The centerpiece of that strategy was a shutdown of all Westinghouse plants in western Pennsylvania. The Westinghouse Electric and Manufacturing Co., Westinghouse Machine Co., and Pittsburgh Meter Co. plants located in East Pittsburgh were the nucleus of the strike effort. The ACIU surrounded those facilities with picket squads composed of 120 workers under the direction of a squad leader. No attempt was made to achieve a precise ethnic or shop balance on each squad, and yet observers were impressed by the harmony that prevailed on the picket lines. Strikers not involved in picket duty were scheduled to participate in mass marches to unorganized Westinghouse plants in Trafford City, Swissvale, and Wilmerding.[16] Workers at Westinghouse Foundry Company in Trafford City did not join the strike, but Bridget Kenny predicted that workers at Union Switch and Signal Company would join the walkout, and on 12 June more than a thousand men struck the Swissvale plant. At times, the parades had a deceptively festive air as local businessmen served lemonade to the marchers along the parade routes. Local clergymen described the conflict as the "most remarkable strike in four hundred years; more peaceable than a ball game." But anger and suspicion ran deep. Rumors circulated that Westinghouse was importing black strikebreakers and an army of private guards. Fortunately, local authorities had closed all taverns immediately after the initial walkout; shortly thereafter, a clamor arose for them to be reopened. Bridget Kenny warned Allegheny County District Attorney R. H. Jackson, "If you want bloodshed, let them open."[17] Westinghouse had in fact brought 250 men into the East Pittsburgh plants. President Herr assured the public that the men were not strikebreakers but "white guards" of the "best reputation." Thirty of those men, armed with Winchesters, patrolled company property abutting Turtle Creek. The strikers responded with a twenty-four-hour "scab patrol" on land and in skiffs along Turtle Creek. After Westinghouse installed searchlights, the workers responded in kind by erecting their own on Oak Hill overlooking the plant. Company superintendents, foremen, and "picked men" conducted a house-to-house canvass in order to convince workers to return to their jobs. The workers replied with more intensive picketing. Amid this sparring, strikers who were volunteeer firemen extinguished a fire in the Westinghouse Electric plant.[18]

A siege mentality prevailed in the executive offices of Westinghouse. E. M. Herr had no intention of negotiating with the strikers or meeting their demands. Herr told Ralph Easley of the National Civic Federation that Bridget Kenny was an IWW "in principle" if not in fact. He believed the other officers of the ACIU were dyed-in-the-wool Socialists who intended nothing less than the takeover of Westinghouse. E. M. Herr's sentiments were echoed by his brother, H. T. Herr, corporate vice-president and general superintendent of Westinghouse Machine Company. The latter argued that no worker demands for adjustment of grievances had been received during his six-year tenure at Westinghouse Machine. In his opinion, the strike was not due to employee dissatisfaction but rather to the machinations of a "radical socialistic movement which had been developing in the Turtle Creek Valley for a number of years." According to Herr, the ACIU was a stepchild of radicalism and did not reflect the sentiments of Westinghouse workers. He pointed to the repeated failures of strikers to induce Westinghouse Foundry men to leave their jobs in Trafford City, a community little affected by Socialism. Three ballots had failed to produce a strike vote there. H. T. Herr averred that the Trafford men had been "conservative enough to investigate before taking such a radical step."[19]

The Herr brothers' decision to stand fast against all demands bore fruit in less than a month. During the first week of the conflict, the fainthearted among the strikers admitted that they were ready to return to work. Cracks continued to develop in worker solidarity during the second quiet week of the strike. Not even the appearance of such celebrities as Emil Seidel, former Socialist mayor of Milwaukee, stemmed the growing tide of defections. Perceiving a break in the conflict, Westinghouse quietly announced that its main gates would be opened on 13 June for employees who desired to return to work. Workers who entered the plant that day found that some interesting renovations had been made during their absence. Inside the main gates, narrow passageways resembling livestock chutes had been constructed. Only one worker at a time was able to pass through those narrow passageways. Each worker was required to stop at a window in order to reapply for employment. Upon completion of reapplication, each person was asked one question: "Are you satisfied with conditions here?" When word of the procedure reached the outside, the flow of returning workers fell off to a trickle.[20]

Westinghouse had moved too quickly. Management's crude attempt to intimidate the workers clearly prolonged the strike. Nevertheless, that failure did not induce E. M. Herr to assume a more conciliatory posture. It was common knowledge that the strikers were considering compromise. The strike committee had made known its willingness to eliminate the union-recognition clause from the list of demands. However, the committee continued to insist on the abolition of the bonus and piecework systems and demanded pay increases ranging from 15 to 30 percent. Unmoved, management issued a statement on 15 June: Westinghouse shops would remain open shops. Employees might be members of any organization if they so chose. There would be no payment to the unproductive. All employees enjoyed the right of conference with management. Since the interests of Westinghouse and its employees were identical, management implied that the ACIU had no role to play in company affairs. Consultation with employees did not mean collective bargaining. The solution of problems affecting Westinghouse's work force was claimed as the exclusive prerogative of management. E. M. Herr's hard-line intransigence regarding labor relations would endure as company policy for more than three decades. Westinghouse's ardent refusal to engage in collective bargaining assured the company a prominent place in the ranks of corporate America's most strident anti-union "bitter enders." That legacy would live on long after the coming of the New Deal and the adoption of far-reaching labor reforms.[21]

In the days following the company proclamation, the strikers exhibited a growing anxiety about the course of events. Westinghouse began the construction of a cable across Turtle Creek that the strikers believed would become a footbridge for scabs. The strikers took little comfort in the closed meetings held by nonstrikers in nearby Wilkinsburg, or in the announcement by E. M. Herr that the number of employees working in the plant was increasing every day. Rumors also circulated that the company was shipping its dies to its Newark, New Jersey, plant. Although the situation remained peaceful, Sheriff George Richards seemed to have increased his force of deputies and the frequency of their patrols throughout the strikebound Turtle Creek valley. Richards and his men observed but did not interfere as strike committees continued to canvass working-class neighborhoods. But Richards and his men constituted the sole alien police presence in those tension-filled working-class neighborhoods. Herr's security force remained on company property. Local police discreetly maintained a low profile during the conflict. It was a clash between deputy sheriffs and strikers on 24 June that Richards used as an excuse to call in the state constabulary.[22]

Throughout this by-play, the strike committee continued its efforts to bring E. M. Herr to the negotiating table. A grievance committee had been elected at a mass meeting for the purpose of discussing strike issues with Herr. Herr adroitly parried the committee's overtures, citing the union's failure to include nonunion representatives in the grievance procedure as an insurmountable obstacle to a meeting. The union considered Herr's demand, and after voting it down once, finally agreed to nonunion representation on 20 June. Committeeman John C. O'Keefe commented that the workers had always been ready to "meet Mr. Herr halfway," and hoped for no further delay in negotiations. But O'Keefe clearly did not know Herr, for Westinghouse's president had no intention of negotiating with his workers—union or nonunion. Upon receipt of the reconstituted committee's request for a meeting, Herr unveiled a second ploy. He refused to meet the grievance committee at a general conference involving all Westinghouse workers from all plants. Herr insisted that union representatives would have to meet the management of each plant individually, "for any other action would be futile." Herr argued that he could not speak for H. G. Prout of Union Switch and Signal, or for his brother. On 23 June he met with eight delegates from the Westinghouse Electric and Manufacturing Company, and simply reaffirmed the open-shop principles announced on 15 June. The only positive note that emanated from the meeting was an announcement that both sides in the conflict had accepted the services of federal and state mediators.[23]

John Price Jackson, Pennsylvania's commissioner of labor and industry, decided to involve his agency in the strike when the conflict entered its second week. Since Jackson's staff was small, he appealed to the federal secretary of labor, William B. Wilson, for aid. Wilson, a Pennsylvanian, responded quickly by dispatching mediators Patrick Gilday and Charles Mills to East Pittsburgh. The federal mediators were to cooperate with two state mediators, Francis Feehan and Charles Steese, who were assigned to the Westinghouse strike by Jackson. It is clear, however, that the chief responsibility for negotiating an end to the strike fell to Mills. Gilday, president of UMWA District 2, was engaged in concurrent conciliation duties in a Kanawha, West Virginia, coal strike, and spent little time in the Pittsburgh district. There is virtually no evidence of cooperation between the federal and state mediators, for Feehan and Steese remained on the fringes of the mediation effort. Mills eagerly assumed the burden of bringing the sides together. After quietly reconnoitering the Turtle Creek valley, Mills made contact with the strikers and E. M. Herr.[24]

Mills quickly discovered that the workers were far more willing to partake of his persuasive powers than was Westinghouse management. Herr had not requested mediation and was clearly peeved at the government's unsolicited meddling. Herr met with Mills under duress, and it is significant that after his initial meetings with the mediator, he chose to communicate with Mills by letter. On 25 June Commissioner Jackson reported to Secretary Wilson that attempts at mediation were not going well in East Pittsburgh because the "right psychological moment" had not yet been reached. That "moment" would never be reached because Westinghouse was determined to deal with the strike in its own way. On the very day that Jackson wrote to Wilson, H. T. Herr announced that Westinghouse Machine employees would be asked to vote on a return to work when they picked up their pay. The union responded by posting pickets outside the plant carrying banners with the inscription, "Draw your pay but don't vote." Those workers who picked up a paycheck found ballots inside the envelope printed in English, German, and Slavic languages. A local priest, a deputy sheriff, and a worker served as tellers. Of 969 who drew their pay, 686 voted: 518 to return to work and 100 against (the remaining 68 ballots are unaccounted for). The total vote cast represented less than 25 percent of the plant's work force.[25]

Two days later, Westinghouse posted notices throughout the Turtle Creek valley demanding that the men return to their jobs by 30 June or lose their employment. Meanwhile, deputy sheriffs seized control of all bridges and entrances to Westinghouse facilities. Mills informed Wilson that he had attended a strike meeting at which the workers had voted unanimously to reject Herr's back-to-work ultimatum. Mills confessed that he had been unable to move Herr. All that was needed were a few assurances of fair treatment and an adjustment of grievances, and Mills could end the strike in twenty-four hours. But that was not to be. A brawl between the deputies and strikers on the picket line supplied Sheriff Richards with reason to call in the state constabulary.[26]

On a day that the assassination of the Austrian archduke dominated the newspaper headlines, strikers could only watch sullenly as a company of gray-coated Pennsylvania constables filed stoically into East Pittsburgh. One observer marveled that such a "soldierly body of young men, comparable to the Royal Canadian Mounted Police," could generate such resentment among the workers. The strikers were furious that their reward for three weeks of disciplined restraint was an occupation by the hated "cossacks"—strikebreakers on horseback. Mediator Mills also believed that the call for constabulary was unjustified, because the workers had been "orderly and peaceable" for three weeks. Mills concluded that the sheriff had brought in the state police at the instigation of Westinghouse, and that their presence might only serve to provoke the hotheads in the strike zone. Captain Lynn Adams, in command of Troop A, met with the company and then with a delegation of the strikers, assuring the latter of his force's "neutrality." Adams reported that, aside from boos and hisses, the strikers were orderly and that he anticipated no trouble from them so long as the "present committee" was in control. Although he had been in the Turtle Creek valley but one day, Adams claimed that IWW agents had been "circulating" among the "foreign element" but had received only "scant attention."[27] The workers of the Pittsburgh district had good reason to suspect the objectivity of the state police.

Mills temporarily abandoned his attempts to deal directly with E. M. Herr. He informed Wilson that he was attempting to obtain an interview with Boies Penrose in the hope that the senator might intercede with Herr. Mills had good reason to try this end run, because Herr rebuffed him at every turn. Herr answered Mill's offers to mediate the strike by repeating his open-shop principles. Herr asserted that the determination of wages and shop conditions was the exclusive prerogative of management. Workers discharged before the strike would not be reinstated, but no attempts would be made to prevent them from finding employment elsewhere. Strikers had to return to work by 30 June or lose their places. Mills informed Herr that he had attended a strike rally at which not a single voice had been raised for a return to work. The mediator insisted that he could end the strike without surrendering open-shop principles or weakening his position with the workers. "I realize perfectly well the foothold which socialism has acquired in the Turtle Creek Valley," Mills told Herr. "I also realize that this must be stamped out to secure any continued industrial peace, but I believe this can be better stamped out by the removal from the district of the more radical element and the toning down of those less radical, than by a continuance of the strike. Just give me a little encouragement and endorsement and I will swing the tide the other way." Herr flatly refused to make concessions or to involve Mills further in the negotiations. He closed the door on mediation, informing Mills that "there was no way in which he could use his good offices."[28]

Although Mills's attempt to secure intervention by Penrose yielded nothing, he continued his efforts to put pressure on Herr. Mills called Ralph Easley, secretary of the National Civic Federation, asking for contacts in the financial community who might influence Herr. Easley offered to take Mills to J. P. Morgan's offices, and proposed a meeting with Westinghouse board members. Mills wisely rejected the latter offer, but asked Easley to approach Morgan in his name. As it turned out, Morgan's bank was not selling Westinghouse securities. Easley was referred to Paul Warburg of Kuhn and Loeb, but any efforts he may have made in that direction yielded no substantive change in Herr's position. Herr met again with the strikers and extended his return-to-work deadline to 2 July, but the workers refused to return until their grievances were resolved. On 5 July mediator Mills acknowledged his failure, admitting that neither Easley's connections nor his own persuasive powers had been able to move the adamant Westinghouse president.

Herr had reason to stand fast. The sheriff and constabulary had control of the streets, and a suit sponsored by local Socialists to force the withdrawal of those forces was thrown out of court. Picket lines were shrinking, and the number of workers returning to their jobs was growing again. A desperate strike committee petitioned Westinghouse for more time to consider a return to work. Herr responded that the workers had better act quickly, for many job applications had been received. Herr would not guarantee that former employees would get their old jobs back, but he gave assurances that "full consideration" would be given. Local officials were so confident that the worst was over that they allowed the saloons to reopen.[29]

Herr also took measures to rid himself of Mills. He saw Easley and accused the "smoothtalking" mediator of duplicity. According to Easley, informants in the union camp told Herr that Mills had urged the strikers to stand firm against Westinghouse. Mills also assured the workers that he would wring concessions from management. While it is not possible to determine whether Herr's charges were factual or contrived, it is nevertheless clear that Easley believed that Mills's usefulness in the Westinghouse strike was at an end. Easley lost no time in conveying Herr's charges to the secretary of labor.[30]

William Wilson rejected Herr's accusations. Characterizing Mills as "straight forward, level-headed and clean-cut," Wilson assured Easley that Mills had never tried to mislead anyone or misrepresent any situation. Wilson claimed to have signed affidavits made by all the members of the union grievance committee certifying that Mills had never made such statements. Wilson had good reason not to pull Mills out of the Turtle Creek valley, for the strike had reached the brink of collapse. Mills had the ear of moderate elements who were searching for a way to end the conflict. He met with the strike committee on 8 July. Some suggested a return to work for the purposes of sabotaging machinery, but that strategy was rejected by the majority. Mills understood that most of the committee had no desire to prolong the agony. He suggested a letter to Herr. After "considerable argument," the committee agreed, but no one volunteered to write the articles of surrender. The committee turned to Mills, who dictated a rather oblique letter of capitulation to Herr:

> We believe that had the men fully realized and analyzed the signed statements which were issued at the time, they would have returned to work, but owing to verbal statements having been made in addition to the written statements a misunderstanding arose which resulted in the men agreeing to remain out.[31]

Herr accepted the surrender, but not gracefully. Workers who returned to work on 10 July did so with no certainty that old jobs were waiting for them. Each was subjected to the humiliation of the chute and terse interrogation concerning his loyalties by company officials. Rumors circulated that the Chicago IWW was on its way to East Pittsburgh. Socialist Bridget Kenny proclaimed that hard-core workers would walk out again. Neither prophecy proved accurate—the strike was over. In a tribute to the union leadership, the commandant of the departing state constabulary proclaimed that there had "never been a strike so free from disorder." E. M. Herr observed that the strike had been a "severe experience" and hoped that it had been "a valuable lesson to all."[32]

In the months following the strike, the ACIU faded into oblivion, but the unresolved issues that had spawned the strike were not laid to rest. Westinghouse had become a vital cog in industrial war production. The subsequent unrelenting pressures exerted on Westinghouse's mass-production workers exacerbated tension in the shops. By the spring of 1916, tempers had reached the boiling point. The frenzy on the assembly lines pushed workers subjected to Taylorite methods to their limits. Nor did incentive pay schemes respond particularly well to growing inflation. Wartime production also created disparities in wage schedules for workers directly involved in the manufacturing of war materials and those who were not. These problems were not unique to Westinghouse. In 1916 the nation was swept by a series of "munition strikes." The Department of Labor reported 3,789 strikes in that year, 617 of which occurred in May alone. Pennsylvania experienced 574 strikes in 1916, which cost an estimated $15 million in lost wages and more than three-and-a-half million man-days.[33] Western Pennsylvania was especially hard hit as coal miners, aluminum workers, machinists, and steelworkers walked out. Their coincidental walkouts nearly paralyzed some communities, and at times these uncoordinated job actions by diverse groups of workers resembled a general strike. It was in this climate of pervasive industrial unrest that the union movement reappeared at Westinghouse.

In March 1916, dissatisfaction with wage rates caused a walkout at Westinghouse. Workers employed directly in the production of munitions enjoyed higher wages than those who were not. Westinghouse responded with a 10 percent increase, and the men went back to their jobs. For several months prior to the March walkout, representatives of the International Association of Machinists, AFL, had tried without success to organize skilled machinists in the Westinghouse shops.[34] Toolmaker John Hall understood that the great bulk of the unskilled shopmen were hostile to the IAM. Accordingly, in early April he began to organize an independent alternative—the American Industrial Union. On Thursday, 20 April, Hall was discharged, apparently for his union activity. The next day, more than fourteen thousand Westinghouse workers walked off their jobs.[35]

The Good Friday strike was testimony to both the degree of industrial discontent at Westinghouse and E. M. Herr's failure to stamp out the spirit of industrial unionism in his shops. The workers had responded to a strike call by a union not yet a month old. The AIU had not issued a manifesto or a declaration of principles, and it is anything but clear how many of the strikers were actually members of the new industrial organization. Nevertheless, with the exception of the IAM, elements involved in the conflict were essentially identical to those who participated in the 1914 strike. John Hall shared the fate of Michael Barrett. As the strike progressed, the public leadership of Hall and his strike committee was eclipsed by less moderate and more newsworthy Socialists. E. M. Herr remained as intransigent as ever. Federal and state mediators made futile efforts to bring the parties together. Women and foreign workmen directed the picket lines and mass marches. Fred Merrick continued in his role as ideological advisor, but also joined fellow Socialists in the front ranks of the strikers. The AIU appeared to be a logical successor to the defunct ACIU. To observers in the Turtle Creek valley, the strike must have seemed an eerie repetition of the ill-fated conflict that had rocked their community two years earlier.

But the Good Friday strike would have far more tragic consequences than its predecessor, for it was not the product of coherent, long-range planning. No worker associated with the leadership of the 1914 effort reappeared in like capacity during the Good Friday strike.[36] It is not clear whether John Hall and AIU secretary Edgar Donaldson had participated in the 1914 strike or if they supported the ACIU. Whatever continuity of leadership existed may have been provided by the Socialists, but neither the strikers nor the forces of order exercised much restraint. An absence of discipline of the sort that existed on both sides of the picket line in 1914 would largely account for the defeat of the Westinghouse strikers in 1916.

On 22 April thousands of strikers linked arms on picket lines thrown around five Westinghouse plants. The AIU announced four demands: reinstatement of union organizers, no discrimination against union members, fifty-two-hours' pay for forty-eight-hours' work, and a 6 percent wage increase. Mass marches and rallies were held, but the festive air that had often accompanied the demonstrations in 1914 was gone. Scuffles on the picket line between strikers and nonunion workers were common. Anticipating problems with the police, a mass march was made to the East Pittsburgh police station. Chief Adam Sode was warned not to arrest picketers or otherwise interfere with the strike. He discreetly agreed not to employ his small force of police. Picketers on duty outside Westinghouse Electric and Manufacturing watched with bitter frustration as four thousand workers disembarked from commuter trains and entered the plant by crossing a bridge owned and controlled by the Pennsylvania Railroad. The heavily guarded bridge provided a safe corridor that convinced the strikers that the railroad was in league with Westinghouse. Tensions were further exacerbated on 24 April. Strikers led by Socialist Fred Merrick broke down the door of the Wilmerding YMCA in order to disperse a meeting of nonunion shell makers called by Westinghouse.[37]

Merrick's appearance on the streets of East Pittsburgh represented a sharp departure from his advisory role of 1914. As editor of *Justice*, Merrick was the most prominent Socialist in the Turtle Creek valley. The son of a Parkersburg, West Virginia, attorney, Merrick, thirty-five-years old, had moved to the Pittsburgh district in 1909. In addition to his editorial duties, he also dabbled in real estate and worked at a luncheonette run by fellow Socialists Bridget Kenny and George Bradley. Merrick was not a member of the AIU nor was he employed by Westinghouse. He would later claim that he was approached by several workers during the week before the Good Friday walkout and asked to speak on the merits of the eight-hour day. Merrick was not originally recruited by John Hall, and sharp differences surfaced at their first meeting on 15 April. Hall was vehemently opposed to the AFL, and for that reason had founded the AIU. Merrick agreed to speak on behalf of the eight-hour day but not against the AFL, for such a split would serve only Westinghouse. Despite their differences, Hall made no attempt to stop Merrick from speaking. On 17 April Merrick appeared at Turner Hall in East Pittsburgh and delivered a speech more worthy of an incipient anarchist than a convinced Socialist. He defended the eight-hour day but professed to have little faith in the AIU or any organization. Organizations invariably bred "autocracy" among their leadership, and in the process the purpose for which a body was created was forgotten. Merrick urged his audience to be like the "Indians of olden times" and fight for their rights.[38]

Merrick returned to Turner Hall on Easter, 23 April, and delivered a speech that surprised the most militant members of the AIU and appeared to set the public tone for the rest of the strike. After delivering a short, snappy speech about the right of workers to resist industrial oppression, someone backstage handed Merrick a pistol and a shotgun. Merrick held up the weapons, but cautioned his audience to remain calm. He then suggested that the Constitution gave the people of the United States the right to arm themselves when their rights were abridged. Merrick discouraged the indiscriminate use of firearms and the carrying of concealed weapons, but he urged the workers to stockpile guns and ammunition in their homes. He reasoned that such a state of preparedness would dissuade Westinghouse from importing another army of occupation.[39]

Merrick understood the temper of the strikers, and he must have recognized the dangers in using such potentially incendiary props. It is not surprising that his public display of weapons became a major point of contention during the strike. Nor were his protestations of peaceful intent particularly convincing, for Merrick was identified as a leader of the raid on the Wilmerding YMCA on the following day. A local magistrate issued a warrant against Merrick for inciting to riot; he surrendered to authorities on 25 April. On that day, strikers attempted to storm the gates of Westinghouse Airbrake in Wilmerding.

Westinghouse announced that it would hire no strikebreakers, but trainloads of armed security guards were stationed along the boundaries of its five plants. The decision to use armed guards did little to defuse explosive tempers on the picket lines. Picket-line discipline had been maintained with difficulty in 1914, but the mood of the strikers was far less ugly then. When Chief Deputy Sheriff Robert Braun appeared outside Westinghouse Electric, cries of "Lynch them!" emanated from the strikers. The presence of large numbers of non-English-speaking workers among the strikers also compounded the problem of discipline. In most mass marches, non-English-speaking workers probably constituted the majority. That would not have been surprising to anyone

living near the Westinghouse plants. Native-born white persons of foreign-born white parents represented 52 percent of East Pittsburgh's
population in 1910, and nearly 41 percent of Turtle Creek's. In
Wilmerding, their share of the population was 63 percent, and in North
Braddock, their proportion was nearly 66 percent.[40] However, less than
10 percent of those workers elected to union offices and strike committees represented the ethnic community. Ironically, recognition of the
critical role played by this inarticulate majority was largely confined to
public condemnations of strike violence committed by "drunken foreigners."

Women also played a major role in the mass marches and street
demonstrations staged during the week following Merrick's speech.
Anna K. Bell, a twenty-year-old Westinghouse shop worker, marched
shoulder to shoulder with Merrick. Bell, charismatic and vivacious, made
good press and was dubbed the "Joan of Arc of the Westinghouse
Strike." Much to the chagrin of some of the other women, Bell per-
sistently sought the limelight. She apparently had a flair for the dramatic
and appeared at the head of one march in a mask fashioned from
cardboard and was heralded as the "girl in the paper mask."[41]

Anna Bell was not identified with the Socialist movement as Bridget
Kenny had been in 1914, but she was no less militant. She proclaimed,
"We girls will stay out as long as the men do. We know that victory for
them is a victory for us. We have the tradespeople of the valley behind us
and I'm sure the grocers and butchers will see that no persons starve."
Bell publicly repudiated violence, but seemed caught up in escalating
picket-line combat. Picketer Louisa Johnbusky brandished a pistol on the
picket line in Wilmerding and was promptly arrested. Two days later,
Bell was jailed on a charge of assault and battery.[42]

Undaunted by the arrests, the union women intensified their marches,
singing:

Come on, you rounders,
We want you in the AIU.
All we want is an eight hour day
With nine and a half hours pay.

Put a sign on your bonnet
With eights hours on it,
And we don't care what the bosses say.
When the strike is over,
We'll roam in clover,
For we'll work eight hours a day.

What are you? What are you?
We belong to the AIU.
What for? Eight hours.

One-a-zipa, two-a-zipa,
Three-a-zipa, bang.
We belong to the eight hour gang.

Are we in it?
Well, I should smile,
We've been in it
For a hell of a while.
What for? Eight hours.[43]

On 26 April Westinghouse announced the closing of its airbrake plant in Wilmerding. That decision triggered a lull during which mass meetings took the place of street demonstrations. AFL and IAM organizers John L. Lewis, James Roach, and Andrew McNamara joined Fred Merrick and John Hall on the speakers' platform. The AFL pledged support for the AIU and announced that IAM machinists would strike throughout the Pittsburgh district on 1 May. A central strike committee consisting of twenty members representing the AIU and the IAM was elected on 27 April. The committee was directed to seek direct negotations with Westinghouse. This businesslike atmosphere was briefly disturbed when strikers who were members of volunteer fire companies rushed to extinguish a blaze in the Westinghouse shops on 28 April. Mass meetings continued throughout the weekend of 29 April, and an important announcement was made at a Turtle Creek playground on Sunday, 30 April. Strikers were told to report for duty at 5:00 A.M. Monday and to prepare for a mass march on the Edgar Thomson Steel Works.[44]

The decision to expand the strike to plants other than those affiliated with Westinghouse departed sharply from earlier ACIU and AIU strategy. It is not known who originally suggested this change in tactics, but it is clear that it enjoyed broad support. The IAM strike scheduled for the same day involved all manner of industrial plants in western Pennsylvania, and Edgar Thomson workers were a specific target of the march. Big steel was the chief proponent of the open shop in the Pittsburgh district, and its anti-union posture sustained the union-busting work of Westinghouse and the local employers' association. Many AIU strikers believed that U.S. Steel, like the Pennsylvania Railroad (which regularly supplied industrial police to Westinghouse), was guilty of complicity at least in the Westinghouse strike. It therefore took little effort to recruit workers for a march and demonstration at Edgar Thomson.

On the afternoon of 1 May, four thousand strikers led by a Lithuanian band marched from East Pittsburgh through Braddock and Rankin. In less than an hour, the marchers had become a mob. They broke down the gates at Edgar Thomson. A force of eighty "Coal and Iron" police made no attempt to intervene, for they were vastly outnumbered. Attempts by the strikers to recruit the steelworkers failed, for the latter were apparently satisfied with recent wage increases. The strikers stormed out of Edgar Thomson and randomly invaded a number of plants along their line of march. With Merrick in the lead, the mob entered Standard Chain Works in Rankin, American Steel and Wire in Braddock, and McClintic Marshall Construction in Rankin. More often than not, persuasion gave way to intimidation, but few workers joined the strikers. A number of plants closed down rather than face the risk of injury or property damage. That much accomplished, the mob began to break up, stoning a small squad of police in Braddock before finally dispersing.[45]

The strike had taken an ugly, overtly violent turn. Local residents pleaded for protection against a mob of "drunken foreigners." But domestic residences and small businesses had not been, and would not be, a target of the strikers. Their purpose was to shut down the industrial sector of the Turtle Creek and Monongahela valleys. The management of Edgar Thomson refused to shut down and prepared for more violence by reinforcing the industrial police stationed in the plant. Sheriff George Richards seemed unconcerned for the safety of private residences and deployed his deputies near the industrial sites.

On the morning of 2 May, the strikers gathered again in East Pittsburgh and received their marching orders. They moved in a body down Braddock Avenue and then separated into smaller groups,each proceeding to industrial operations along Turtle Creek and the Monongahela. Plants that had closed the day before were left undisturbed except for squads of pickets left behind to prevent reopening. Facilities that continued to operate were invaded. Employees were threatened with clubs and rocks. By midmorning the industrial district along the Monongahela and Turtle Creek was in a state of paralysis.

At noon the strikers returned to Edgar Thomson. Company guards armed with rifles and riot guns stood behind stacked billets inside the company fences. Jeers and taunts were exchanged between a crowd of strikers estimated at four thousand and the force of nearly two hundred Coal and Iron police, sheriff's deputies, and railroad detectives. Rocks were thrown; shots were exchanged. (Each side later claimed the other had fired first.) A striker fell wounded. The demonstrators responded with a furious charge at the guards and were repulsed by volleys of gunfire. As male strikers tried to tear through a board fence, women dragged off the wounded. The workers then retreated, regrouped, and

charged several more times, only to be repelled as before. When the
violence subsided in the late afternoon, three persons lay dead and at
least thirty others were wounded.[46]

In the hours following the bloody confrontation, Governor Martin
Brumbaugh ordered in the National Guard. Warrants were issued for
the arrest of John Hall, Fred Merrick, and other strike leaders on
charges of inciting to riot and accessory to murder before the fact.
Deputies swept the strike zone searching for snipers who had allegedly
fired on them from buildings located near Edgar Thomson. The deputies encountered no more resistance, for the bloody encounter had
snuffed out the American Industrial Union's ability and will to resist.
Workers remained in their homes, treating the wounds of their comrades while awaiting the vengeance of what one Socialist commentator
called Pennsylvania's "trust-made criminal law."[47]

While Pennsylvania cavalry and infantry detachments patrolled the
streets, and sheriff's deputies served scores of John Doe warrants, state
and federal mediators moved to insure a final settlement of the strike.
State mediators Patrick Gilday, Francis Feehan, and Charles Steese had
been dispatched to East Pittsburgh on 24 April. They met with E. M.
Herr on 27 April and remained in the Turtle Creek valley as interested
observers. Federal mediator Clifton Reeves arrived in the district on 30
April. Reeves reconnoitered the strike zone and quickly developed an
aversion to Fred Merrick and his radical friends. Like Charles Mills,
Reeves was more inclined to do business with reliable, predictable trade
unionists. On 2 May, while violence raged at Edgar Thomson, Reeves
and Gilday were huddled with organizer Andrew McNamara at IAM
headquarters in East Pittsburgh. McNamara had pleaded with AIU vice-
president Edgar Donaldson to force Merrick to call off the second march
on the Edgar Thomson works. Though his efforts were in vain, they
absolved McNamara and the IAM of responsibility for the 2 May debacle. Reeves held Merrick solely responsible for the bloodshed.[48]

McNamara arranged for Reeves and Gilday to meet with members of
the original central strike committee that had been elected on 27 April.
The membership of that committee reflected a tenuous alliance consisting of the AIU, IAM, and independent workers. Reeves and Gilday
hoped that a smaller committee of five would be chosen for the purpose
of meeting with E. M. Herr. If that procedure had worked, the IAM
would probably have dominated the proceedings, for the AIU was in a
state of disarray. Its president, vice-president, secretary, and financial
secretary had been arrested. None of that really mattered, however, for
E. M. Herr had no intention of negotiating with representatives of any
labor organization.

Reeves and Gilday were received by Herr on 4 May. He rejected the workers chosen for the negotiations and proposed a method of choosing committee members that he knew the workers would refuse. Herr stalled, much as he had in 1914. He met Governor Brumbaugh at Pittsburgh's William Penn Hotel and listened politely to his offers of mediation. But Herr had no reason to accept mediation or to negotiate. The AIU had been smashed, its members intimidated and dispersed, and its leadership jailed and publicly discredited. All of that had been accomplished without a hand being raised or a shot being fired in anger by Westinghouse. Reeves was dealing with representatives of the IAM, a union that enjoyed minimal credibility among Westinghouse workers. Not even the efforts of Detroit IWW organizer Emil Richter and Socialist Sarah Jane Tate were enough to induce the workers back to the picket lines. Herr refused to consider the demands of the strikers, and confidently awaited their capitulation. On 8 May Reeves reminded Herr that a "reasoned settlement" would be better for all concerned, but Herr was not moved. On that date, fifteen hundred toolmakers and sharpeners marched in a body into the Westinghouse Electric plant. Herr casually informed Reeves that his services were not needed, for he knew that the returning men had been in the vanguard of the strike.[49]

On 10 May the withdrawal of troops began and saloons were reopened, a clear sign that the trouble had passed. The IAM attempted to carry on the strike, but few workers seemed interested. Mass meetings called by the machinists drew fewer than two thousand participants. On 17 May Andrew McNamara admitted that 90 percent of the strikers had returned to their jobs, and he called off his strike. In the end, craft unionists were no more successful than industrial unionists in their attempts to organize Westinghouse.[50]

The wheels of criminal justice turned with uncharacteristic speed in May 1916. Sheriff George Richards served more than thirty warrants issued by Coroner Samuel Jamison on 3 May. Following perfunctory hearings on 4 May, more than thirty defendants were rushed before Judge Ambrose Reid a day later. Fred Merrick, Anna Bell, and several others were denied bail so that they would not "go out and incite workers to further riot." On 9 May thirty-seven defendants were herded before a grand jury. Judge Reid ordered the jurors to indict the defendants because it was "not necessary that they actually participated in the rioting, for they usually do not have the courage to enter the fray." The jury complied by indicting the strikers a week later.[51]

Judge Reid's prejudicial outburst seemed to substantiate charges by the Iron City Trades Council that the civil authorities were merely instruments of corporate repression. Lawyers hired by the Trades Council accused the court of railroading their clients, but Reid just brushed them aside and speeded the trial on its way. Westinghouse published reports in the press stating that the thirteen-day strike had cost $1,285,000 in lost wages. The employers' association joined West-inghouse in condemning the strike and the eight-hour day. The associa-tion argued that the latter would cripple productivity, rob workmen of wages, and ultimately undermine local prosperity. The employers' asso-ciation capped off their anti-union campaign with a virulent xenophobic attack aimed at alien workers in the strike district. The association announced that it had created an investigative team to examine the role of alien workmen in the strike. If those men applied for American citizenship, any evidence gathered by the investigations would be placed at the disposal of the naturalization authorities. Deportation proceedings would eventually bring about the desired result.[52]

The first of two riot trials opened on 26 May, Judge Reid presiding. Merrick, Hall, Bell, and fourteen others were tried on the basis of evidence presented at a coroner's inquest on 23 May. L. J. O'Neill, superintendent of safety at Edgar Thomson, testified that the strikers were responsible for initiating the violence and bloodshed. Bridget Kenny, a spectator at the inquest, was arrested there and subsequently stood trial with fellow Socialists Fred Merrick and Anna Goldenberg. John Hall and Edgar Donaldson, president and vice-president respec-tively of the AIU, provided the only other surprises during two weeks of testimony. Each pleaded nolo contendere and testified for the state. Hall admitted that he had doubts about Merrick's participation in the strike, but he accepted responsibility for Merrick's involvement. Hall and Don-aldson each confirmed Merrick's Easter Day Gun speech at Turner Hall.[53]

Fred Merrick was the focal point of the trials, but he seemed rather subdued on the stand. Merrick explained that he had lost faith in labor unions and expressed a preference for direct action by workers. When questioned about his Easter Day speech, Merrick explained that he had not used the guns as an incendiary device. He claimed that the guns were used to explain to the workers their constitutional right of self-defense. The jury was unimpressed. Merrick and a dozen others were sentenced to the Allegheny County workhouse on several counts of riot and incit-ing to riot. Anna Bell and Bridget Kenny were acquitted. All charges against John Hall and Edgar Donaldson were dropped. The state also determined that insufficient evidence prevented the prosecution of the defendants on the charge of accessory to murder.[54]

The Westinghouse strikes were conducted by the first industrial unions to emerge outside the coalfields in western Pennsylvania. The ACIU produced what was perhaps the most eloquent expression of industrial solidarity ever articulated by mass-production workers in the region. The Westinghouse workers were clearly disenchanted with the performance of AFL affiliates. But it was not the structure of craft unionism or proletarian ideology that moved them to action. Economic issues, including pay cuts and inflation, and changes on the shop floor brought about by Taylorism provoked them to action. No doubt the new egalitarianism accounted for much of the unprecedented unity displayed on the picket line. However, it was the militant participation by formerly docile aliens that strained the union's ties to the community. Both the ACIU and AIU enjoyed reasonably amicable relations with local civil authorities, police, and businessmen. They had access to the streets, parks, playgrounds, and meeting halls. But when events turned ugly, it was easy to blame everything on "drunken foreigners."

If the position of the new unions in the community was ambiguous, they encountered nothing but hostility from organized labor. Both the IWW and the AFL questioned the legitimacy of the new movement, thereby robbing it of much of its power. Right or wrong, both the Left and the Right identified the ACIU and AIU with rogue agitator Fred Merrick—any organization associated with or dominated by him could not act responsibly. Nearly two decades passed before Westinghouse workers marched again under the union banner. In 1919 steelworkers took to the field in the region's next great industrial strike. They discovered that murder and the repression of labor would be widely regarded as acts of patriotism.

2

Black Valley: Organizing Coal Miners and Steelworkers in the Alle-Kiski, 1901–1922

FROM DEEP IN THE FORESTS OF WESTERN PENNSYLVANIA'S LAUREL HIGH-lands, clear rivulets descend and create the Conemaugh River. At Saltsburg, fifty miles downstream from Johnstown, the Conemaugh joins the Loyalhanna, forming the Kiskiminetas River. The Kiskiminetas enters the Allegheny River twenty-eight miles northwest of Saltsburg, uniting the Allegheny and Kiskiminestas valleys. Strategically located and richly endowed by nature, the Alle-Kiski[1] played an important role in the economic and social evolution of the Greater Ohio River Basin. Fur trappers, salt miners, the Pennsylvania Canal, and the Pennsylvania Railroad moved west through the Alle-Kiski Valley. Orange sulfur water, slag piles, and subsidence problems bear mute testimony to the area's recent industrial past. Coal and steel interests exploited the region's natural resources without regard for environmental consequences. The labor force of the Alle-Kiski fared little better.

For World War I–era union organizers, the Alle-Kiski was Black Valley. Its antilabor tradition began with an abortive Apollo mill strike in 1893. The local lodge of the Amalgamated Association of Iron, Steel and Tin Workers refused to accept the wage scale offered by the Apollo Iron and Steel Company. The union men also demanded the right to establish work rules within the plant and walked off their jobs when management refused to accept their demands. The timing of the strike was not fortuitous, for Henry Clay Frick had broken a major strike by the Amalgamated at Homestead a year before. George McMurtry, president of Apollo Steel, ordered the strikers to come to terms within ten days or face the consequences. When the union failed to comply, McMurtry hired local farm boys to break the strike and led them through the picket lines himself. In ensuing decades, the anti-union tradition became firmly entrenched in the valley. In 1901 Amalgamated organizers were dogged by detectives and denied accommodations in Vandergrift. Eight years later, Amalgamated organizers reappeared in Vandergrift only to be beaten by a mob led by company officials. Landlords who offered them lodgings were threatened with arson. In New Kensington, scab labor and the threat of plant closings accounted for the failure of Amalgamated's campaign to organize steelworkers. An advance guard of UMWA organizers who reconnoitered the Alle-Kiski prior to 1913 also discovered that Black Valley's reputation was well deserved.[2]

Situated north of Pittsburgh, the Alle-Kiski region emerged as an important coal- and steel-producing center during the three decades preceding World War I. The Pennsylvania Railroad, which ran the entire length of the valley, had always been an important coal consumer. However, the establishment of steel mills in Saltsburg, Apollo, Vandergrift, Leechburg, Natrona, Brackenridge, and New Kensington sharply increased the demand for coal. By 1900 coal mines operated in or near all Alle-Kiski mill towns. Such independent coal operators as Lewis Hicks owned more than a dozen mines in Leechburg, Avonmore, Apollo, and Vandergrift. "Captive" mines, such as Allegheny Coal and Coke, owned and operated by Allegheny Steel in Natrona, also flourished in the valley.

The availability of coal, undeveloped real estate, navigable rivers for barge traffic, and access to the Pennsylvania Railroad encouraged an industrial boom in the Alle-Kiski during the 1890s. Steelmaker George McMurtry created Vandergrift and moved his operation there in 1897. Within two decades, that facility became American Sheet and Tin Plate Company, employing more than five thousand workers in its thirty-two mills. In 1891 not a single heavy industry existed in New Kensington. By 1901 more than a dozen aluminum, glass, steel, and heavy-machinery plants operated in the community.[3] The sudden concentration of industrial operations not only stimulated the growth of the local coal industry, but also brought about dramatic changes in the demography of the Alle-Kiski.

Prior to the industrial boom, the population of the Alle-Kiski was relatively homogenous. Workers of English, Scots-Irish, and German ancestry left local farms for the mills and mines of the region. Industrialization, however, attracted southern and eastern Europeans to the valley. Polish and Lithuanian workers displaced the native-born American founders of East Vandergrift to the degree that Polish sometimes replaced English at school board meetings. North Vandergrift became a Slovak hamlet. Large Italian communities were established in Vandergrift Heights and Arnold. Calabrians who did not work in the mills went into the mines. The UMWA local in Apollo conducted its meetings in Italian, and organizers were fluent in that language.[4]

The American-born population of the Alle-Kiski was clearly uneasy about the rush of alien workers to their valley. The *New Kensington Dispatch* felt compelled to warn its readership against "imported labor" scares generated by "newspaper sensation-chasers" in the Pittsburgh press. The utilization of foreign workmen as scabs reinforced the nativism of established resident workers. In 1902 a howling mob of fifteen hundred persons attempted to lynch three Italians in New Kensington. The three men were scabs in a local mine and were harassed by strikers. They responded by shooting two striking miners during a fight. Local authorities saved their lives by barricading the Italians in the local railroad station until a train was able to carry them to safety. Black workers—scab or otherwise—were no more welcome in the Alle-Kiski than were Europeans. Local citizens complained bitterly about a hundred "bad negroes" employed at a federal dam project near Barking, located on the Allegheny River below New Kensington. The encampment represented the single largest concentration of black workers in the valley, and local authorities wanted them to leave.[5] When the UMWA entered the Alle-Kiski in force, it would find that race and ethnicity were barriers to unionization no less formidable than the opposition of the coal operators.

By the turn of the century, the Pittsburgh district had become a UMWA stronghold. Its major coal operators had signed union contracts in 1898, and the UMWA had achieved de facto jurisdiction in many of the pits. Attempts by the UMWA to expand into the coke fields of eastern and southern Westmoreland County were brutally repulsed in 1911. Two years later, the leadership of UMWA District 5 mounted an organizing campaign northward along the Allegheny River. The initial target was the miners of Harwick district, site of the infamous mine disaster of 1904, in which 180 miners died.[6] Harwick was located at the southern end of the Alle-Kiski, and the importance of a union victory there was clear to both coal operators and the UMWA. The Harwick strike was a prelude to a maximum union organizing effort in the Alle-Kiski. A UMWA success at Harwick was not merely a matter of establishing the first union foothold in Black Valley. Many Harwick district mines straddled the Bessemer and Lake Erie Railroad, which hauled coal, coke, and ore to the mills of U.S. Steel. A union success at Harwick could have been construed by unorganized miners only as a victory against an industrial titan. Determined to avert such a victory, coal operators brought thugs and strikebreakers in. The miners retaliated with picket lines and sabotage. After three years of protracted violence and deprivation at Harwick, the union reported that only one of the original striking miners remained in the battle.[7]

A union contract ended the Harwick conflict in September 1916. The favorable Harwick settlement was timely, for UMWA morale and unity were at a low ebb. In March 1916, the union plunged into the heart of the Alle-Kiski, even though it had not yet signed a contract with the Harwick operators. Although weakened by a three-year war of attrition at Harwick, the UMWA gambled, vowing to recruit every miner in the valley. Local coal operators not involved in the Harwick struggle had watched the conflict with interest and were poised for a counterattack when the union struck their mines. However, the operators were not prepared for the strike fever that swept across Pennsylvania in 1916.

New Kensington, the largest city in the Alle-Kiski, was virtually paralyzed by a series of strikes in May. Aluminum workers, laundry women, box makers, garment workers, machinists, foundry men, and steelworkers at two American Sheet and Tin Plate plants walked off their jobs. Burgess Daniel Burns quickly shut down all taverns and clubs because so many of the strikers were "foreigners." Those "foreigners" persuaded the Alcoa women to leave their jobs, and the latter had in turn convinced laundrywomen and garment workers to quit working. On the opposite shore of the Allegheny, all steelworkers except rollers and heaters walked out of the West Penn Mill near Natrona, demanding higher wages. They were joined on the picket lines by striking workers from the Penn Salt Copper Works in Tarentum. Local officials in Tarentum feared bloodshed, for a strike begun in 1913 by streetcar men against the Allegheny Valley Street Railway Company had involved widespread violence directed at strikebreakers and equipment. That bitter conflict had endured for three years; only intervention by the Allegheny County sheriff, local businessmen, and civic leaders brought an end to the hostilities. Wage increases brought a swift end to most of the strikes in the Alle-Kiski, but the walkouts fed the fires of discontent in its coalfields. Coal operators believed that their striking miners received "no little impetus" from the Braddock riots and the general atmosphere of industrial chaos. The operators also complained that "some powerful influence" had instilled an uncharacteristic militance in the ranks of the theretofore docile foreign-born in the mining camps.[8]

The coal barons launched a furious counterattack against the union miners. Their efforts were aided substantially by internal dissension and a failure of leadership within the union camp. The history of the UMWA is marked by factionalism, localism, regionalism, clashing personalities, and conflicts born of individual ambition. District 5, which encompassed Pittsburgh and most of southwestern Pennsylvania, reflected the national experience of the union. The UMWA had come in force to southwestern Pennsylvania at the turn of the century. A bitter internal power struggle developed in 1906 when Francis Feehan defeated incumbent Patrick Dolan for the district presidency. Feehan was committed to an aggressive organizing campaign in his district, and he began a drive to win nonunion miners in the Greensburg area of Westmoreland County. UMWA national president, Thomas Lewis, criticized the timing of the strike. Dolan loyalists also opposed it, and their locals did all they could to disrupt the organizing drive. The guerrilla warfare continued long after Feehan's vice-president, Van Bittner, assumed the district presidency in 1912.[9]

Bittner was no less committed to organizing nonunion miners in his district than Feehan had been. Although his locals were in a chronic state of revolt, he expanded the UMWA campaign into Harwick in 1913, and to the Russellton, Tarentum, New Kensington, Leechburg, Apollo, Vandergrift, and Saltsburg areas in 1916. The Dolan forces continued to cripple the campaign and were aided in their efforts by Al Hamilton, publisher of the *Coal Trade Bulletin*. Hamilton, a reputed friend of Dolan, fed insider union information supplied by Dolan's spies to the coal operators when it suited his purposes. Although the precise nature of his loyalties is not clear, this "shady entrepreneurial character" sowed the .seeds of dissension wherever he went. Van Bittner, a fighter, met the challenge. This tough and aggressive UMWA advocate pressed the Harwick strike for three years in defiance of the machinations of union defectors, fixers, and coal operators. However, his personality and leadership qualities were not assets in a situation that required tact as well as courage. Bittner appeared unable to solve problems that demanded conciliation and compromise. In July 1916 Harwick district coal operators finally came to the bargaining table. Bittner was unable to obtain an agreement on a uniform wage scale from his locals.[10]

The controversy precipitated a major upheaval in District 5. A wage-scale committee headed by John L. Lewis, union statistician, editor of the *United Mine Workers Journal,* and future president of the UMWA, was sent in by union headquarters to settle the dispute. A uniform scale was adopted. Van Bittner resigned and took a staff job with the union national office. Philip Murray was appointed president of District 5. From that point on, District 5 assumed a demeanor not unlike that exhibited by neighboring District 2. That district, which included Cambria, Clearfield, and Somerset counties, had 40,000 miners dispersed among 170 locals. Under the consistent and firm leadership of its district president, John Brophy, internecine strife had been virtually eliminated. With Philip Murray, a man of "easy and conciliatory manner," internal peace would at last come to District 5. Murray was a man inclined "to steer his way carefully through a mess" rather than "push things to a showdown."[11]

The leadership crisis and district reorganization had weakened but not broken the recruiting campaign in the Alle-Kiski. Although Philip

Murray had replaced Bittner's hard-line approach with one that was more conciliatory, he was no less committed to the struggle than his predecessor had been. Under his leadership, controversies concerning internal union problems simmered but rarely reached the boiling point. Murray succeeded in subordinating hierarchical questions to the needs of union expansion. He supported Bittner's Alle-Kiski strike, which began on 3 March 1916. Fifteen hundred miners struck Alle-Kiski mines, demanding recognition of the UMWA, an eight-hour day, a checkweighman at the tipple, and better wages. By late summer, estimates placed the strikers' numbers at eight thousand.[12]

The coal operators struck back with spies, scabs, armed guards, and thugs, some of whom were deputized. The strike soon assumed the proportions of a small but earnest guerrilla war. Company thugs attacked and shot union miners; union miners attacked company guards, scabs, and property. Organizer Steve Kiewicz was shot in the neck while picketing mines near Avonmore. Organizer Louis Federkiewicz, a founder and secretary of the Allegheny Valley Central Labor Union, was accused by colleagues of betraying the strike by supplying the names of union miners to the operators of the Cornell Coal Company. Beleagured union miners responded by bombing the homes of nonunion miners employed in the Cornell mines. On 22 October organizer J. J. Kilpatrick, riding a white horse, led a thousand striking miners across the New Kensington Bridge to a union rally scheduled at Glassmere, located near the Cornell mines. The rally was directed at Cornell Coal, and guest speakers included John P. White, Frank Hayes, and John L. Lewis. During the speeches, Earl Iseman, son of the president of Cornell Coal, appeared on the scene in the company of five deputy sheriffs. As Iseman began to jot down the license plate numbers of cars parked on company property, he was punched by a miner. Iseman pulled a gun and began shooting (he later claimed they were blank cartridges) at the aroused miners. The miners quickly produced their own guns and opened fire on Iseman and the hopelessly outnumbered deputies. Iseman and his associates fled the scene aboard a trolley amid a hail of miners' bullets. Miners were the targets of violence on and off company property. Guards and deputies found miners lodged in company housing fair game, and were only slightly less bold on the public streets. Deputies attacked a brass band composed largely of miners as it marched along a public road near West Apollo. More often than not, the union men responded in kind, for bombings and beatings were commonplace. Kiewicz and Kilpatrick were arrested for beating a nonunion miner near Freeport. Kilpatrick was also arrested for attacking a black miner in New Kensington while intoxicated. Unfortunately, impartial law enforcement was virtually nonexistent, and the violence continued to escalate.[13]

Armed confrontations were particularly prevalent at mines operated by Lewis Hicks. Alle-Kiski miners who worked for Hicks generally earned sixty-three cents per day less than their unionized brethren in the Pittsburgh district, even though their workday was two hours longer. Many of the Hicks operations were situated in extremely remote areas, and the forces of law and order in those isolated camps were little more than vigilantes. Hicks also pioneered the use of black scabs in the region, and armed confrontations were more often than not race riots. It was the "slave-like conditions" and the strikebreaking techniques used that generated violence. Hicks operated fourteen mines in the valley and enjoyed access to economic resources that were not available to smaller operators. His father, Alfred Hicks, a Welsh immigrant, had helped to found Allegheny Steel and held important interests in local banks. Lewis Hicks understood that his mining operations had been selected as a special target by the UMWA. He responded by hiring the largest private army in the valley and by importing trainloads of strikebreakers. In Saltsburg, Avonmore, Apollo, and Leechburg, Hicks's hirelings beat, shot, and intimidated miners and their families, virtually unrestrained by local authorities.[14] Other operators imitated Hicks on a smaller scale. Union organizers were forced to employ their skills against Alle-Kiski coal operators who were virtually unanimous in their commitment to an armed suppression of the strike.

Foremost among UMWA operatives in the Alle-Kiski was Fannie Sellins. An activist in the tradition of Mother Jones,[15] Sellins had participated in coal strikes in Follansbee, Buffalo, and Yorkville, West Virginia. Prior to that, she had been a garment worker and a union organizer in that industry.[16] When and why she took up residence in New Kensington is not known. According to one source, she moved there after being pardoned by President Woodrow Wilson after a conviction resulting from her union activities in Fairmont, West Virginia. She was active at union rallies sponsored by the Allegheny Valley Central Labor Union in March 1916 and made militant speeches to laundrywomen and aluminum workers during the great wave of strikes in May of that year. Sellins prevented violence between union and nonunion coal miners working in the Penn Salt pits during the spring of 1916, and she apparently joined the UMWA as a full-time organizer sometime during January 1917.[17]

Sellins directed her initial efforts at the mining operators of Cornell Coal Company, located near Creighton on the west bank of the Allegheny River, opposite New Kensington. Superintendent Iseman used gunmen so liberally that his commission as deputy sheriff had been revoked by the Allegheny County sheriff several months before. Following a scuffle with Iseman and his men, Sellins charged him with assault, but lost the case. A month later, Deputy Joseph Murray arrested Sellins in Creighton because she called him a "scab."[18] The use of scab labor was an established tradition in the Alle-Kiski, and Sellins and her colleagues had no choice but to defeat that tactic if they were to be successful. Strikebreakers of diverse ethnic backgrounds—including English, Germans, Italians, Greeks, and blacks—had been brought into the valley. But nothing incited Alle-Kiski coal miners to a frenzy as did the presence of black strikebreakers. For many Alle-Kiski workers, the mere fact that a man was black was presumptive of being a scab.

On 24 February 1917, union organizers received word that a special trainload of black strikebreakers was approaching Pittsburgh. The black workers had been recruited in Birmingham, Alabama, and lured north by the promise of high wages. They apparently had not been informed that they were bound for scab duty in the coal mines of Lewis Hicks, but were instead told that they would work in newly opened mines. Union organizers rushed to Pittsburgh hoping to talk the blacks off the train, but were prevented from approaching the coaches by guards. As the train moved north from Pittsburgh along the Allegheny River, it was forced to stop at a block signal near Tarentum. There, Fannie Sellins and other organizers ran alongside the cars and induced about a hundred men to leave the train. Many blacks scrambled out of the coach windows, for the doors remained locked. With a pledge of train fare, food, and shelter, the entire contingent paraded across the Tarentum Bridge to New Kensington, where temporary lodgings were provided at the Polish Falcon Hall. With that small success in hand, Sellins continued her assault on the coal barons and their accomplices. She accused the Allegheny County sheriff of hiring thugs as deputies for the purpose of attacking miners and urged all miners to vote against him. She then shared a rally platform with district president Philip Murray at New Kensington's Garibaldi Hall and helped lead a parade across the river to Creighton and back.[19]

And suddenly the strike ended. Upon American entry into World War I on 6 April 1917, Alle-Kiski miners and coal operators fell in behind the flag. The Hicks interests even came to an agreement with the UMWA that included a 50 percent increase in pay for its miners. Ironically, war brought more than a year of labor peace to the Alle-Kiski. War also brought administered prosperity to the nation's coalfields. Strikes were forbidden. All labor disputes were subject to arbitration by the War Labor Board or Federal Fuel Administration. In an unprecedented move, the United States government became a third party to a basic national wage agreement signed by bituminous coal operators and the UMWA in October 1917. Under that agreement, Alle-Kiski miners temporarily surrendered their goals of free collective bargaining and the right to strike,[20] but escaped the rigors of unemployment and wage cuts traditionally a part of life in the coalfields. However, the agreement did not protect the miners from the consequences of inflation.

The 1917 agreement bound the UMWA not to renegotiate its terms before the war officially ended or 1 April 1920, whichever came first. Although the armistice was signed in November 1918, the United States Senate did not ratify the Treaty of Versailles, and the war did not end officially until July 1921. Adjustment of miners' wages had never kept pace with accelerating wartime inflation, and the UMWA rank and file had begun to clamor for a new wage scale long before the shooting ceased in Europe. Uncertainty concerning the peace treaty did little to sustain UMWA confidence in the 1917 agreement. Many coal operators had signed the 1917 accord under duress and never recognized the UMWA as the legal bargaining agent for the miners. Operators of that mind chafed under government controls and longed for a return to unregulated, nonunion conditions. By early spring 1919 there were abundant signs that labor relations in the Alle-Kiski were returning to prewar conditions. Coal operators abrogated the 1917 agreement. Alle-Kiski miners attempted to use the modest achievements of 1917 as a foundation for future negotiations with the operators. They demanded an adjustment of their wage scale and an affirmation of the union recognition that they knew had not been won before the war.

The year of the Red Scare—1919—was replete with charges of radicalism, Bolshevism, and sedition. Labor unrest exacerbated the hysteria that swept the nation, and industrial workers in the Alle-Kiski proved to be ripe targets for red-baiting. The disproportionate number of aliens in their ranks and a surprising postwar militance seemed to threaten the established order. The UMWA had begun a concerted antiradical campaign prior to American entry into World War I. The Industrial Workers of the World and its "one big union" idea was a particular target of the UMWA. Samuel Gompers had assigned John L. Lewis to aid UMWA president John White in ridding their union of its radical elements. Lewis and Gompers were both political conservatives, and each believed labor "visionaries, doctrinaires and insurgents" to be threats to the established order as well as to their own place and power. After he ascended to the UMWA presidency, Lewis ordered his union to purge itself of its "progressive" and pro-Soviet elements. In that spirit, he tried to persuade John Brophy to expedite the expulsion of Socialists from the Pennsylvania Labor Council. Lewis also supported immigration restriction and declared that Americanization programs would strengthen rank-and-file solidarity. In fact, Lewis and local red-baiters had little to fear from radical labor in the Alle-Kiski coalfields in 1919. The IWW presence in the valley was confined to the occasional distribution of pamphlets,[21] and Communist miners did not appear until 1923. However that may be, the absence of an effective radical presence in the coalfields and the Lewis purge did not secure immunity from Bolshevik-baiting for the UMWA.

The region's steelworkers, who had not shown an interest in unions for nearly two decades, were also caught up in the events of 1919. A year before, Samuel Gompers had been pushed into a campaign to organize the nation's steel mills. On 1 August fifteen international unions affiliated with the AFL met in Chicago and formed a national committee for organizing the ironworkers and steelworkers. John Fitzpatrick, president of the Chicago Federation of Labor, served as chairman. William Z. Foster, secretary-treasurer, directed the organizing drive and conceived the tactics for the subsequent strike. The constituent AFL unions that comprised the national committee were supposed to supply money and organizers for the campaign. After steelworkers were signed up by the national committee, they were to be sorted out and assigned to an AFL international according to the appropriate jurisdiction.[22] In short, the purpose of the campaign was not the establishment of a single industrial union for all steelworkers. Craft unionism would once again be superimposed on an industrial domain.

In the Alle-Kiski, most steelworkers were recruited by the venerable Amalgamated Association of Iron, Steel and Tin Workers. Amalgamated lodges were established in every community in which a mill existed. Such special "floating" organizers as Fannie Sellins supplemented the work of the Amalgamated organizers. By early summer of 1919, it was clear to all that a strike in the mills had become a real possibility. The Amalgamated had enjoyed particular success recruiting foreign-born steelworkers. That "alien" presence, coupled with public revelations of Foster's past associations with the IWW, fed the fires of nativism, prejudice, and xenophobia. Given the ingredients at hand, it was not difficult for the steelmakers to portray the strike as un-American. Indeed, the region's steelworkers would prove to be more vulnerable to the charges of subversion than their brethren in the mines.

The common destiny shared by Alle-Kiski miners and mill workers became tragically clear in the late summer and fall of 1919. On 26 August organizer Fannie Sellins and Joseph Starzeleski, a miner, were shot and killed by Allegheny Coal and Coke Company deputy sheriffs in West Natrona. Sellins had been active on the west bank of the Allegheny for several years. She had directed picketing at Allegheny Coal and Coke, a subsidiary of Allegheny Steel, for several months. Less than a week before her death, she participated in an open-air rally for the recruitment of steelworkers held in Natrona.[23] On the day of her death, Sellins had been meeting with the wives of Slavic miners and mill workers in West Natrona, known locally as Ducktown. Situated on the bluffs above the Allegheny River, its predominantly Polish and Slovak residents kept large flocks of waterfowl in the tradition of village life. Most of the men worked at nearby Allegheny and West Penn Steel companies. Those who did not worked at the Allegheny Coal and Coke mine, whose portal entered the bluff immediately below West Natrona. Slavic workers were a tough nut for union organizers to crack, but Sellins addressed that problem successfully by appealing to their wives as well as to the men themselves. Sellins also continued to enjoy a reputation for recruiting black workers, a source of industrial labor normally beyond the reach of union organizers.

Few blacks lived in the Alle-Kiski. Racial hostility made living and working in the valley difficult for them. Some mills, including American Sheet and Tin Plate in Vandergrift, employed blacks in menial jobs, while others, such as Apollo Steel, refused to hire them at all. Black miners worked in small numbers throughout the district, but were not welcomed, particularly by UMWA miners. Crosses burned and white-robed figures marched in the night as the Ku Klux Klan appeared throughout the valley in the postwar years. In an atmosphere of hysterical xenophobia and racism, few people could discuss rationally the reasons for the appearance of black scabs in the valley. The unions were never able to mobilize public opinion against their use. Fannie Sellins and other UMWA organizers searched for and found a weakness in the strikebreaking tactics of the operators—many blacks had been hired under false pretenses. They rioted in Avonmore and Leechburg after being informed that they had been recruited for scab duty in Hicks's mines. In Creighton, blacks not only deserted the operators but defected to the UMWA.[24]

Fannie Sellins was both audacious and persuasive. After the war, she went back to work in Creighton and convinced the black strikebreakers there to join the union. In July 1919 she and a dozen of those men appeared on the union picket lines at the mine of Allegheny Coal and Coke, which had been founded by Captain Alfred Hicks. Members of the Hicks family managed the mill, and the appearance of black picketers at its nearby mine must have been a rude shock. Company complaints concerning the black picketers were quickly rebutted by the UMWA. Union organizers reminded the local press that it was hardly appropriate for the Hicks interests to make race an issue in the strike, since Lewis Hicks had been the chief importer of black laborers into the Alle-Kiski.[25]

Fannie Sellins's tactics at Allegheny Coal and Coke were a modest success. Company miners walked out, and black strikebreakers refused to cross the picket lines. According to union sources, the company then imported "a bunch of lousy, scabby Greeks," and advertised for "free born American" miners to replace those who had been misled by "outside agitators."[26] The Allegheny Coal and Coke strike became a stalemate that reflected conditions at most mines in the valley. Sellins divided her time between service on the picket lines at the mines and organizing the steelworkers of Allegheny and West Penn Steel. She was easily the most visible member of a crack organizing team sent into the Alle-Kiski by the UMWA. Her successes undoubtedly made her a target for violence, and rumors circulated that she was in imminent danger. It is not possible to prove or refute William Foster's charge that her death was managed from beginning to end by the "Steel Trust."[27] Nor is it probable that the actual sequence of events that occurred on 26 August will ever be entirely clear. Newspaper, eyewitness, and official accounts are often contradictory, but available evidence suggests that the Sellins killing was not simply the result of spontaneous violence.

According to local newspapers, Fannie Sellins was killed on picket duty. As the afternoon shift left the mine at five o'clock, with an escort of company deputies, the guards and pickets exchanged angry words. In the ensuing melee, shotguns and buckshot were employed against the strikers. Guards claimed that Sellins was shot while leading a riot. They maintained that they had acted in self-defense and that they resorted to the use of deadly force only after being pelted with rocks and sticks. Miners protested that there had been no such provocation. Some claimed that Sellins was clubbed and shot after giving aid to the fallen Joseph Starzeleski. Most believed that her death was the result of a premeditated attack.[28]

Eyewitness accounts dispute both newspaper reports and the official version of the Sellins episode. Stanley Rafalko was running an errand for his father when the Sellins incident occurred. According to Rafalko, there were no picket lines or shouting mobs in his neighborhood on that hot August afternoon. Several local steelworkers, towels tied around their necks, made their way down the hill to the mill below. Evening turn was about to begin. As Rafalko approached the local grocery, he noticed a maroon touring car parked not far away. Its top was down, and Rafalko had no difficulty seeing Joseph Czarnowski and another steelworker seated in the car, engaged in conversation with three uniformed officers. Rafalko entered the store, and when he emerged a few minutes later, a wild brawl had erupted.

The officers used blackjacks on anyone who came within reach, and then began to fire their handguns at any available target. Joseph Czarnowski was wounded in the arm, but escaped with his life by scrambling down the hill toward the mill. The gunfire apparently attracted the attention of Fannie Sellins, who arrived on the scene in the company of neighborhood women and children. Sellins appeared to know the officers and attempted to remonstrate with them, citing the obvious danger to innocent bystanders. The officers were not moved. A black hunchback emerged from a nearby company shack carrying an armful of shotguns, which were quickly brought into play with deadly effect as another local resident was shot. Again, Sellins approached the officers and protested, but they cursed and struck her savagely with a gun butt. She scrambled to her feet and attempted to flee the scene through a gate leading to the property owned by Konstanty Rafalko, Stanley Rafalko's grandfather. As she ran, the officer shot her at point-blank range. Sellins fell, mortally wounded, her false teeth lying in a pool of blood.[29]

Following her death, the violence ended as quickly as it had begun. At least nine persons had been shot, two fatally. One deputy was treated for bruises. The officers picked up the body of Fannie Sellins by the head and heels and stacked it with that of Joseph Starzeleski on the floor of the touring car. Joseph Czarnowski was present when the bodies were dropped unceremoniously on the floor of the Allegheny Steel infirmary. Czarnowski's wound had been discovered by deputies on patrol, and he had been taken to that facility for medical attention. According to Czarnowski, the chief deputy rejoiced that the "whore" had finally received the treatment she deserved. His only regret was that one of the men shot by his officers was a company spy.[30]

Ensuing official investigations by the Allegheny County coroner and sheriff did little to establish the facts in the Sellins case. In fact, the cursory character of those inquiries give credence to the charges made by miners that local authorities were covering up the deeds of the coal operators. Local miners insisted that deputy Joseph Murray had threatened Sellins and the Creighton justice of the peace, who had shown leniency toward miners in his court. Sellins and Murray had been involved in altercations while he worked in Creighton in 1917, and he had allegedly sworn "to get her." Orders for Murray's arrest were issued, apparently by the local justice of the peace. Sheriff William Haddock ordered the justice's warrant rescinded and appeared to retaliate by ordering the arrest of James Oates, a union organizer, for "conspiracy."[31]

The political by-play was followed by a shoddy investigation and inquest conducted by the coroner.[32] His investigator apparently ignored deputy Murray's possible connection to the Sellins incident and rejected a county detective's recommendations that murder warrants be issued against specific company deputies. Investigators seemed content to interview miners and deputies. According to the investigators, the pickets, many of whom spoke broken English, did not have their stories straight. The explanation of the deputies contained no contradictions or conflicts, and the coroner accepted their testimony without question or further review. Reports to the coroner concluded that "the pickets" were solely responsible for both the violence and the bloodshed.[33]

The reports and medical evidence were presented to a coroner's jury that was convened in Pittsburgh a month after the shooting. The jury found that Fannie Sellins's death was caused by a gunshot wound in the left temple that was inflicted during a riot. The shooting was done in self-defense and was therefore justifiable. The mine guards had simply done their duty. The jurors were "certain that there was a riot" and that "there were no innocent bystanders." "Everyone in the crowd was guilty of rioting."[34]

The antilabor bias of the jury was made clear in posthearing statements to the press. The jury deplored and condemned "the foreign agitators who instilled anarchy and Bolshevik doctrines into the minds of un-American and uneducated aliens of the district."[35] Even as those sentiments were being made public, several miners who had attended the inquest were arrested for inciting to riot. If Fannie Sellins and Joseph Starzeleski had fallen victim to Black Valley's legacy of industrial violence, justice had succumbed to Red Scare hysteria.

The Sellins case never evoked public indignation or moral outrage in the Alle-Kiski. Editorial comment in the local press was only slightly less subdued than the union response to the killings. Fannie Sellins received a martyr's funeral. Local miners marched in protest, but her death received scant coverage in the *Amalgamated Journal* and *United Mine Workers Journal*. Philip Murray dashed off angry telegrams to the president and governor demanding an investigation, but that short flurry of protests by union officials was followed by little else. The UMWA leadership may well have been preoccupied with preparations for the impending national coal strike that would be called on 1 November.

In the months following the inquest, the Sellins case assumed a grotesque character, as antilabor spokesmen used her death to denounce the steelworkers' union. Sheriff Haddock spared no effort to break the steel strike that had erupted during September in Allegheny County. Employing a policy of arbitrary arrests and numerous suspensions of civil liberties, the sheriff imposed his own special brand of law and order in the Pittsburgh district. The Sellins case presented a unique opportunity to further discredit the strike. Forty-three days after the Sellins funeral, the sheriff wrote to a senate labor committee and complained that Sellins's body had been exhumed and mutilated by radicals. Their ghoulish acts were designed to smear local authorities and furnish propaganda for "anarchists and revolutionaries." According to the sheriff, unrest and disorder existed in the region because of the "presence in the community of dishonest, revolutionary Bolshevistic agitators whose sole purpose [was] to prey [upon] the unintelligent foreigner and goad him into deeds which the American worker [would] not tolerate."[36]

John Fitzpatrick, chairman of the national committee for organizing iron and steelworkers, believed that Fannie Sellins had been killed in order to instill the "fear of God" in the strikers. If those responsible for her death were so motivated, their strategy failed. The steelworkers understood that the attack on Sellins was also an attack on them. Nevertheless, despite an atmosphere of fear and uncertainty generated by the killings,[37] steelworkers in Apollo, Vandergrift, Leechburg, Brackenridge, Natrona, and New Kensington walked out on 22 September. All the major steel plants in the Alle-Kiski, including Apollo Steel, American Sheet and Tin Plate, Allegheny, and West Penn Steel were temporarily paralyzed by the strike. Steelworkers in the district were organized into five lodges of the Amalgamated Association of Iron, Steel and Tin Workers. The Amalgamated was never very strong in the valley, for it had traditionally served only the interests of white, American-born, skilled steelworkers. Efforts to attract Italians, Poles, Lithuanians, and Slovaks appeared to promise not only a change in image but in direction for the Amalgamated.

William Foster claimed that on 30 September, more than 14,000 men had signed union cards: 4,000 in Vandergrift, 1,500 in Apollo, 3,000 in Leechburg, 5,000 in Brackenridge, and 1,100 in New Kensington. Those results were not altogether encouraging. The union could boast that most of the foreign-born workers in the Vandergrift, Natrona, and Brackenridge areas supported the strike. Few Slavic or Italian men worked in the Apollo mill. Nevertheless, it closed down completely for ten days, even though organizers complained that the commitment of the Apollo men was thin because many of the rollers and heaters were "veteran scabs." The native-born strikers of Apollo were clearly the exception to the general strike pattern of 1919. In most mills, the skilled Americans stayed on the job and out of the Amalgamated. A veteran American Sheet and Tin Plate roller in Vandergrift refused to join the strike because he believed it poorly timed and doomed to failure. A New Kensington roller and former member of the Amalgamated admitted that he was no union man or striker in 1919. He believed the steel companies would simply resort to their old policy of plant shutdowns or removals.[38] Their feelings probably reflected the opinion of skilled steelworkers in most communities in the valley. It is clear that throughout the strike, company spokesmen, newspapers, and union organizers quoted strike statistics that suited their own purposes. The situation was so fluid in the Alle-Kiski that it seems improbable that anyone had accurate numbers of strikers and nonstrikers. However, no one questioned the fact that the foreign-born constituted the bulk of the strikers at most mills.

The ardent support given to the strike effort by traditionally "docile" Italian and Slavic steelworkers was a pleasant surprise to the Amalgamated, and a rude surprise for the rest of the community. Most ethnic workers were confined to common labor in the mills, and most endured the twelve-hour day. But that had been true for two generations. Occupational hardships alone did not account for their new militance. Radical ideology was not a factor. Workers confessed that they knew virtually nothing about the IWW or Socialist doctrines and had but the most remote knowledge of Foster and his radical connections. Interviews for the Interchurch Commission of Inquiry concluded that Bolshevism was not a factor in the strike. Some of the Slavic and Italian men had acquired American citizenship. Others had served in Europe during the war. These men were determined not to suffer the indignities of the past. Humiliation on the job and in town was a common ingredient of the new militance. A Lithuanian-American from East Vandergrift, six years a citizen, told Interchurch investigators that his chief grievance was "discrimination and contempt." Younger "American" men were promoted before him. Two Poles from the same community cited exploitation by heaters and rollers as their chief complaint. Another complained bitterly of bias against his family and his inability to raise his status in the mill and community. A Neapolitan from New Kensington echoed the sentiments of the Slavs. The events of 1919 did not simply constitute a strike—it was in fact a community revolt. In a quiet act of defiance, the burgess of East Vandergrift ordered the constabulary out of his town in order to protect his people from humiliation and intimidation by men on horseback. William Foster was correct when he characterized the strike as a revolt against industrial serfdom.[39]

Throughout the valley, the strike was viewed primarily for and by "hunkies" and "foreigners." That apparent alien quality stigmatized the entire conflict as un-American. The union was never able to deal effectively with the charge of un-Americanism or radicalism. As mills in Apollo, Vandergrift, and Natrona advertised for hardworking, loyal, American men, union organizers protested that the national origins of the strikers of the district were evenly divided. They also complained that American-born strikers were being relegated to the "Uncle Tom" class.[40] Local organizers had anticipated the issue of alien-inspired radicalism and worked diligently to recruit war veterans in order to insure respectability for their cause. That tactic did not succeed, and radicalism remained a consuming issue throughout the strike.

The local press exhibited an acute interest in radicalism long before the strike.[41] During the strike, however, antiradical editorial comment intensified. The *Valley Daily News* observed that "so much apparent radicalism" existed because "there were grievances to correct in the present economic system." Those injustices could best be alleviated without the assistance of "Fosters, Trotskys, and Lenins." "Inequality of hours and working conditions could be remedied—propagation of Red Doctrines could not." The solution to industrial strife was to be found in collective bargaining and government arbitration. "Americanization," editorialized the *New Kensington Daily Dispatch*, "was the best antidote for radicalism."[42]

There is little evidence to support the charge that radicals had inspired labor unrest in the Alle-Kiski. The United Mine Workers had campaigned effectively against the International Workers of the World and its "one big union" idea. IWW agents passed out literature in the coalfields,[43] but had little influence in the valley. Federal agents swept down on the New Kensington Polish Singing Society, arresting its officers while confiscating liquor and radical literature. That hardly represented an epidemic of radicalism. Yet it seemed to be a problem. A. Mitchell Palmer, radical-hunting attorney general of the United States, made a personal appearance in the valley pleading for an absolute industrial armistice.[44] American society appeared to be under attack. For many in the Alle-Kiski, "Americanization" represented a patriotic solution by which all citizens might contribute to the defeat of internal subversion.

An Americanization Club was established in Leechburg in February 1919. It sponsored a program of English instruction for the diverse ethnic community. The avowed purpose of the club was the reduction of hatred for foreign-born members of the community. "If we are to receive full value from our alien and foreign born subjects," commented the editor of the *Leechburg Advance*, "we will have to educate them." The local burgess organized the Americanization Day Parade. Italian, Slovak, Polish, Greek, Jewish, and Hungarian miners' societies supported the parade and its theme: "America First—One Flag for All."[45]

The advent of the strike brought forth calls for the adoption of Americanization programs throughout the Alle-Kiski. The *New Kensington Daily Dispatch* supported Americanization programs such as that sponsored by the American Legion, an avowed open-shop organization. Removal of William Z. Foster and a government roundup of other "IWW types" would supplement the assimilation of aliens. Suspicious persons who refused to become American citizens would be deported to the land of their birth.[46] The rival *Valley Daily News* lamented the return of ethnic prejudice:

> Since the end-of-the war Americans are lapsing into the old careless habits of alluding to foreign speaking laborers as "Hunkies," "Wops,"

"Guineas," and "foreigners." When the war was at its height and several thousands of these individuals were in the American Army, public speaking managers, newspapers and the like referred to them in terms of the highest dignity.

Why shouldn't this decency of language be continued? It is true these men are aliens in the sense that they were born in foreign countries. But now that they are in America and largely through an industrial system that is constantly seeking cheap labor, it is the duty of that industrial system and of the country wherein located to Americanize the workers. There will be "Hunkies," "Wops," and "Guineas" just so long as they are not taught American ways.[47]

In an atmosphere charged by allegations of treason, subversion, radicalism, and un-Americanism, steelworkers failed to build a union in the Alle-Kiski. The defeat of the "Great Strike" crushed the hopes of the millworkers for nearly two decades. Strike committees that attempted to expedite the return of the men to the mills were rebuked by management. Steelworkers were hired or blacklisted individually. Company unions appeared throughout the valley. Not even a receding Red Scare softened the blow. While editorials blasted the "blundering deportations," "gag laws," and "tomfoolery" produced by the "Red Menace,"[48] local coal operators intensified their efforts against the coal miners who had walked out in a nationwide strike on 1 November. By mid-November, the steel strike had collapsed, and the UMWA alone remained on the field of battle. The union miners would enjoy that dubious distinction for more than a decade.

John L. Lewis, the new president of the UMWA, had given the strike order reluctantly. Lewis had a keen sense of politics, and he knew that the fall of 1919 was not the time for a coal strike. His presidency was, however, the result of fortuitous circumstances rather than election. Union rivals and a militant rank and file forced his hand. Coal operators, buoyed by the success of the steel industry, did not budge. Federal court injunctions made the UMWA position untenable. Union miners in the Alle-Kiski took months to straggle back to work following a Lewis order to return to the pits.

The miners of the Central Competitive Field, of which the Alle-Kiski was a part, were influenced by two new forces during the 1920s. The first was John L. Lewis. Lewis was a man of exquisite intelligence and ruthless ambition who was determined to make himself absolute master of the UMWA. To that end he built a machine utterly loyal to his person. Union rivals accepted sinecures or were purged. Local district autonomy was systematically eliminated. Most of the men connected to western Pennsylvania's UMWA District 5 went along with the Lewis program. District presidents Philip Murray and Pat Fagan were Lewis loyalists.

The rank and file of the valley forgave Lewis his mistakes and remained faithful through thick and thin. Not even his occasional egregious abandonment of their interests drove them from the fold.

If the 1920s brought the miners John L. Lewis, it also gave them depression. While Lewis established an iron grip on the UMWA, depression became the established economic reality in the northern bituminous fields. There were simply too many miners and mines, and too much coal. Comparative advantage had been lost to nonunion operators in West Virginia, Kentucky, and Tennessee. Southern operators enjoyed lower freight rates and a nonunion scale. Oil and natural gas also invaded established energy markets. In 1920, 29 percent of the nation's coal was mined in union fields; by 1924 the union share fell to 24.6 percent. Between 1920 and 1927, the market share of Pennsylvania and Ohio fell from 60 percent to 39 percent. The price of coal fell to $1.78 per ton in 1929. Coal miners averaged 220 workdays a year in 1920, 149 in 1921, 174 in 1924, and 191 in 1927. In 1921 bituminous operators employed 663,754 miners in 8,078 mines. By 1928 the number of miners fell to 522,150 in 6,450 mines.[49] None of the trends augered well for the bituminous industry, but the situation was particularly bleak for northern union operations, which were losing markets in an inter-regional competition with the south.

In 1921 bituminous was a sick industry in the Alle-Kiski. A local operator attributed eleven cents a bushel to the "chimes of normalcy." Although Westmoreland County led Pennsylvania in coal production, and Allegheny County ranked fifth, bituminous miners worked fewer than 150 days that year. There was plenty of coal to be mined. The commonwealth estimated 1.4 million recoverable tons of coal in Allegheny, 3.2 million in Westmoreland, and 2.4 million in Armstrong counties.[50] But markets had dried up. It was therefore a surprise to no one when the Freeport Thick Vein Coal Operators' Association refused to accept a continuance of the union wage scale in 1922. Henry Kinloch, superintendent and part owner of the Valley Camp Coal Company, emerged as the association's chief advocate for an adjusted union scale. Valley Camp operated two large mines near New Kensington. Kinloch had operated on a union scale since 1917 and enjoyed a particular rapport with the union miners in his employ. Valley Camp made no attempt to force the issue and simply allowed its mines to shut down on 1 April 1922. Maverick Lewis Hicks operated a dozen mines in the Alle-Kiski Valley and was determined to stamp out the UMWA in his mines. Hicks imported trainloads of black strikebreakers, and vicious riots between white union and black miners erupted at Edri and Foster in January 1922. The savage fighting, which endured through the summer, resulted in several killings.[51] The violence at Hicks's mines was the exception, however. In the Alle-Kiski, the 1922 coal strike proved for the most part to be a peaceful affair. Most operators chose to emulate Valley Camp's policy of watchful waiting.

On 1 April 1922, fifteen thousand miners of Subdistrict 7, UMWA District 5, went out on strike. Those Alle-Kiski miners joined forty-five thousand of their brothers in ten western Pennsylvania counties. Fifteen thousand miners aspiring to be union men also struck mines in the Connellsville coke fields and other mines in Somerset County. The UMWA demanded union recognition, preservation of the then-present wage scale, and the checkoff. The strike proved to be a disaster for the UMWA, and some were inclined to attribute its failures to John L. Lewis. Lewis, however, had not favored a strike that flew in the teeth of depression and shrinking union resources. In 1922 Lewis continued in his efforts to wrest control of the union from rivals, and a strike effort beset by financial problems entailed risks he was reluctant to take. But, as in 1919, his hand was forced from below. At a special convention in February, rank-and-file militants pushed a broad program including nationalization of the mines, establishment of an independent labor party, a six-hour day, expansion of the union, and wage increases. Lewis understood that he did not have sufficient money to finance union expansion, particularly in such antilabor bastions as the coke fields of Fayette and Westmoreland counties. Lewis rightly identified the cries for nationalization and the establishment of a labor party with left-wing rivals in the UMWA. He was content to call for federal regulation of coal production and pricing. By the time the union walked out on April, UMWA demands had been reduced to a maintenance of the status quo in wages, the checkoff, and the organization of the nonunion fields.[52]

After 1 April most of the major mines in the Alle-Kiski were shut down. Exceptions were the West Penn Power Company mine in Barking, Penn Salt and Allegheny Coal and Coke near Brackenridge, Hicks's mines, and a few other small operations. Throughout April tranquillity prevailed in most of the valley. A great deal of the violence was centered in the coke region, where more than a thousand deputy sheriffs fought striking miners. At Logans Ferry, two hundred UMWA miners tried to prevent thirty strikebreakers—the majority of whom were black—from entering the mines. State police and deputy sheriffs kept the men apart. On 25 April the UMWA shut down half a dozen small "country mines" along Bull Creek for allegedly supplying coal to West Penn Steel. On 4 May the apparent serenity was shattered by an explosion at the Patterson mine on the west bank of the Kiskiminetas River, opposite Apollo. Patterson was not Hicks's mine, but it supplied coal to Apollo Steel and was thus under seige by the UMWA. Stanley Meilke, Andrew Borniak, and Frank Ridgski, strikebreakers from Natrona, were sleeping in a bunkhouse when someone threw dynamite through an open window. The men were killed instantly.[53] Following that spate of savagery, relative serenity returned to the Alle-Kiski and remained for the rest of the summer. The situation remained so orderly that Governor Sproul exempted the valley from occupation by the National Guard.

By mid-July it was also apparent that the solidarity of the coal operators was dissolving. President Warren G. Harding offered his offices to both parties, suggesting that the standard wages be $7.50 for daymen, $.94 a ton for machine-cut coal, and $1.16 for pick miners. The Pittsburgh Coal Producers countered with the 1917 scale, including $5.00 for daymen, $.70 a ton for machine-cut coal, and $.88 for pick miners. The Freeport Association seemed ready to go along with their counterparts in Pittsburgh. Henry Kinloch was evidently displeased with the tone of the proceedings and bolted the association. When Lewis extended an olive branch and offered to negotiate with operators in Cleveland, Kinloch accepted. On 6 August Kinloch, A. R. Pollock of Ford Collieries, and John H. Jones representing Bertha-Consumers Coal signed a UMWA contract *status quo ante*. The agreement put 3,600 miners back to work. Many operators continued to hold out for elimination of the checkoff, but it is clear that the united front of the operators was irrevocably smashed.[54]

The fading resolve of the operators proved to be of small comfort to John L. Lewis. He abandoned hope for a national, uniform union contract. Valley Camp and the other operations that signed with the UMWA in Cleveland did so on the basis that miners would return to the pits. This move defied UMWA tradition, which demanded that all union miners stay out until a uniform contract was reached for the entire membership. In effect, Lewis abandoned his membership in the Kiskiminetas Valley, southern Indiana County, Somerset, and the coke regions, for operators there did not expect to sign a union contract of any kind. Lewis's decision was not an act of wanton faithlessness or craven cowardice, but an effort to make the most of a deteriorating situation. Striking miners could not replenish a union treasury already depleted by a membership stricken by an industrywide depression. The Valley Camp local was not much impressed with Lewis's change of course and attempted to adhere to the tradition of one union, indivisible.

On 16 August the Valley Camp miners met at their union hall near Kinloch. "Conscientious objectors" at Valley Camp and Ford Collieries in Curtisville had refused to heed Lewis's order to return to work. At Ford Collieries, union miners cast votes three to one against returning to work until a uniform contract was signed. James Paisley, president of Valley Camp Coal, and Superintendent Henry Kinloch attended the meeting of Local 1230 and attempted to persuade the men to return to work. Individual miners thanked Kinloch and Paisley for their good faith, but collectively the miners did not budge. A member of the local's policy committee added that Valley Camp had extended credit to the strikers, had promised to end evictions, and had refused to call for soldiers, deputies, or police. The miners freely acknowledged that all of that was true, but remained adamant. Local President Peter Haser then pulled out and read a telegram from John L. Lewis ordering the men to work. In 1922 a telegram from Lewis did not carry the weight that it would in later years. The men balked, deferring action until a meeting called for the following day.[55]

On 18 August the union men at Ford Collieries were back on the picket lines despite a union contract signed by their international president. These men were reinforced by roving pickets from the Connellsville district. International organizer F. P. Hanaway assured the men that 140 operators in the district had signed with the union, and all but 12 had signed for the first time. The picketers were not impressed, and a zealous foreman who tried to bring matters to a head suffered a broken arm and several broken ribs. Roving pickets disrupted outdoor meetings held by the Valley Camp locals on 19 and 20 August. Peter Haser moved the meetings indoors and posted guards at the entrances on 21 August. The men voted to return. On the same day, the district Vice-President, Pat Fagan, presided at a meeting of 1,500 Ford Collieries miners in Curtisville, and they voted to return. Following the settlement at Valley Camp and Curtisville, other operators also began to sign with the UMWA. Holdouts continued to protest the checkoff, but most signed by 29 August. By 1 September the strike was over in the Alle-Kiski, and most of the valley's operators had been pulled back into the union fold. In January of the following year, both the Pittsburgh and Freeport Thick Vein operators signed a UMWA contract, effective April 1923 through April 1924. Those associations controlled 20 percent of the soft coal mined in western Pennsylvania, and a contract seemed to offer a measure of security to the UMWA.[56]

In fact the 1922 coal strike opened a deep internal schism in the UMWA. The Kiskiminetas Valley miners had been cast into the wilderness like their brothers in the coke fields.[57] The Somerset miners would fight on for another year, but alone they were doomed to failure. Their bitter struggle generated charges of betrayal against the international and especially against Lewis. Lewis was perceived not only as a grasping despot, but as a traitor to the rank and file as well. The loss of Somerset and the coke regions was bad enough, but those regions had just been organized. Many of the Kiskiminetas Valley locals had been established in the lean days prior to World War I. The struggle with Lewis Hicks had been long and bitter, and after 1922 it was difficult for an Allegheny Valley miner to look a brother from the Kiskiminetas Valley in the eye.

The 1922 coal strike encouraged a revolt against John L. Lewis. On 2 June 1923, an organization calling itself the Progressive Miners International Committee met at the Labor Lyceum in Pittsburgh. The participants included UMWA insurgent Alex Howat, Communist miner Thomas Myerscough, William Z. Foster, and radical Socialist Fred Merrick. Five coal mining states and two Canadian provinces were represented. The organization eschewed "dual unionism," but promised much "boring from within." Its radical agenda included the ouster of Lewis, nationalization of the mines, establishment of a labor party, a six-hour workday and a five-day workweek, justice for Fannie Sellins, and the reinstatement of Lewis's archrival, Alex Howat. The Progressive Miners organized districts that coincided with those which already existed in the UMWA, but they added District 4 representing miners in the Pennsylvania coke fields. The elected officers of the Progressive Miners were all western Pennsylvanians, and Pittsburgh became its headquarters. Lewis condemned the proceedings as the work of a motley band of UMWA traitors, Communists, IWWs, and dualists.[58] The Progressive Bloc would never be able to defeat the Lewis organization in western Pennsylvania, but it would deny the UMWA the internal unity that it would so desperately need during the vicious coal strike in 1927.

Across town at the Allegheny County Courthouse, events also transpired that undermined the standing of the UMWA in the community. On the very day that the Progressive Bloc opened its convention, the Sellins murder trial began. Due solely to the persistence of the UMWA organizer, James Oates, murder indictments were issued against three Allegheny Coal and Coke deputy sheriffs on 15 February 1922. On 2 June 1923, almost four years after Sellins's death, deputies Edward Mannison, D. J. Riley, and John Pearson were tried for murder. The forty-six months that had elapsed made a fair trial impossible, and it is not clear why the court permitted it to proceed. Witnesses had moved away, and one defendant—John Pearson—was never located.

Medical evidence presented in open court disputed the coroner's findings in 1919. The Allegheny County medical examiner testified that Fannie Sellins had been shot twice in the head, not once. New Kensington mortician A. H. Hemer testified that he received the body after the postmortem and claimed that he found two head wounds and a back wound. He also claimed that Sellins's skull had been crushed. A New Kensington physician examined the body before and after it was exhumed on 13 October 1919. On both occasions, he found two head wounds and a single back wound.[59] The medical evidence presented cast grave doubts on the quality of the Allegheny County coroner's work. If the state managed to discredit official medical evidence, determining who actually fired the shots proved to be much more difficult. UMWA organizer James Oates testified that Deputy D. J. Riley had shot Starzeleski. But a woman who had witnessed the events of 26 August claimed that neither Mannison or Riley had done the shooting. It was believed that both Sellins and Starzeleski were hit by buckshot fired from a riot gun. Witnesses claimed that only the absent John Pearson was armed with such a weapon. Sheriff William Haddock also weakened the prosecutor's case. He claimed that James Oates had originally charged deputies Thomas (Joseph) Murray and Meyer von Lewin with the shootings.[60] If nothing else, the Sellins incident demonstrated the fluid quality of law enforcement when deputy sheriffs patrolled the picket lines.

The trial dealt with not only the guilt or innocence of the deputies, but also with whether their use of violence was justified. Deputies Thomas Ford and R. J. Schrandt testified that vile language had precipitated the violence. They had simply defended themselves against a mob led by Sellins. "Surprise witness" James Bradley of Tarentum had not testified at the coroner's inquest. He corroborated the deputies' claims that they had acted in self-defense. Retired steelworker Mike Rafalko and his nephew Frank Rafalko claimed that there was no angry mob of strikers near their backyard on the day in question. The Rafalkos argued that the gathering consisted of women and children and a few men. They denied that the mob charged the deputies or that the officers had been fired upon from nearby homes. Resident Martin Symkoviak corroborated the Rafalkos' testimony that the rampaging mob was a fiction created by the deputies.[61]

The trial was over in a week. Visiting Judge Henry C. Quigly ordered a directed verdict of acquittal. The jury complied in less than an hour. It is questionable whether Sellins or her killer could have received justice in 1923. Why the district attorney or the courts permitted such a prolonged delay in the proceedings is not known. Perhaps it was because violence was an expected and accepted result of industrial strife and was accordingly assigned a low judicial priority. With that in mind, it should also be noted that the murder of the three Patterson miners was subject to only a perfunctory investigation. The perpetrators were never found, and no one seemed to care. The official response to the Sellins affair did little to reduce the likelihood of further violence in the coalfields. In fact, four years later the coalfields would be subjected to violence so flagrant and pervasive that the 1927 bituminous strike would, at times, verge on local civil war. Internal dissension and systematic repression would make the Great Coal Strike the supreme test for the UMWA and for the survival of industrial unionism in western Pennsylvania.

3

The Great Coal Strike, 1925–1928

BITUMINOUS WAS AN AILING INDUSTRY THROUGHOUT THE 1920S. INDUS-trywide expansion peaked during World War I, but demand declined after 1920. In 1927 coal production fell 60 million tons below 1920 levels. Between 1924 and 1926 more than two thousand bituminous mines closed and 116,000 miners were discharged. The price of coal fell 24 percent during that period. In 1929 only 35 percent of all bituminous producers reported profits, compared to 90 percent in 1920. Operators in the Central Competitive Field bore the brunt of the depression in bituminous. In 1920 Pennsylvania and Ohio produced 60 percent of the nation's bituminous coal. By 1927 northern production had been re-duced to 39 percent. The chief culprit so far as the northern operators were concerned was interregional competition. The advantages enjoyed by southern operators were both relative and absolute. They produced a high-quality industrial steam coal. Mining was expedited by new seams located close to the surface. Southern freight rates were significantly lower than those paid by their northern competitors. Wage differentials also gave southern operators a distinct advantage. In 1926 West Virginia surpassed Pennsylvania in bituminous production. During that year, West Virginia miners, paid on a tonnage basis, averaged $5.85 per start compared to Pennsylvania's $6.18. Alabama miners earned $4.57, and those in Kentucky, $5.18.[1]

It was this difference between union and nonunion wages that brought the Pennsylvania operators and the UMWA into conflict. In 1924 John L. Lewis met with the operators in Jacksonville, Florida, and negotiated a wage agreement that became known as the Jacksonville scale. Under that agreement, the $7.50 wage for daymen established in 1922 was retained, and wages for tonnage men remained above $6.00. There was, however, widespread dissatisfaction with the Jacksonville scale. In September 1924 operators in central Pennsylvania shut down, claiming they could not pay the "impossible wage scale." Charles O'Neill, secretary of the Central Pennsylvania Coal Producers' Association, requested a meeting with the UMWA for the purpose of reducing wages. Operator associations in western Pennsylvania made the same request in March 1925.[2] On both occasions, the UMWA refused the operators, and No Backward Step became the battle cry of the union miners.

Some operators wished to return to the 1917 wage scales. Others desired less extreme measures and called for a "continuously competitive" scale in which miners' wages would be adjusted according to the price of coal.[3] The eventual direction of the operators was charted by Pittsburgh Coal Company, one of the largest bituminous producers in western Pennsylvania. In 1925 control of Pittsburgh Coal was acquired by the Mellon family of Pittsburgh. Following the UMWA rejection of wage adjustments, Pittsburgh Coal closed all of its mines in western Pennsylvania. On 10 August its mines were reopened on a nonunion basis. Pittsburgh Coal had done business with the UMWA for thirty-five years, and most of its 17,000 miners were union men. Pittsburgh Coal simply abrogated the Jacksonville agreement. In so doing, it attacked a vital bastion of union strength. Pittsburgh Coal was not alone: Bethlehem Mines; Buffalo, Rochester and Pittsburgh Coal; and others also repudiated the UMWA in 1925. By the end of the year, 65 percent of the nation's soft coal, and 61 percent of all bituminous miners, were nonunion.[4]

Industry analyst Basil Manley was employed by the *Pittsburgh Press* to provide independent commentary on conditions in the coalfields. Manley believed that the operators presented a strong case for wage reductions because salaries paid in the south were 30 percent below the Jacksonville scale. But wage scales were, according to Manley, the least of the bituminous industry's problems. "Overdevelopment and cut-throat competition" also plagued the industry. According to Manley, railroads exacerbated the problem of overproduction by encouraging the opening of new mines in order to get traffic, even though additional mines produced a glut. Railroads also consumed more than 25 percent of all bituminous, and they demanded lower prices. Purchasing agents for the Pennsylvania Railroad told two Ohio coal operators that their coal would not be bought if they paid their miners union scale.[5]

The operators also made war on each other, and those closely tied to banking interests enjoyed a distinct advantage. Manley found some evidence that operators willing to continue paying union scale found their credit lines eliminated. The experience of John Jones, president of Bertha-Consumers Coal Company, bespoke the dog-eat-dog competition in the Pittsburgh district. Jones believed in a union contract because he thought it insured a measure of stability for the industry. He continued to operate under the Jacksonville agreement until it expired on 1 April 1927. Local competition forced him to abandon the union, but he continued to believe that all operations could make money under a union scale if cooperation replaced rapacity. But that sort of salvation was not forthcoming, and in 1927 Bertha-Consumers Coal was placed in receivership. Jones's chief creditor was Pittsburgh Coal. Jones paid a visit to William Warden and tried to sell out, but the president of Pittsburgh Coal rebuffed Jones. "Our policy," Warden informed Jones, "is to mind our own business and run our business to suit ourselves and make money." Warden's competitive rationale was designed to crush such independents as Bertha-Consumers and "buy their properties for a song."[6]

Pittsburgh Coal set the competitive standard for bituminous in western Pennsylvania in the mid-1920s. William Warden openly subscribed to the doctrine of "survival of the fittest," arguing that the well-being of Pittsburgh Coal depended upon how well management used its "brains and physical strength." Other industry spokesmen were only a bit less harsh. John D. Rockefeller of Consolidated Coal opined that wage cuts were simply a "temporary expedient." Charles Schwab of Bethlehem Steel hinted that the open shop was merely a device whereby 200,000 excess miners might be culled from the industry. Basil Manley suggested that what the soft-coal industry needed was not collective intransigence, but a J. P. Morgan to eliminate ruthless competition and a Henry Ford to make the industry efficient.[7]

Such remedies were not forthcoming, and conditions in the soft-coalfields continued to deteriorate. Through 1925 and most of 1926, many mines in western Pennsylvania operated at less than 50 percent of capacity. In October 1926 some activity developed in the wake of the British General Strike, but domestic markets for soft coal remained sluggish. Miners worked under three different scales: Jacksonville, continuously competitive, and 1917. Wages fluctuated wildly, sometimes soaring above the Jacksonville scale. Even the wages at the nonunion Hicks mines and Pittsburgh Coal mines rose above the Jacksonville scale due to the temporary opening of British markets. But the general tendency was for wages to fall. There was growing resentment among the UMWA rank and file about their union's adherence to the Jacksonville agreement while part of their membership had been subjected to the open shop. For some miners, the languid response of their international to Pittsburgh Coal's open-shop plan was a repeat of the Lewis sellout of 1922. Insurgent candidacies began to develop in District 2 in central Pennsylvania. On 20 January 1927, Horace Baker of Pittsburgh Terminal Coal announced that the open shop would be adopted in his companies' mines when the Jacksonville agreement expired on 1 April. Everyone even remotely connected with the bituminous industry was predicting a showdown in soft coal after 1 April.[8]

A preview of what was to come was played out at the mines of Bethlehem Steel and Pittsburgh Coal in the winter and spring of 1926. The men who occupied the boardrooms of those corporations understood that the open shop would not be established by executive fiat. Union miners were a hard-bitten lot and were expected to resist. The coal magnates therefore perceived their first chore to be the establishment of firm physical control over their mines and property. Miners who would not conform to the new regime were to be driven out. This meant that the operators had to increase mine security and obtain a reliable source of nonunion labor. Guards and strikebreakers were an established tradition in the soft-coal fields of western Pennsylvania. But the Great Coal Strike ushered in important changes and refinements in the tools of repression to be used against the UMWA.

Strikebreakers were introduced into the area's coalfields during the final two decades of the nineteenth century. Henry C. Frick brought black strikebreakers into the coke district during that period. Lewis Hicks imported trainloads of blacks into the Kiskiminetas Valley before and after World War I. In 1921 Pennsylvania's secretary of internal affairs counted only 3,430 black miners in the commonwealth's 1,236 bituminous mines. In 1927 some operators employed more black miners than white. In most cases, that condition would not endure, but it is nevertheless clear that the Great Coal Strike changed forever the racial composition of the bituminous fields in Pennsylvania.[9]

Until 1925 the soft-coal operators customarily relied upon sheriff's deputies to enforce their will. These men were hired by the operators or sheriff, sworn in by the sheriff, and paid by the coal companies through the sheriff. The deputies were mostly transients; some had dubious pasts and lived on the fringes of the law. Some, as in the Fannie Sellins case, were trigger-happy. Many were undisciplined and unreliable. After Pittsburgh Coal declared itself an open shop, its management decided to abandon deputy sheriffs for a private force of industrial police. Such men, known widely as the Coal and Iron police, held commissions granted by the state, but their activities were directed solely by their employer. The Coal and Iron police had been widely used in the anthracite fields. In western Pennsylvania their activities had been confined to the railroads, steel mills, and manufacturing complexes such as those owned by Westinghouse. Bethlehem Steel had long employed industrial police, and the conversion to their use at Bethlehem Mines posed no problem. Pittsburgh Coal had no industrial police of its own, and in January 1927 it set about to find a man to organize its force. Major Lynn Adams of the Pennsylvania State Constabulary recommended Captain J. G. Searsch, head of the Pennsylvania Railroad security police, to William Warden. Warden wrote to Pennsylvania Railroad President

W. W. Atterbury asking for Searsch, and he lost no time in granting the captain a leave of absence.[10]

In April 1927, the press reported that Pittsburgh Coal had more than two hundred industrial police in the field. Searchlights were mounted in gun towers, and around-the-clock patrols were instituted. The purpose of the industrial police was to protect company property. They did so by isolating the miners in their company towns. Strangers were not admitted without a pass. A special effort was made to detect and intercept "union agitators." Through their use of industrial police, Pittsburgh Coal was reasonably successful in closing off their properties. But their use of scab labor was not immediately successful. Many of the strikebreakers were professional "bounty jumpers," who took bonuses or advances and then fled the scene after a few days. The chief of Bethlehem Mines' industrial police told his superiors that it was "needless for [him] to comment upon the type of employee [required] to answer the need of the hour. Keen supervision and surveillance was needed at all mines. No one was permitted to leave the camps until they had settled their just debts."[11] Not all operators followed Pittsburgh Coal's lead to the letter. Some retained the services of deputy sheriffs. Others hired white strikebreakers exclusively. But the general pattern of repression established at Pittsburgh Coal appeared throughout the soft-coal fields in one form or another.

On 1 April Valley Camp and Pittsburgh Terminal Coal joined the nonunion camp. They were joined several months later by Clearfield Bituminous Coal, which was owned and operated by the New York Central Railroad. Other companies that had closed under the Jacksonville agreement reopened nonunion in the spring and summer of 1927. The UMWA reeled under the growing tide of repudiation. Only the Central Pennsylvania Coal Operators' Association held out an olive branch to the union. It rejected the Jacksonville scale and called for a continuation of collective bargaining and a resumption of negotiations. The Pittsburgh operators were far less conciliatory. J. D. A. Morrow of Pittsburgh Coal told Basil Manley that so far as he was concerned there "was no strike and there were no problems." His company was "done with the Union." It would not sign a contract with the UMWA "no matter what wage reductions they might prepare to accept."[12]

The anti-union movement was strongest in the lower Allegheny Valley, the Pittsburgh district, and Washington County. A common view prevailed that the area within a thirty-five-mile radius of Pittsburgh would provide the crucial test of strength and will of both the operators and the UMWA. All eyes were focused on the mines of Pittsburgh Terminal Coal at Coverdale, a few miles south of Pittsburgh. Following Horace Baker's open-shop proclamation on 1 April, guards were brought in and barracks for strikebreakers were constructed. Eviction proceedings were brought against striking union miners. Pittsburgh Terminal had done business with the UMWA for three decades and lived up to its obligations under the Jacksonville agreement until it expired. To what extremes Pittsburgh Terminal would go in order to shed the UMWA had been a matter of open speculation, but by June it was clear that it had emulated its chief rival, Pittsburgh Coal. Thirty miles north on the Allegheny River, two large Valley Camp mines also acquired open-shop standing. James Paisley had run a union operation since World War I and, like Pittsburgh Terminal, had adhered to the provisions of the Jacksonville accord until its expiration on 1 April. On 21 May the Valley Camp mines reopened—nonunion. Seventy-five strikebreakers, said to be largely foreign-born whites and a dozen blacks, marched to work under the watchful eye of five state police and a dozen deputy sheriffs. In normal times the two mines employed 900 miners and had a payroll of $1.5 million a year. Union miners lodged in 180 company houses were offered the jobs first, and upon refusal faced eviction. The Paisley interests were based in Cleveland and appeared no more subservient to the Mellons than Pittsburgh Terminal had been. They claimed, however, not to be able to compete against nonunion scale. In June and July mines in Harwick, Harmarville, Russellton, and Curtisville also rejected the union. A. R. Pollock of Ford Collieries had joined the management of Valley Camp in restoring the union contract in 1922. No such return to the union fold was forthcoming in 1927. In August the Freeport Thick Vein Association joined the central Pennsylvania and Pittsburgh operators in a final repudiation of the UMWA. By 1 September all but a few small operators in the lower Allegheny Valley had turned their backs on the union miners.[13]

Although the first two months of the strike were relatively peaceful, the decision of the operators to employ strikebreakers supported by guards assured widespread violence. As the presence of scabs and their yellow-dog protectors increased, so did the incidence of physical conflict. Even though Bethlehem Mines achieved open-shop status in 1926, the head of its Coal and Iron police reported more than five hundred separate incidents involving guns and dynamite in 1927. And so far as he was concerned, UMWA organizers were a force for peace—violence was the work of even more inflammatory elements in the miners' ranks. Destitution and deprivation brought on by job displacement fed the fires of hatred on the picket lines. As the strike wore on, Basil Manley reported that differences over the wage scale were almost forgotten. For union miners, guards and scabs were deadly instruments employed to force their imminent extinction. Their endurance was thus pitted against the seemingly inexhaustible resources of the operators.

There is little doubt that most operators would have preferred to keep their regular miners on the job; they accordingly offered jobs to employees of long standing. Most union men refused, and even some foremen and supervisory personnel quit rather than face a nonunion industry. For a miner to surrender his union status was considered a display of abject cowardice. It was also exceedingly dangerous. A union miner who scabbed on his fellows was subject to abuse both on and off the job. Name calling, beatings, and "accidents" awaited turncoats. Shootings were not uncommon, and many a defector's home was burned or dynamited. Moreover, a scab's family could expect permanent pariah status. Tales of familial ostracism that endured for generations are legend in the soft-coal fields. Impoverishment brought on by months of attrition forced many to scab in 1927. Some changed their names and moved around. Others with families moved to mines where they were not known. But the hard core of the union stood fast, and Basil Manley reported the "union wives" were often more militant than their husbands. The soft-coal miners' loyalty to the UMWA and fear of reprisals forced the operators to rely upon strikebreakers, particularly during the first six months of the strike.[14]

Available evidence suggests that those strikebreakers were drawn from every ethnic community, race, and geographic region in the nation. Nevertheless, public attention and subsequent opprobrium fell chiefly upon the black strikebreaker. The UMWA lost no time in making race an issue in the conflict. Philip Murray claimed that Pittsburgh Coal had imported more than 50,000 black scabs since 1925, a figure undoubtedly inflated for effect. Murray complained to the Pittsburgh Council of Churches that the presence of the blacks was a menace to society because they engaged in widespread dope peddling and bootlegging. Murray also pandered to social fears by accusing the black miners of "mingling" with white women. Murray's rhetoric could not obscure his union's failure to deal with the issue of race. In 1921 a black delegate to the District 5 convention warned his white brothers that black strikebreakers were the product of UMWA racism. He demanded equality of opportunity for the black miner and claimed "that when the black man is treated as the other races of men and given the privilege of making a livelihood, you and every other man in this hall will say that the black man stands for something. But how in the name of God can we stand for anything when you have closed the door and avenues of life against us."[15]

The UMWA had apparently learned little from the widespread use of black strikebreakers in 1922 and by Pittsburgh Coal in 1925. The editors of the *National Labor Tribune,* an UMWA nemesis, chided Lewis, Murray, and Fagan for their failure to put an end to jim crow. The *Tribune* was an organ of the coal operators, but its delight at this union failure reflected reality. Black strikebreakers who had belonged to the union waved their cards in the faces of strikers, saying, "You would not work with me before the strike. Now I have your job and I'm going to keep it." A young black miner employed at the Pittsburgh Plate Glass mine near Creighton on the Allegheny River cited job discrimination as his reason for abandoning the UMWA. He was barred from day jobs and was never able to increase his tonnage by receiving assignments at the best faces in the mine. Such men saw the strike as an opportunity to improve their station in the soft-coal industry without giving much thought to long-term consequences. A researcher at Pittsburgh Coal observed black men working as motormen, fire bosses, and checkweighmen, jobs that were largely closed to blacks before the strike. It would be a mistake to conclude from all this that the purpose of the open shop was the advancement of racial democracy in the mines. A leading company reported 900 black and 800 white miners in its employ in January 1928. The following September, after the union had been broken, the same company reported 1,500 white and 750 blacks on its payroll. As red-neck union miners returned, the proportion of blacks receded, but never to pre-1927 levels.

The condition and status of blacks within the UMWA and the Pennsylvania bituminous industry was not altogether clear-cut. Despite charges by the *National Labor Tribune*, a hard-line policy of jim crow did not exist in the UMWA. John H. Jones, president of Bertha-Consumers Coal, the sixth-largest operator in the Pittsburgh district, reported that he had employed black union miners long before the strike. Black and white miners lived in separate patches, but a black man had been elected as president of a local union representing his miners. Clearfield Bituminous Coal, operating in Indiana County, represented the other extreme in the black miner's condition. Superintendent F. D. Welsh testified before a Senate investigating committee that his company never hired "colored men," "Spaniards," "Mexicans," or "people of that class." His company believed that there were many efficient black miners, but they were not welcome in his mining camps. Welsh explained that the employment of blacks would decrease the "standing of the community, particularly its schools."[16]

The Reverend John Skrak, pastor of Saint Clement's Church in Ellsworth, documented the changing racial demography in his parish for the Senate committee. Skrak served parishioners in Ellsworth, Bentleyville, and Cokeburg in Washington County. Many of his congregants were employed by Bethlehem Mines, a force so dominant in Ellsworth that the only properties not owned by that company were the railroad station, post office, and church. Skrak knew the region well and claimed that before 1925 there were only three black families in his parish. In March 1928 he estimated that the black population had grown to as much as 50 percent of the community. Despite efforts to keep him away from the strikebreakers, he discovered that many of the men trucked in at night by Bethlehem Mines were professional scabs or misinformed innocents who knew nothing about mining. Superintendent H. H. Calloway of Pittsburgh Terminal Coal's No. 3 Mine at Coverdale indicated that most of the black miners in his employ were also inexperienced. It is likely that that was the case everywhere. A survey of 173 blacks working in the mines during the strike established that 75 had found work there simply as a temporary measure to escape unemployment. There were 23 local steelworkers, 26 common laborers, and 26 listed no specific occupations. Some were hired right off the streets of Pittsburgh and left quickly when they discovered the rigors of mining, the hostility of the union men, and the Spartan life offered by the coal patches. At one time Pittsburgh Coal acknowledged that 45 percent of the miners employed in its eighteen mines were black. Black miners employed by Pittsburgh Terminal rose to 42 percent of its total. Company officials admitted that many of those men were "floaters" and that "turnover" did little to increase productivity. It is probable, then, that most black strikebreakers were not renegade unionists victimized by a racist UMWA, but were simply desperate men in search of a decent job. Most did not find such a job in soft coal. Given the circumstances, it is not surprising that the companies welcomed back their union red-necks once the strike was broken.[17]

The UMWA had no official strategy for dealing with strikebreakers, black or otherwise. The work of Fannie Sellins apparently had not been carried on. The traditional response of the union rank and file to the use of scabs was violence, on and off the picket lines. Events that transpired in New Kensington in June 1927 were probably typical of the labor and racial violence that occurred throughout the coalfields. Valley Camp Coal Company operated two mines—Puckety Creek and Kinloch—near New Kensington. Under the Jacksonville agreement, 950 men, 100 of whom were black, worked in relative harmony. Fred Broad, Fannie Sellins's son-in-law and local real estate entrepreneur, established Lincoln Beach in 1925. This "exclusive city for colored folks" was located three miles from the Kinloch mine. The Reverend Guy Johnson, a black miner, was Broad's chief salesman. Fred Broad was a staunch ally of the UMWA, and his community was not designed to provide a haven for strikebreakers. Nor was it just another black coal patch carefully tucked away in some remote hollow. It was a diverse community that abutted a major highway. Neat homes situated on residential lots enabled Broad to make a statement on race. Unfortunately, a stable black community closely connected to the UMWA made little visible impact on the conduct of local union miners.[18]

On 3 June three black men arrived by train in New Kensington. The local union miners had the passenger station under constant surveillance. When the men entered, they were asked, "Where are you going?" They replied, "To work at Kinloch." Angry words followed, and fists flew. As the fight spilled out into the street, an angry mob joined the miners. Two of the strikebreakers were armed, and Homer Brooks of Homestead began shooting, wounding a man. As the mob scattered, the black men ran for their lives. The fortuitous arrival of the local police spared the community more bloodshed. The blacks were charged with weapons violations and spirited off to the county seat. Seventeen other blacks were ordered to leave town by the chief of police. Sheriff William Feightner took control of the community, posting orders forbidding more than two persons from congregating on the public streets at any one time. Feightner had twelve deputies on duty at Kinloch, but he called upon the state constabulary for assistance. Fifteen gray-uniformed troopers patrolled the streets of New Kensington for several weeks. Strikebreakers were escorted to the mines under heavy guard. In February 1928 Kinloch Superintendent J. H. Schweinsburg reported that 450 were working, half of them black.[19]

Violent incidents involving striking union miners and scabs were so commonplace that they defy precise enumeration. Ambushes, beatings, and bombings were daily events, but labor violence took on new meaning at Pittsburgh Terminal's Harmony No. 4 Mine, near Broughton, Allegheny County. Strikebreakers employed there were subject to all sorts of abuse. The children of union miners enjoyed stoning the men, while chanting "Scab" and "Yellow Dog." According to Herbert McCrory, a photographer for the *New York Daily News,* thirty black strikebreakers stationed themselves on a railroad trestle above the public school at Broughton and opened fire on the building that served local children. McCrory, an eyewitness, disputed the findings of a state police investigator sent in by Governor Fisher that attributed the shooting to the union miners. An incredulous McCrory told a Senate committee that the Coal and Iron police, who had watched his every move, were conspicuous by their absence. After the shooting, the scabs retreated to the company patch. When the company police finally appeared, they did nothing.[20]

Robert Vann, black editor of the *Pittsburgh Courier,* observed the escalating violence in the soft-coal fields with growing concern. Vann had a keen understanding of the economic factors that had brought about the strike as well as the racial issue that exacerbated the conflict. He had monitored Pittsburgh Coal and the implementation of its open-shop plan since 1926. Vann warned his readership of the dangers that awaited inexperienced blacks from the agricultural South. Such novices could expect exploitation, injury, or worse in nonunion "death-traps." Vann advised black miners that the UMWA was an alternative to the "trickery of calculating employers." Unorganized workers had no chance of getting fair treatment. Vann acknowledged that the UMWA was guilty of racist practices, but since it prohibited membership in the Ku Klux Klan, it offered genuine hope. Vann argued that the fate of all miners—white and black—would be determined by the Great Coal Strike. An open-shop victory for the operators meant the reestablishment of "industrial feudalism" in the coalfields.[21]

The editor of the *Pittsburgh Courier* was a civil rights activist. He believed that the strike and the black miners' role in it were part of a greater struggle for human dignity. Blacks were being made scapegoats in the conflict. "No real man," Vann mused, "wanted to be called scab." Vann was convinced that real competition between Northern and Southern operators did not exist, for he believed the entire industry was controlled by an interlocking directorate. What mattered most was that black miners not become fodder in an industry in which both black and white miners were victims. He urged the UMWA to desist in its distortions about black scabs, and urged the employment of more black organizers. Vann believed that there were enough loyal black union men in the pits to do that job, and he was probably right. Although the UMWA did not respond, the *Courier* continued to call the "race miners" to the union colors. Vann's editorials must have had some impact, for the *Courier* was banned in many mining camps.[22]

Robert Vann was also troubled by the caliber of law enforcement in the nonunion camps. Black miners were just as likely to suffer abuse at the hands of the Coal and Iron police as union miners. Vann began to document those abuses, citing the vigilante quality of private industrial police. On that issue, neither the *Pittsburgh Courier* nor the UMWA could have any quarrel. The *United Mine Workers Journal* condemned the Coal and Iron police as a private army of vicious thugs. The union preferred the state constabulary, which was efficient but neutral in most industrial conflicts. Basil Manley agreed. The constabulary kept order with "a minimum of friction and violence," but the work of the Coal and Iron police produced "bitterness and brutality." Manley would not allow himself to be drawn into the futile debate produced by charges and countercharges concerning company and union violence. He believed that it would be impossible "to sift out the facts." But he knew that private police would do little to enhance labor peace, for they were "a survival of the condition of industrial feudalism which should not be tolerated in a civilized community." Manley was personally aware of several cases in which Coal and Iron police had been jailed for their excesses, only to be returned to active duty immediately following their release. He believed that the only solution to this scandal in law enforcement was the abolition of all privately paid police forces as recommended by the United States Coal Commission in 1923.[23]

Condemnation of private police forces was not confined to the newspapers and union rhetoric. In August 1927 sixty-five New Kensington businessmen headed by Fred Broad petitioned Governor John Fisher for relief from the depredations of local deputy sheriffs. According to the petitioners, women and girls had been abducted and assaulted. It was alleged that private citizens had been arrested on trumped-up charges of disorderly conduct. The businessmen warned the governor that if the brutal assaults were not stopped, the law-abiding citizenry would be driven to desperate measures. Businessmen in Monongahela, Washington County, and Bruceton, Allegheny County, sent the governor similar petitions during the same month. Even the district attorney of Allegheny County joined the chorus of protest, denouncing the outrageous conduct and illegal methods employed by officers in Castle Shannon. But no reply was forthcoming from the governor's mansion. The private police system remained in place long after the Great Coal Strike had ended.[24]

The Coal and Iron police and company-paid deputy sheriffs went about their business apparently indifferent to the public opprobrium that they evoked. These men were a hard lot, and their job was difficult and dangerous. Two of their number were murdered near Denbo, Washington County, in February 1927. Many more were injured on the job. But these men did not inspire sympathy. They were in fact outcasts in most communities, widely regarded as mercenaries of the lowest type. The success of the open-shop drive was utterly dependent upon the work of these men and their charges, the strikebreakers. The relationship of the Coal and Iron police and the strikebreakers hardly constituted an alliance, nor was it particularly amicable, for race and temperament were perpetual problems. It was always difficult to determine whether industrial police were protecting the strikebreakers or guarding them as prisoners. In most cases they were probably doing both. In such circumstances their working relationship was extremely tenuous. Reporter Lowell Limpus of the *New York Daily News* concluded that the majority of the men he observed in the mines near Pittsburgh were working in a state of debt peonage: They owed the companies money and could not leave. Limpus faced drawn revolvers on several occasions and was admitted only because he was a newspaperman who had cajoled company officials into giving him a pass. Limpus visited

forty mines in Pennsylvania's bituminous fields and managed to interview some of the strikebreakers. At a Pittsburgh Terminal mine, he
learned that a hundred blacks had deserted to the union. They stole out
of camp to attend a union meeting a few miles away, but were observed
upon their return. They were subsequently beaten by the guards and
dragged before a "judge," a company official who meted out further
punishment. It is understandable why such men defected. A captain in
the Pittsburgh Terminal police acknowledged that one of his chief duties
was to patrol two strings of boxcars in which several hundred, predominantly black, strikebreakers were housed.[25]

Despite such deplorable conditions and practices, the widespread use
of guards and strikebreakers was a huge success for the operators. Coal
production fell off dramatically, but the mines were pumped and equipment maintained. The companies seemed content to trade the short-
term expenses for guards and strikebreakers for the lower wages and
higher profits in the long run. The strategy succeeded despite friction
between guards and strikebreakers and the earnest efforts of the union
to defeat them. Guards and strikebreakers enabled the operators alone
to dictate conditions in the coal camps. No matter how brutal coal camp
life became, the Commonwealth of Pennsylvania declined to intervene.
In the end it was the unity of the operators and the untrammaled use of
guards and scabs that accounted for the victory of the open-shop forces.

In many coal camps, miners lived in company housing and shopped in
company stores. Company stores and housing had been established long
before the 1927 strike. If a company wished to open a mine in a rural
area, the establishment of a store and housing for its miners became a
necessity. The companies also controlled the utilities, the roads,and
often the churches and school buildings. Such conditions clearly worked
to the advantage of operators when they converted to the open shop.
However, they did encounter one unexpected snag. Union miners who
refused to work without a union contract often would not vacate their
homes when ordered to do so. The UMWA posted thousands of surety
bonds with local courts in order to forestall evictions. That tactic brought
time for the UMWA, but worked a severe hardship on its treasury. The
operators quickly filled vacant housing with strikebreakers, and used the
guards to prevent harassment by union neighbors. The water and elec-
tricity of striking union miners were shut off, and roofs were even pulled
off their houses. Credit was denied at the company store, and the camps
were closed to outside salesmen and peddlers. The services of company
doctors were withheld, and access to the camps was all but closed to relief
agencies.

Even in the best of times, life in the soft-coal camps rarely rose above
bare subsistence. Years of depression reduced paychecks, and savings

dwindled. The strike brought new levels of "destitution, misery and brutality." Writer Fannie Hurst claimed that she had observed "human degradation" in the coal camps that exceeded anything she had seen on a recent trip to the Soviet Union. Senator Frank Gooding of Idaho, chairman of a Senate committee investigating the coal strike, believed that the hovels, squalor, and suffering in the camps constituted "fertile fields for the source of communism and other doctrines." The misery that mining families were forced to endure was a "blotch on American civilization" and should not be "tolerated in the heart of one of the richest industrial centers in the world." A local physician quietly toured the coalfields and concluded that malnutrition was a major problem. Milk, butter, meat, and fresh vegetables were scarce. "Bulldog gravy" (a mixture of flour and grease), bread, molasses, and tea had become staples. Colston Warne, assistant professor of economics at the University of Pittsburgh, reported that UMWA strike relief averaged $1.00 a week for adults, and $.40 a week for children. Maximum benefits per family were $5.00 a week in western Pennsylvania and $3.00 in central Pennsylvania. In December 1927 Warne estimated that 200,000 of 275,000 persons involved in the strike zone were "noncombatants." Feeding and clothing miners' families proved to be an impossible task for the UMWA. Warne also estimated that because of their impoverishment, fewer than 60,000 union miners remained on the picket lines in the Northern Competitive field at the end of the year.[26]

Despite public denunciation of conditions in their industry, the coal operators stepped up the pressure on the union miners in their camps. Strikebreakers were moved from shanties, tents, and boxcars into newly constructed camp barracks. The companies also filed suits requesting the courts to enforce the eviction of union miners from company housing. The operators stopped at nothing to break the spirit of the union miners. The Pittsburgh Coal Company evicted the Reverend William G. Nowell from his company house located in Hills Station, near its Montour No. 4 Mine. The pastor of Fawcett Methodist Episcopal Church had not preached "the gospel of company." He was, in fact, both a union sympathizer and a graduate student in sociology at the University of Pittsburgh. Nowell compiled data on conditions in the coal patches and testified before a special commission of the Pittsburgh Council of Churches. He was also seen in the company of union pickets. Nowell attempted to bring about a reconciliation of the UMWA and Pittsburgh Coal, but was told by mine superintendent H. M. White that his efforts were futile. The company had no intention of cooperating with the UMWA or any group of workmen. Company spokesman J. D. A. Morrow reiterated that position six months later. The UMWA had missed its opportunity to consider "remedial action" in 1925. Company spokesmen seemed unmoved by the suffering that the strike had wrought. When asked about the misery in his camps, R. B. Mellon replied coldly that he had not personally observed conditions at his mines. That was the function of the coal office, and he was not in the coal office.[27]

Not all operators were that cold-blooded, and some people questioned whether conditions in the nonunion camps were as bad as the union said they were. A reporter for the *Pittsburgh Post-Gazette* was hired on as a strikebreaker at the Coverdale No. 8 Mine, operated by Pittsburgh Terminal Coal. On 9 March 1928, he was escorted under armed guard from the Wabash Railroad station waiting room in Pittsburgh to a bunkhouse near the mine. He claimed that he was fed roast beef, potatoes and gravy, and was treated well. He was not sure how well his deception worked, but he casually questioned his newfound comrades in the pits. He encountered no resentment toward the Coal and Iron police. Indeed, most claimed they had never had any contact with the guards. Others claimed that they feared only the red-neck union miners. The reporter concluded that Coverdale people were not any different than workers in other industrial communities. His assumptions are, however, open to question. Coal miners were not inclined to pour out their hearts to strangers, for it was well known to all that the operators employed a network of spies. Complaining to strangers about the industrial police or conditions in the mines would not have prolonged a man's time on the job. By March 1928 most companies, including Pittsburgh Coal, had cut back their police forces, a sure sign that the strike was winding down. If the *Pittsburgh Post-Gazette* had acted six months earlier, its reporter might have had a significantly different impression. Had he entered a Bertha-Consumers mine, he might have concluded that the operators and the UMWA were just troubled friends. John H. Jones preferred the union, but competitive conditions forced him to abandon it. He insisted that his miners accept nonunion scale, or leave. They refused. He served eviction notices. He doubled, tripled, and quadrupled rents. He threatened to attach furniture and personal belongings in lieu of payment of back rent. All of these ploys were bluffs, for his heart just was not in it. Finally he offered to exempt the men from back rent and legal costs if they would leave. The men left.[28]

It is improbable that roast beef and gravy became a standard benefit derived from the open shop, but it is clear that most operators were in dead earnest when evicting their miners. During the last six months of 1927, twelve thousand Pennsylvania miners and their families were driven from the coal camps. Pittsburgh Terminal Coal served its initial eviction notices in April, and Valley Camp followed in May. The UMWA struck back with surety bonds and the construction of union barracks, both of which were disastrously expensive alternatives to company housing. In the weeks following the eviction notices, explosions destroyed mining equipment throughout the coalfields. Even the homes of supervisory personnel were the target of the dynamiters. A union miner claimed that the dynamite campaign in the Kinloch area was the work of agents provocateurs hired by the Paisley interests, but that would have been a terribly expensive method of discrediting the union.

In August mines operated by the Republic and Iron Steel Company near Russellton began evicting their miners. The furniture of the Russellton miners was auctioned in September to pay back rent. Fred Broad redeemed the belongings of 120 families, spending $7,500 in the process. But few such "angels of mercy" were available to the UMWA. As the union treasury was depleted, construction of union barracks failed to keep pace with evictions. As winter approached, 250 mining families were housed in schools and churches in the Russellton district, and the union issued a plea for clothing. When the first snow fell, some miners' children were barefoot, and one woman died of pneumonia during a transfer to the rude union barracks. By mid-December 3,000 persons lived in union barracks, often without heat, in the Russellton district alone.[29]

In the end, the courts were responsible for the mass evictions from the camps. In August 1927 Pittsburgh Terminal Coal filed suit in the superior court of western Pennsylvania, requesting the execution of eviction notices sent out in May and June. Judge F. P. Schoonmaker heard testimony of both coal operators and the UMWA. Witnesses for Pittsburgh Terminal testified that since 1 April the company had spent $15,000 a month for guards, $135,000 for barracks construction, and had suffered a total loss of $1.5 million since the strike began. Since the living quarters of loyal workers were "frequently in the midst of the houses of union strikers," the company asked the court to act decisively on evictions. It also asked the court to restrain the UMWA, for working miners had to run a "gauntlet of attacks" every time they went into the mines. Their families were also subject to "abuse, insults, systematic heckling and annoyance." On 30 September the judge issued an order enjoining the National Surety Company from granting additional appeal bonds from the UMWA. The union was forbidden to disburse its funds for that purpose, and its miners were ordered to move out of company housing. Union picketing was also limited. Picket stations of no more than three persons were to be set up no closer than one hundred feet from company property. Congregating, parading, and intimidation were forbidden. Since Valley Camp, Union Collieries of Renton, and Consumers' Mining of Harmarville had supplied supportive testimony on behalf of Pittsburgh Terminal, it was widely assumed that further litigation on the question of evictions and picketing would be futile for the union. The Schoonmaker injunction had brought a decisive turn of events to the strikebound Pittsburgh district, but public attention was quickly diverted to events that transpired in a court fifty miles northeast of Pittsburgh.[30]

In November 1927 J. N. Langham, presiding judge of the Indiana County Court of Common Pleas, issued an injunction against UMWA miners on strike at the Clearfield Bituminous Coal Company mine located at Rossiter. The order was so sweeping and punitive that it could be construed only as an invitation to the union to disband. Under its provisions, the UMWA was forbidden to do anything common to an industrial strike. The union could not picket, march, or gather for meetings or rallies. It was prohibited from dispersing union funds as relief for striking miners. The judge's prohibitions on vile language and physical intimidation were understandable, but his order forbade the union men "from saying or doing anything to cause the men [who were] working to quit or cause men seeking work to refrain [from doing so]." Communication by billboard, signs, or newspaper advertisements was deemed a violation of the order. All of this quite naturally raised questions about the violation of First Amendment rights, but that was not terribly unusual. What raised a furor was the judge's prohibition against the singing of hymns and the holding of church services on two lots owned by the Magyar Presbyterian Church, situated directly opposite the drift mouth of the mine.[31]

Judge Langham's prohibitions against hymn singing account for the instant notoriety of his "Rossiter injunction," and in ensuing months *Rossiter* became synonomous with repression. That was ironic, because Clearfield Bituminous Coal Company did not qualify as the most vicious strikebreaker in the soft-coal fields. Unique circumstances rather than ruthlessness catapulted the Rossiter scenario into the national headlines. Prior to the discovery of coal deposits in 1898, the Rossiter area had been inhabited by German, Scots-Irish, Welsh, and Scandinavian farmers. Clearfield Bituminous, a subsidiary of the New York Central Railroad, built the town at the turn of the century, and named it for E. W. Rossiter, treasurer of the railroad. During the next quarter-century the company, its union miners, and the town prospered. The company abided by the Jacksonville agreement until it expired on 1 April 1927. Like most other western Pennsylvania operators, Clearfield Bituminous hoped for a readjustment of wage scales. When negotiations with the union did not materialize, the mines were reopened on a nonunion basis in midsummer. Some union miners returned to work while others went on strike, thereby splitting the community into bitter factions. Strikebreakers, all of them white, were imported. Deputy sheriffs patrolled the town and the mines under the nominal supervision of County Sheriff John Malcolm.[32]

Rossiter was a company town, and virtually everything in it belonged to Clearfield Bituminous. The only properties to which striking miners had access were the two lots owned by the Magyar Presbyterian Church. The titles to those lots had been donated by Clearfield Bituminous to the original congregation years before the strike. When the original congregation faded away, the property was ceded to a lay preacher and his flock. That minister, A. J. Phillips, just happened to be vice-president of the Rossiter UMWA local. The strategic value of the church properties was immediately apparent, for strikebreakers had to pass it on their way to work. It was more than mere chance that many of the "church services" coincided with the shift changes at the mine. The Rossiter strike lasted more than a year and a half, and the prolonged suffering that it produced no doubt inspired deep resentment and bitterness. Christian charity must have been strained to its limits, and passing scabs probably had things said to them that were not to be found in hymnals or prayerbooks.[33]

"Onward, Christian Soldiers" and "I'm on the Winning Side with Jesus" were traditional hymns. But Langham was probably correct when he perceived that "We'll Get You Bye and Bye" was sung in a way designed to intimidate strikebreakers. He was clearly embarrassed by the flap over his injunction, and even sent a check to the church in order to buy hymnals for "religious purposes." Langham's heavy-handed insensitivity was not the only thing that invited attack. He had based the injunction upon allegations contained in a bill of particulars presented in his court by attorneys for Clearfield Bituminous Coal on 30 August. The November injunction was issued ex parte. Hearings would not be conducted until 10 May 1928, and the injunction did not become final until 21 May 1928. Although the question of a hearing escaped national attention, the *Pittsburgh Press* claimed that the "Rossiter injunction" was the most drastic ever issued in that coal strike or any other labor dispute in the history of the commonwealth. The *Press* averred that Judge Schoonmaker's injunction was "mild" by comparison. The publicity generated by Langham's injunction eventually attracted out-of-state journalists and a U.S. Senate investigating committee to Rossiter during the winter of 1928.[34]

The senators came to Indiana County after touring mining camps and taking testimony in the Pittsburgh district and the lower Allegheny Valley. After establishing their headquarters at Indiana's Moore Hotel, they began holding public sessions. The committee heard testimony given by coal operators and union officials concerning conditions in the region. But Rossiter was their chief interest. Newspaperman Lowell Limpus had whetted their appetites in earlier testimony about his trip to Rossiter in December 1927. He likened his visit to a journey among isolated, destitute medieval serfs. Limpus professed shock at the degradation of "good American types," "New England Yankees," whose womenfolk were "cultured, refined and educated."[35] Limpus described a guardhouse that had been erected in front of the church so that Judge Langham's prohibition against hymn singing could be enforced. Limpus had good reason to remember the guard station, for the deputy on duty had drawn his gun on the newsman. Intrigued, the committee made a quick trip to Rossiter. They visited the Magyar Presbyterian Church, and the Reverend Mr. Phillips and his congregation put on a hymn-singing demonstration.[36]

Company officials expressed few regrets about their actions in Rossiter. They had tried to negotiate with the union. They had not imported black or Mexican strikebreakers, nor had Coal and Iron police been employed. The termination of a thirty-year relationship with the UMWA was predicated upon economic necessity, not union busting. Vice-president A. J. Musser did not believe Judge Langham's order was particularly drastic. Clearfield Bituminous had originally given title to the church lots to a genuine religious denomination. Unfortunately, control of the church had fallen to a union constituency that had not used the churchyard for hymn singing before the strike. Langham's order was not a violation of freedom of worship, but a blow against a union subterfuge.[37]

Clearfield Bituminous attorney James Mack was subjected to rigorous questioning by the Senate panel. Several members of the committee had served in the supreme courts of their respective states, and they made it clear that an application for an injunction that employed such broad language would never have passed muster in their courts. Implying that Judge Langham was merely a rubber stamp for the coal operators, Montana's Burton Wheeler argued that the court had no right to issue even a preliminary injunction that employed such broad language. The injunction prevented the union from employing "any scheme, ways, means, or methods," or from "doing any acts or uttering any words" to prevent the mine at Rossiter from operating. Mack countered that the injunction was proper, and that the UMWA did not even have the right to express its point of view in newspaper advertisements. An irate Senator Frank Gooding of Idaho sputtered that "songs couldn't hurt anyone," and Wheeler warned that wholesale denial of civil liberties would "breed anarchy." The incredulous senators also learned that Judge Langham had issued not one but three blanket injunctions in 1927, and that he had issued his first repressive order in 1925. Blanket injunctions were not new in Indiana County. It was the religious twist and not the denial of civil liberties that had thrown Rossiter into the limelight.[38]

The committee members seemed more subdued when Judge Langham appeared before them. Langham said that his original purpose was to get the parties into court so that he could determine the facts in the conflict. He admitted that he had issued the injunction solely on the basis of affadavits supplied by Clearfield Bituminous Coal, ex parte. Senator Robert Wagner of New York asked the judge why a hearing had not been held. Langham replied that the union had never asked for one, an accusation that union organizer John Ghizzoni repudiated as "a flagrant, glaring untruth." Wagner asked Langham if he could even recall a case in which an organization was restrained from advertising in a newspaper. The judge admitted that he could not. Wagner asked Langham if a striker had no right to speak to someone who was employed at a place where a strike had been called. Langham replied that no one had the right to persuade or restrain anyone who wanted to work. Langham also defended his prohibitions against congregating and singing at the Rossiter church. It was a defense against union intimidation and was not meant as an attack on religious freedom.[39]

The editors of the *Indiana Evening Gazette* were quick to defend their judge against charges made by outsiders. In their opinion, Judge Langham was as "just and fair a jurist" as ever served on the court of common pleas. Another commentator quipped that the Senate committee was always accompanied by "an able force of newspapermen [who bugled] their every unconsidered remark to the outside world long before their findings could possibly reach the authority that sent them." Pennsylvania's politicians were less than ecstatic about the arrival of the committee or the sensational publicity it generated concerning the strike. The senators were, after all, uninvited guests, who would only embarrass the powerful Mellons, a major force in the Pennsylvania Republican party. With the exception of Gifford Pinchot, who was in temporary retirement, most prominent politicians—Republican and Democrat—refused to become involved in the conflict. Pinchot was a champion of the UMWA, but limited his comments to condemnation of the Coal and Iron police, an old enemy. Governor John Fisher scrupulously avoided involvement in the strike. He met with Philip Murray and Pat Fagan in April 1927, and announced that he would not "inject himself" into the bituminous strike. In December of that year, John L. Lewis invited Republican Senator David Reed to sponsor a call for a federal investigation of the strike. Reed acknowledged the "distress in Pennsylvania," but declined to sponsor the resolution for an investigation. Reed told Lewis that by "taking sides," he would "destroy his usefulness" in the commonwealth.[40]

Governor John Fisher was perhaps the most pathetic political figure during the strike. Fisher was born and raised in the coalfields of Indiana County. He had served as a director and attorney for Clearfield Bituminous Coal. Fisher was probably the first governor in the history of the commonwealth really to understand the bituminous industry, yet he chose to remain aloof from the conflict in soft coal. Critics charged that Fisher was a tool of the Mellon interests and simply stood by and allowed the operators to work their will in the coal camps. Others suggest that he was simply a conservative politician who disdained government interference in the private sector. Fisher never revealed his reasons for remaining aloof from his state's most serious labor conflict. His papers do reveal, however, that he was forced to intervene in a limited fashion when the public outcry became impossible to ignore. In November 1927 New Kensington's businessmen demanded that Fisher prevent the eviction of miners from their lodgings at the Inland Coal Company, situated at Indianola, in Allegheny County. Fisher intervened, and requested the coal company to defer the evictions until union barracks were completed. The attorney for Inland Coal grumbled that the union men were interfering with the work of the nonunion miners, but promised the evictions would not be "pre-emptory."[41]

Fisher was also unable to avoid the growing controversy concerning the Coal and Iron police. It was well known that his predecessor, Gifford Pinchot, had revoked many of the commissions for industrial police. A reporter for the *Pittsburgh Press* announced that under Fisher the ranks of the industrial police had swollen to more than 3,000 men, and that the administration of these commissions by the state was in shambles. The UMWA complained that Coal and Iron police records had been arbitrarily closed to union investigators. Fisher responded by appointing a veteran officer in the state police as a full administrator of the industrial police system. His job was to investigate applicants for commissions and eliminate the bad apples. This satisfied no one. Critics continued to complain that the operators had an army of "private gunmen" at their disposal, and that the governor's reforms were little more than cosmetic. Fisher countered that legislation was the only remedy. He acknowledged that the Coal and Iron police system was "wrong in theory" but argued that the 305-man state police force was insufficient to control industrial strife and criminal activity at the same time. Only the state legislature had the power to eliminate the industrial police and expand the constabulary.[42]

Fisher bristled when U.S. Senate investigators got into the act. An advance guard of that committee arrived in Pittsburgh during the first week of February 1928. Fisher was no doubt aware that Senator James Couzens of Michigan had refused to serve on the committee because he "did not want to be part of a travelling circus." Although a majority of senators on the committee were Republican, Pennsylvania's political establishment suspected that the committee's whirlwind tour through the coalfields had been arranged in the interests of publicity. Democrat Burton K. Wheeler did nothing to allay Fisher's suspicions about his committee's intentions. After taking a brief tour of some mining camps in the Pittsburgh district, Wheeler made it clear that the committee on which he served would not maintain a low profile. The hills of western Pennsylvania were "the most fertile breeding grounds for Bolshevism" the senator had ever seen. It was inconceivable to him that "helpless women and children" were being evicted from their homes in the dead of winter. Wheeler also failed to understand how the state of Pennsylvania had turned over law enforcement in its mining villages to Coal and Iron police employed by the coal operators.[43]

John Fisher understood that Wheeler's final allegation was aimed at him, but his anger soon gave way to acute embarrassment. After the committee completed its work in Pittsburgh, it moved to Indiana where it focused upon the Rossiter injunction and its author. Judge Langham and the governor were old friends, and both were deeply pained by the grilling to which the judge was subjected. Democrats Robert Wagner of New York and Burton Wheeler were polite to the judge—perhaps excessively so—but their disapproval of his injunction verged on accusations of judicial incompetence. Long before the Senate hearings, Langham had assured his political friends that his order did not curtail religious freedom. Apparently dazed by the intensity of the interrogation of his friend, Fisher wrote Langham and admitted that he had never heard of the "Rossiter injunction." Fisher expected that he would also be called as a witness and asked the judge to brief him. Langham avowed that his order had been distorted by misrepresentations in the press and by the prejudice of Wagner and Wheeler. He insisted that the prohibitions against hymn singing on the church lot were not aimed at religious practices but at union intimidation. He simply was protecting the rights of men to work. He also claimed that his order did not preclude the distribution of food and clothing, but prevented the use of union funds for the "furtherance of a conspiracy to prevent persons from going to work."[44]

Fisher had no intention of enduring the kind of public interrogation to which his friend Judge Langham had been subjected. He informed Senator Reed that if he received a subpoena from the Senate, he would "throw it in the wastebasket." Fisher advised Reed that if the Senate was sincerely interested in rescuing the bituminous industry from its "deplorable state," it should convene a conference composed of the governors of the bituminous states, representatives of Congress, and the secretary of labor. The aim of such a conference would be the establishment of uniform wages in the bituminous industry, wage arbitration, the equitable adjustment of freight rates, and the regulation of coal production. If the Senate continued on its present partisan course, the situation in the soft-coal fields was hopeless.[45]

Fisher was annoyed by reports that he would be called before the committee. In March he made a speech to the Easton Board of Trade in which he broke his "customary silence" and blasted the Senate investigation committee as a tool of partisan political opportunists. The governor wondered why Pennsylvania had been singled out for special criticism; it was common knowledge that bituminous was in trouble throughout the Central Competitive Field. The solution to the problems in soft coal could be found "in the brain of the states, not in the small minds of petty politicians." Fisher called for the national bituminous conference that he had suggested to Senator Reed, and encouraged his constituents to ignore "rumors" concerning his impending appearance before the Senate. Fisher was in fact engaged in a game of cat and mouse with that body. Throughout March and April he led the senators on a merry chase. He asked for a list of specific questions in advance. Had invitations been given to governors of other bituminous-producing states? Would wages, freight rules, and regulation of production be discussed? Did the Senate invitation imply that the governor of a sovereign state was accountable to that body? Fisher made it clear that he would "not go to Jerusalem to pay tribute." The Senate committee responded that it did not claim the right "to supervise the acts of a governor of a sovereign state," but its assurances yielded nothing. Fisher had no intention of appearing. That refusal and his "emphatic chastisement" of the Senate committee earned him the praise of old friends. Fisher never appeared, and on 1 May the Senate investigation drew to an unspectacular close in Washington. Only two senators and a handful of spectators were on hand, for interest in the soft-coal strike had waned. The work of the committee neither yielded reform legislation nor alleviated the suffering in the mining camps.[46]

During the first week of May, the Federal Council of Churches also issued a final report of its findings on the coal strike. The report condemned the unilateral abrogation of the Jacksonville agreement as "bad business ethics." It repudiated the industrial police and recommended a resumption of collective bargaining. But the Council of Churches went far beyond holding hearings and issuing reports. The Reverend F. Ernest Johnson had set the council's strike investigation in motion in December 1927 and was instrumental in organizing its miners' relief program in the following spring. Eleven Protestant denominations were joined by Roman Catholic and Greek Orthodox parishes, as well as the Jewish community, in a joint relief effort. Food and clothing were distributed by such parish priests as the Reverend James Cox of Saint Patrick's and by social workers representing fifteen agencies. The work of the church council was supplemented by a Pittsburgh Businessmen's Relief Committee, headed by A. K. Oliver. By mid-April fifty mining villages in the Pittsburgh district were being served from four substations by the Joint Relief Committee.[47]

Although miners outside the Pittsburgh district did not enjoy the services of a blanket organization like the Joint Relief Committee, they did receive relief from diverse sources. Local businessmen extended credit and put on benefits for the miners. Veterans' organizations, ethnic associations, churches, clubs, and central labor unions also contributed funds. Private philanthropy was carried on by such men as Fred Broad, who saved miners' furniture from the auction block, and Dr. E. W. Cross of Tarentum, who treated the miners and paid for their medicine out of his own pocket. The UMWA encouraged community participation in the relief effort, for its miners could not survive on the meager strike benefits they received. Lewis and his associates were also acutely aware of the charges made by critics within and without the UMWA that the union was not taking care of its own. By December 1927 the UMWA verged on bankruptcy, a condition some attributed to official incompetence and corruption. The Pennsylvania and Ohio Relief Committee, a body composed of UMWA dissidents, the Progressive Miners Bloc, and Communists, entered the coal camps and distributed food, clothing, and anti-Lewis propaganda. By the end of January 1928 the distribution of relief had become a political football. The enemies of John L. Lewis were determined to drive a wedge between the union president and his miners. Food was their weapon, and destitution their ally.[48]

As winter turned to spring in 1928, it was clear to everyone that the UMWA had lost the strike. The union's avowed purpose had been maintenance of the status quo, not expansion into nonunion fields or mines. Critics were quick to assail the strategy as a repetition of that used in 1922. But had Lewis failed to adhere to those limited objectives, the 1927 strike would probably have collapsed even more rapidly than it did. A union strike fund, estimated at more than a million dollars in March 1927, was totally depleted by the dispersal of relief and the posting of appeal bonds to forestall evictions. The ranks of union organizers were far too thin, and the experiences of "floater" George Medrick are instructive. Medrick had an automobile, and a typical day carried him to Perryopolis, Banning, White Valley, Jacob's Creek, McKeesport, Brownsville, Youngwood, Fayette City, New Kensington, Duquesne, and Russellton. Medrick met regularly with parish priests and fickle boarding bosses, who rented rooms to miners, in a futile attempt to keep local miners in line. He spent much of his time haunting "scab joints": taverns, hotels, pool halls, and employment offices situated in downtown Pitts-

burgh. Such organizers as Medrick were tireless, courageous, and re-
sourceful, but they simply did not possess enough thumbs to plug the
growing number of leaks in the UMWA dikes.[49]

In July 1928 the Great Coal Strike ended in defeat, and the Jacksonville scale passed into oblivion. The collapse of the strike was not caused
by pusillanimous leadership, corruption, or mismanagement. Lewis had
drawn a clear line in the sand. Sick or not, the coal industry was asked to
maintain wage levels, and the union president had hardly assumed a
"soft" position. The policy of No Backward Step was probably unrealistic
and no doubt contributed to the intransigence of the operators. As the
conflict wore on, control of the industry became the unspoken issue. In
such a contest, the UMWA simply could not match the resources mar-
shaled by the bankers, steelmakers, and railroads who stood behind the
operators. If Lewis had equivocated or compromised in the face of that
formidable opposition, rivals and critics would undoubtedly have accused him of cowardice and betrayal. By standing firm against seemingly
insurmountable odds, Lewis did insure the loyalty of the rank and file to
the UMWA, if not to himself.

The union miners of western Pennsylvania were not a capricious lot,
and their loyalty to the union ran deep. Lewis, Murray, and Fagan spoke
their language and implemented a strike policy that the rank and file for
the most part supported. The union miner perceived no betrayal in
1927. Unlike in 1922, Lewis left no one to die on the vine; the men
understood that they had simply been beaten by a stronger party. Although the union miners were dispersed and their union reduced to a
shell, Lewis and the UMWA were not destroyed. The union would lie
dormant for six years and then erupt again when better times arrived in
1933.

Union insurgents and radicals had watched the decline of the UMWA
with interest. The Progressive Bloc had not appreciably weakened the
"Lewis machine." Nor had the dissidents effectively cultivated the dis-
affection of the UMWA rank and file from its union president. But the
failure of the Great Coal Strike seemed to offer new opportunities to
dislodge Lewis. The insurgents recognized that the disastrous strike
might well be their final opportunity to seize the UMWA from within.
Their best hope seemed to be John Brophy, whom they supported for
the union presidency in 1926. Brophy, who championed the restoration
of participatory rank-and-file democracy in the UMWA, had maintained
a low profile during the Great Coal Strike. He was never enthusiastic
about the Left, and always managed to keep it at arm's length. However,
when the insurgents invoked his name to "Save the Union," Brophy did
nothing to stop them.

4

Save the Union

INSURGENCY WAS NO STRANGER TO THE UNITED MINE WORKERS, BUT THE dissent promoted by the Progressive Miners Bloc during the early 1920s had a definite leftist flavor. The Progressive Bloc was in fact the first of the three organizations that advocated the seizure of the UMWA from within. The organization was dominated by Pat Toohey, Vincent Kemenovich, Anthony Minerich, and Tom Myerscough, all Communists. In 1926 they supported the candidacy of John Brophy against UMWA incumbent president John L. Lewis in the name of union democracy; Brophy lost. The Progressive Bloc had little to do with the planning and direction of the Great Coal Strike that erupted in April 1927. The Left did, however, attempt to maintain a high profile in the coalfields. The Sacco and Vanzetti controversy offered them an opportunity to state their case.

Nicola Sacco and Bartolomeo Vanzetti, Italian anarchists, were tried and convicted of armed robbery and murder in Massachusetts. The trial, which was conducted in 1921, took place in the wake of the Red Scare. Critics, some of them radicals, charged that Sacco and Vanzetti had been convicted because of their unconventional politics and nativist bigotry. Pittsburgh attorney Michael A. Musmanno, a friend of organized labor, helped to defend the two men. Powers Hapgood, a close friend and associate of John Brophy, was active in the Sacco and Vanzetti crusade. Toohey, Kemenovich, and Minerich organized parades and demonstrations throughout the coalfields. John Brophy, who was occasionally seen in their company, condemned the Sacco and Vanzetti affair as an attempt to "intimidate the masses."[1] Lewis, Murray, and Fagan managed to steer clear of Sacco and Vanzetti. They had a serious strike on their hands, and it was an issue that belonged to Brophy and his "Bolshevik friends" anyway.

Sacco and Vanzetti was the kind of controversy that the UMWA did not need in 1927. Lewis, Murray, and Fagan enjoyed the reputation of being conservative trade unionists. The local press lauded their union's refusal to call for recognition of the Soviet Union and the formation of a labor party as "fresh evidence of the essential conservatism" of the UMWA. Lewis had no reason to tamper with that image, but his radical enemies did not cooperate. Sacco and Vanzetti gave them an opportunity to agitate, to lead, and to exercise a measure of control. In districts where the radicals were influential, Sacco and Vanzetti rallies were often indistinguishable from strike activities. The radicals were reasonably strong in the Harmarville-Harwick-Cheswick district; 1,500 persons, many of them miners, attended a Sacco and Vanzetti rally there on 22 August. The rally was scheduled for 11:00 A.M. at Guido Grove, near Acmetonia. As speakers mounted a platform covered with American flags and signs carrying radical slogans, state police moved in to disperse the crowd. A lieutenant announced that the meeting violated the Allegheny County sheriff's order banning strike meetings, but the crowd refused to disperse. Tear gas was brought into play, and mounted officers charged into the crowd swinging billies. The crowd, blinded by the gas, broke in panic. In the view of some who were present, the officers pursued their duty a bit too zealously. They apparently continued to charge and beat persons who had clearly left the field of battle. In one such incident, a man pulled a revolver and shot Private J. J. Downey to death. Pat Fagan wasted no time in putting distance between the UMWA and the "Cheswick Riot." Fagan announced that "it was a Sacco-Vanzetti meeting and not a strikers' meeting. Our local union there had been asked to join in it, but had refused to do so as a body, leaving it up to individual members to do as they pleased. It was not in any sense a strike meeting."[2]

The radicals understood that opportunities such as the Cheswick riot might temporarily embarrass John L. Lewis, but sporadic acts of protest would never break his grip on the UMWA. The Left correctly perceived that the UMWA strike was going badly and reported almost gleefully at times on the depletion of union resources. UMWA operatives like George Medrick complained that the "Bolsheviks" seemed more committed to the destruction of the UMWA than to the defeat of the coal operators. The radicals emphatically denied this, claiming that the "Lewis machine," "election stealing," and "arbitrary explusions" were their targets. The insurgents also argued that they enjoyed a mandate rooted in the union rank and file. The movement to defeat the "Lewis dictatorship" was not therefore a plot hatched by "dual unionists," but was well within the established democratic traditions of the union.[3]

The inability of Lewis to feed his striking miners presented the Left with a promising opening. It responded in October 1927 by creating the Pennsylvania-Ohio Relief Committee. This committee was the second of three attempts by the Left to take control of the UMWA from within. Spawned by the Progressive Bloc, it also espoused militant leftist doctrine. However, its immediate purpose was to capture the allegiance of striking miners and their families. Feed the miners and their loyalty would soon follow. Since the Left had access to even fewer resources than Lewis, Pennsylvania-Ohio Relief failed. It served only to breed false hopes and to exacerbate bitterness and disillusionment in the coal camps.

Pennsylvania-Ohio Relief appeared at a time when strike discipline was eroding. As fall turned to winter, evictions accelerated and destitution became the rule. As hope faded and tempers grew short, control began to slip away from "safe and sane pacificists" in the UMWA. Pennsylvania-Ohio Relief not only promised relief, but goaded UMWA officials into open defiance of court orders. Mass picketing led to mass arrests and violence. The latter, more often than not, was directed against the agents of Pennsylvania-Ohio Relief; the UMWA could admit no loss of strike leadership. Unfortunately, the internecine struggle between "American" and "Bolshevik" miners also spawned random, wanton attacks of the sort that so often accompany a breakdown of order.[4]

Pennsylvania-Ohio Relief had, by February 1928, penetrated more than thirty mining towns in western Pennsylvania that had previously been the exclusive domain of the UMWA. The organization was most active in the Ellsworth, Bentleyville, Broughton, Renton, and Harmarville districts. It proclaimed a six-point program: mass picketing, defiance of court orders, nationalization of the coal mines, a six-hour day, a five-day workweek, formation of a labor party, and a nationwide coal strike. From its headquarters in Pittsburgh's Lyceum building, it distributed a trickle of relief, copies of its newspaper *Coal Digger,* and much anti-Lewis propaganda. Critics were quick to charge that its relief efforts were a fraud. Local clergymen complained that relief was used as bait, and miners who accepted it were expected to attend speeches by radical orators. Children of those miners were obligated to join youth groups that taught Communist ideology.[5]

Philip Murray dismissed Pennsylvania-Ohio Relief as just another Communist front organization, "boring from within." But Republican Senator Frank Gooding of Idaho, chairman of the Senate investigating committee, warned that Pennsylvania-Ohio Relief was a front for the Industrial Workers of the World. Gooding had fought the IWW while governor of Idaho and claimed that he had picked up the trail of the "I.W.W. monster" everywhere he went in the Pennsylvania coalfields. Gooding charged that repression by the operators was driving good UMWA miners into the arms of the IWW. Local clergymen also placed the IWW in the coal camps and alleged that Wobbly organizer W. J. Winger was working as an agitator for the coal operators. Investigative reporter Max Henrici did not link Pennsylvania-Ohio Relief to the IWW, but claimed that it spoke for a diverse radical community. Funds for its work were supplied by Norman Thomas, Oswald Villard, John Dos Passos, Sherwood Eddy, Amos Pinchot, and Samuel Untermeyer. Henrici also claimed that the organization was closely associated with International Labor Defense and the *Daily Worker*. Henrici alleged that UMWA exile John Brophy, recently returned from a tour of the Soviet Union, was also active in the organization.[6]

The Pennsylvania-Ohio Relief Committee was a loose confederation of Communists, Socialists, and other dissenters. Its supposed connections to the IWW were largely illusory, for there is no evidence to substantiate the presence of Wobblies in its ranks. Actually, Minerich, Kemenovich, and Toohey ran the organization, just as they had the Progressive Bloc. John Brophy was never a "member" of Pennsylvania-Ohio Relief, although he was occasionally seen in the company of the leadership. Although Brophy supported the nationalization of the coal industry, he was not a doctrinaire leftist. He, like many UMWA miners sympathetic to him,[7] correctly viewed Pennsylvania-Ohio Relief as a fragmented, transitional body, unable to deliver anything but propaganda. Ever the practical miner, he knew that the new body was simply an organization for and by radicals that enjoyed little credibility beyond that small circle of dissidents. Brophy was never comfortable with the Left and had avoided joining the Progressive Bloc and Pennsylvania-Ohio Relief. Both, he believed, flirted with dual unionism. Brophy was forever loyal to the UMWA and his estrangement from the union was due to political differences with Lewis rather than to an attraction to the ideological nostrums of the Left. Yet for all that, Brophy accepted the chairmanship of the Save the Union Committee when the radicals offered it to him.

The Save the Union Committee, which was organized in January 1928, was the third and final attempt by the UMWA dissidents and radicals to take control of that union from within. Its tactics and objectives differed only slightly from those established by the Progressive Miners Bloc in June 1923. The insurgent agenda remained the same: removal of John L. Lewis, recognition of the Soviet Union, expansion into the nonunion coalfields, creation of a labor party, nationalization of the mines, district and local autonomy, and rank-and-file control of the UMWA. Like the Progressive Bloc, Save the Union eschewed dual unionism. It issued no charters, collected no dues, and did not levy per capita taxes. The Progressive Bloc was created in the name of worker education. Its elected executive board was drawn exclusively from UMWA locals in western Pennsylvania, but the Left clearly dominated the organization. Communist William Z. Foster was its founder. Tom Myerscough and Vincent Kemenovich, fellow Communists, directed it. Save the Union was also dominated by the Left. John Brophy was its titular chairman, but Minerich, Kemenovich, and Toohey supervised the daily activities of

Save the Union. On 4 June 1923, the Progressive Bloc reported assets in the amount of $43.37. Save the Union was just as destitute, but it finally managed to bring Brophy into the fold.[8]

For nearly five years, Brophy had scrupulously avoided direct association with the Left. He had declined to attend the Progressive Bloc conference in 1923 and had counseled Powers Hapgood to do likewise. Brophy was simply not comfortable with Communists and regarded "boring from within" as one short step from dual unionism.[9] Brophy was a Roman Catholic, but he never expressly opposed the Left on religious grounds. His call for nationalization of the coal mines easily placed him in the left wing of the UMWA, but he was first and foremost a practical trade unionist. Doctrinaires controlled both the Progressive Bloc and the Pennsylvania-Ohio Relief Committee, and Brophy remained aloof from both. He was not, however, above accepting the aid of the Left when it served his purposes.

The bespectacled, slightly built, soft-spoken Brophy offered a sharp contrast to the robust Lewis. Brophy was born and bred in the coalfields and was a seasoned union fighter. He was widely respected in union circles, and his courageous leadership during the Somerset strike in 1922 enhanced his reputation. Brophy was among the first to charge Lewis with bad faith and desertion of the rank and file in 1922. That blast at Lewis earned Brophy the praise of the Progressive Bloc and many UMWA locals, particularly those in central Pennsylvania. Brophy also attempted to defend Powers Hapgood against retaliation by Lewis. Lewis ordered Brophy to drive Hapgood out of the UMWA, because the young Harvard reformer had "traitorously consorted" with the enemies of the UMWA by attending the conference of the Progressive Bloc. Brophy anticipated that Lewis's revenge against Hapgood would be swift and certain. And Brophy knew that as president of District 2, the one in which Hapgood worked, he would be asked to do the dirty deed. Brophy stalled, deferring Hapgood's dismissal to the district executive board. Hapgood had attended the Progressive conference knowing full well that Lewis was as "ruthless in the suppression of minorities as any king." Hapgood was a Socialist and had many friends in the Communist party. Brophy's defense of Hapgood not only solidified an already firm friendship, but also provided Brophy with a permanent, if unsolicited, link to the radical community.[10]

If John Brophy and Powers Hapgood differed in political temperament, each was nevertheless dedicated to union democracy and justice for coal miners. They believed the Lewis administration to be inimical to those ends. Brophy charged that Lewis had panicked in 1922 by sacrificing thousands of new union men in order to secure tonnage for the union. Each resented the iron grip that Lewis was fastening on the

UMWA—anyone who opposed the UMWA president was quickly labeled a "dualist, communist, or I.W.W.," and expelled. Both Brophy and Hapgood viewed the economic decline in the soft-coal fields with alarm. Brophy characterized the situation in his district as the worst depression in thirty years. In 1925 Buffalo, Rochester and Pittsburgh Coal Company, Buffalo and Susquehanna Coal Company, and Bethlehem Mines abrogated the Jacksonville agreement. Those companies had demanded relief from the Jacksonville scale for more than a year before adopting the open shop. They had appealed to the UMWA through the Punxatawney businessmen's association, but Brophy had refused to budge. Hapgood witnessed suffering in 1926 that presaged events in 1927. He visited Sagamore, a small, remote mining town in northeastern Armstrong County. A year before, the miners there had been asked to accept the 1917 scale. They refused. The mines were closed, and scabs were imported. Hapgood was moved to tears as striking miners' children, buffeted by gusting wintry winds, sang a hymn, composed by a local schoolteacher, to passing scabs:

Oh, stranger, why did you come here
and take our homes and bread away?
Oh, won't you quit your work today
and join us now, we pray.

We need you in our ranks today
Men brave and true with courage bold.
Now come and be a man, we say,
and join our happy fold.

In Union there is strength and might
So why oppose a cause that's right?
For God will lead us in our fight
and victory is assured.

Won't you join us, won't you join us
In fighting for our rights today?
We're going to win, we know we will,
So join us now we pray.[11]

Brophy and Hapgood suspected that far greater hardships lay ahead for UMWA miners. Unless Lewis was deposed, union miners might well lose everything that they had gained in thirty years of struggle. Hapgood decided to remain in Pennsylvania and aid Brophy. Lewis had brought an acute internal crisis to the UMWA and Hapgood perceived opportunities for "constructive work" within the union. What he had in mind was a plan to run John Brophy against John L. Lewis for the UMWA presidency. Brophy met with Hapgood and leftist editor Art Shields at Brophy's home in Clearfield on 5 July 1926, and plotted campaign strategy. Brophy apparently did not agree immediately to oppose Lewis. The reasons for his hesitancy remain a mystery, but the job of persuading Brophy to run fell to Hapgood. Two weeks after the Clearfield meeting, Hapgood made a journey to Pittsburgh and met with the Progressive Bloc. The clandestine meeting was "held in the quiet, so as not to draw the guns of Lewis" before the Brophy faction was ready. Less than a week later, Hapgood attended a meeting of International Labor Defense, another Communist organization. Hapgood learned that the Communists had planned to field a slate of candidates against Lewis. However, if Brophy chose to run, the Communist candidate would be withdrawn, and their support thrown to Brophy. Hapgood acknowledged that he was working closely with the Communists, but declined to join the party. If Brophy had refused to run, Hapgood was ready to support the Communist party candidate on principle. Brophy eventually agreed to oppose Lewis, but he never acknowledged this Communist connection privately or publicly.[12]

The support of the far Left was hardly sufficient to insure a Brophy victory. Lewis controlled the *United Mineworkers Journal,* chief organ of the union. He used that periodical to red-bait Brophy and his associates to good effect. Lewis also controlled the union treasury and patronage, and his disciples were no less zealous than Brophy's. Brophy had barely announced his candidacy before his supporters were considering the possibility of election fraud. The ballot boxes would be in the sole custody of the UMWA, and thus under the exclusive control of the incumbent. But the insurgents pressed their campaign anyhow. Since he had no access to the union journal, Brophy's camp issued news releases and open letters, written by its candidate. In these messages, Brophy promised to organize the unorganized, to restore UMWA integrity, and to press for nationalization of the mines and creation of a labor party. Brophy speeches were usually delivered with an accompaniment supplied by Lewis hecklers. The UMWA president left much of his legwork in western Pennsylvania to Phil Murray and Pat Fagan. By and large, western Pennsylvania was Lewis country, but there were pockets of Progressive support. Avella, in Washington County, was one such place. Fred Siders, Progressive candidate for the presidency of District 5, and Powers Hapgood "debated" Pat Fagan there for three and one-half hours in October. Hapgood was written off as a Harvard dilettante and not even a bona fide member of the UMWA. Siders and Brophy were dismissed as fellow travelers, dualists, traitors, and dupes of the coal

operators. In November Hapgood appeared in New Kensington in be-
half of Brophy. The president of the local union there attacked
Hapgood as a mischief maker and meddler who had earned less than
$500 in the mines, and he repudiated Save the Union as a contrivance
promoted by union-busting operators, Communists, and the anti-union
National Labor Tribune. Despite his popularity, Brophy's campaign never
took off. His supporters attributed his defeat to vote stealing by the
Lewis camp, particularly in locals situated in the lower Allegheny Valley.
Electoral chicanery was no doubt a factor in the campaign, but the
resources available to Lewis were simply too formidable for the Brophy
forces to overcome.[13]

The Brophy camp did not accept defeat gracefully. Following their
defeat in December 1926, they caucused and planned a second assault
against Lewis at the UMWA convention scheduled for Indianapolis on
25 January 1927. A week before the convention, Hapgood was expelled
from the UMWA by the District 2 executive board, which had been
prodded by its new district president James Mark, a Lewis man. (At
about the same time, Hapgood was elected as a delegate by the rebellious
local in Cresson, Pennsylvania.) Brophy was declared persona non grata
in his old district. Undaunted, Brophy, Hapgood, and Communist organizer Pat Toohey appeared at the convention but were refused delegate
status. Each was given time to speak, but was booed off the speakers'
platform. An attempt by the Cresson local to censure Lewis was crushed.
Motions calling for the recognition of the Soviet Union and the founding of a labor party were defeated. In a final display of mastery, the
Lewis forces declared Brophy a traitor and expelled him from the
UMWA.[14]

Brophy withdrew from the battle and moved to Pittsburgh, leaving the
opposition to Lewis in the hands of Hapgood and the Communists. The
latter never tired of what seemed to be a futile struggle. In May 1927
Hapgood acknowledged that they alone remained on the field of battle.
He praised their "courage, devotion and enthusiasm," but like Brophy,
he declined to join their ranks. Hapgood remained active, attending
Communist meetings and writing occasionally for the *Daily Worker.* Eventually, he was hired as a field-worker for the Pennsylvania-Ohio Relief
Committee. The Communists continued to claim Brophy as their own
long after "the rightful president of the UMWA" had retreated to the
sidelines, but Brophy seemed a bit demoralized by his exile. He not only
cut himself off from the Left, but he also refused to visit friendly locals
for fear of bringing Lewis's wrath down on them. In August he traveled
to Europe and the Soviet Union, where he met Trotsky and other
Bolshevik officials. Upon his return, he spoke to the University of
Pittsburgh economics department about conditions in the coalfields. He

also attended a Workers' Education Forum and an AFL conference in Pittsburgh. He toured the strikebound coalfields around Pittsburgh, but not once did he raise his voice against John L. Lewis.[15] For all the world, it appeared that John Brophy had quit the miners' fight.

But Brophy had not abandoned the struggle. During the first week of January 1928, he suddenly appeared at Pittsburgh's Walton Hall with 125 dissidents and organized the Save the Union Committee. Brophy never explained his renewed interest in opposing Lewis, but he later acknowledged that the committee was dominated by Communists. The Save the Union Committee of 1928, was not, according to Brophy, an organization, but a movement. He was "called chairman because he was the most prominent spokesman for its platform, which was his platform." Anyone could hold a meeting in the name of the committee. He guessed that most of the "public outcry" in the name of the committee was in fact the work of a "little, but incredibly hard working faction of communists who were trying to build themselves a base in the miners union." Hapgood, Pat Toohey, Vincent Kemenovich, Anthony Minerich, Ella Reeve ("Mother") Bloor comprised its leadership. With few exceptions, the program of the Save the Union Committee remained the same as that of the old Progressive Bloc. The "new movement" added mass picketing in defiance of court injunctions, a tactic borrowed from the still-active Pennsylvania-Ohio Relief Committee. It also announced that it would undertake a campaign to recruit all miners—black and white—working in both union and nonunion coalfields.[16]

The Save the Union Committee threw down the gauntlet to John L. Lewis and all his "conservative" supporters. "Liberal muckraker" Basil Manley was dismissed as a "dummy in the lap" of the UMWA dictator because Manley characterized Save the Union as a Communist and operators movement. A visiting Senate committee was also condemned. The editors of *Coal Digger* damned liberal reformists, the Coal and Iron police, the state constabulary, courts and injunctions, arbitration, and the established political parties. The last, and the ludicrous investigating committee that they spawned, were simply tools of the capitalists. Only an independent labor party, representing the laboring classes, was free to carry on the class warfare necessary to end exploitation in the coalfields. Save the Union took dead aim at 235 locals in UMWA District 5, as well as mines in the coke fields that had never been affiliated with the union. Party officials informed Powers Hapgood that it had strong representation in 29 UMWA locals, a substantial base from which their message might be carried to the union rank and file. The party made Save the Union its chief priority in western Pennsylvania. The efforts of such party field organizers as Rebecca Grecht were diverted to the coalfields, and party organizing became indistinguishable from Save the

Union recruiting. Grecht scoured the mining towns of Westmoreland, Allegheny, and Washington counties for recruits, and in doing so ran afoul of the state sedition law. Bail was quickly raised, and she immediately rejoined the fray.[17]

Save the Union made a direct appeal to black miners, a constitutency largely neglected by the UMWA. This effort featured black field organizers. Charles Fulp, an officer of a UMWA local in Washington County, was among the first. S. C. Nelson conducted secret meetings in the Kiskiminetas Valley, one of which was held in a black church on the mining property of Lewis Hicks. Isaiah Hawkins, son of a Baptist minister, was the most prominent black recruiter in western Pennsylvania. Hawkins's father was pastor of the Mt. Lebanon Baptist Church in Brownsville and was active in the relief committee in nearby Vestaburg. His son was a Progressive miner, determined to rid the UMWA of the "perfidious Lewis and his supine henchmen." Lewis expelled Hawkins, according to the *Pittsburgh Courier,* because Lewis feared his growing popularity:

> We white members cannot tolerate this sort of thing. This man Hawkins is getting too strong a hold. He has already attained the leadership of a large group of whites throughout western Pennsylvania, West Virginia, and Ohio. He must be stopped before his following spreads throughout the country and creates an embarrassing situation. He must be stopped now and thereby be prevented from getting into any of our meetings. It would not matter so much if his work attracted simply negroes, but he has a large and growing following among the whites.[18]

According to Hawkins, he joined Save the Union because Lewis had attempted to "delude and double cross" the rank and file. He never specifically cited racism as his chief target, although it was clearly an issue in the Save the Union crusade. The Kinloch disaster of February 1928 presented the Left with a delicate problem. All of the miners killed there were scabs, and half of their number were black. In the Allegheny Valley, *black* meant *scab.* T. J. O'Flaherty, a writer for the *Daily Worker,* covered the disaster and carefully skirted the issue of race. He acknowledged the callousness of local miners toward the misfortunes of those who would "never scab again," but he never directly addressed the racial issue that was clearly present. O'Flaherty opined that "a sentimentalist might slobber over such hardness," but not him. The conflict was "a war and belligerents don't wail over the enemy's misfortunes." "Yet the men were workers . . . hauled to Kinloch by union trainmen." Perhaps the Left was wise in making Kinloch a workers' issue rather than one of race, for in reality it was primarily a labor problem. Race would undoubtedly have obscured what Kinloch meant for all miners. All of this did not mean that Save the Union would always duck the issue of race. In April the movement made a point of electing five blacks to its executive board. It also pledged to end all discrimination against blacks in the UMWA.[19]

John Brophy, not race, emerged as the chief issue connected to Save the Union. He toured the coalfields in the company of the Left, sometimes with Socialists like Norman Thomas or Powers Hapgood, other times with Communists. Lewis and his following delighted in condemning the "traitorous" Brophy as a tool of the Left. Other misfortunes befell Brophy. James McGrew, editor of *Labor World,* appeared before the Senate investigating committee and accused Brophy of receiving money from Joseph Vitchestrain, editor of the anti-UMWA *National Labor Tribune.* McGrew charged that the money was delivered in a brown satchel during a secret meeting at a Pittsburgh hotel. The source of the cash was, according to McGrew, the Pittsburgh Coal Company. Brophy vehemently denied the charges, but never had the opportunity to rebut the charges before the committee, which was winding down its investigation. The brown-satchel affair has a rank odor about it, for its exquisite timing and seamy character resemble another incident that allegedly occurred in a Pittsburgh hotel in 1923. Less than a week after he had attended the Progressive Miners Conference, Alex Howat was accused of "mistreating" a five-year-old boy after enticing him to his room. Howat claimed that he had been "framed," but he never specified by whom.[20]

Brown satchels were not the only source of Brophy's problems. In March, he and Pat Toohey responded to an invitation to speak issued by UMWA Local 811, in Renton, Allegheny County. The Progressive Bloc had penetrated the local several years before, and Local 811 became a prominent thorn in the side of district president Pat Fagan. When Brophy and Toohey arrived for the meeting, they were greeted by deputy sheriffs and the state constabulary, and warned against giving "radical speeches." Brophy was introduced by the local union president, and delivered a speech on the aims of Save the Union. Toohey then took the platform and delivered a "two hour harangue" on all that was wrong with industrial America. He charged that the Mellons and Charles Schwab were attempting to "Mussolini-ize" the nation by using the Coal and Iron police to suppress the working class. After attacking the state and federal governments as tools of the capitalists, he condemned the American presence in Central America as imperialism. The United States Marines, Toohey explained, ought to "get the hell out of Nicaragua," At that point, a burley corporal in the state constabulary, apparently an ex-marine, stepped forward and knocked Toohey down. The meeting was dispersed. Brophy and Toohey were arrested for inciting to riot, a charge that was later dropped after the American Civil Liberties Union intervened.[21]

Brophy's final act as chairman of the Save the Union Committee, was an appearance at its first and only convention held in Pittsburgh on 1 April. A reporter for the *Valley Daily News,* drawn to the convention by reports of the "Red Menace," described what transpired at Pittsburgh's Labor Lyceum:

> Pittsburgh, huge mills, dark, overgrowing, stretching for miles along the banks of streams running full; many trains, narrow streets, slipping from a misty rain; towering structures against a black sky; slums climbing bleak hills . . . Here in the slums, the meeting.
> Labor Lyceum. Emblematic of Pittsburgh, City of Steel, great steel girders support the roof, and a balcony too, clings to them. This balcony . . . grim mass of workers, shapely men . . . held up by steel. No rafters shaking here from the cheers; the mighty steel is too solid.
> On the stage, a group of men, gaunt faces, tired, a youth or two among them. Stern jaws, protruding cheek bones. Downstairs, rows of men, many rows. But in the front, women: A queerly silent crowd, roared to anger only against Lewis.

The reporter went on to describe the ragged band of participants. Anna Mondell of Renton, standing by her rebel husband, had little more to lose. They had suffered eviction. Their furniture had been confiscated. The Lewis machine had denied them access to UMWA relief. The Communist Pat Toohey, "boyish, Irish, square-jawed and golden tongued," joined in the denunciations of the Lewis machine and its corruption. The aging Ella Reeve Bloor declared that her constituents, the miners of Indiana, were starving. Only Save the Union held out hope to them. The journalist questioned whether people who could not afford to buy lunches during a convention would be able to feed starving miners in the state of Indiana. Nor did Toohey and Bloor appear to be much of a menace, "red" or otherwise. The reporter was even less impressed by Brophy, whom he found to be "laboriously formal" and ineffectual on the speakers' platform. Brophy's appearance was apparently not one of the prouder moments of his life, for he rarely spoke of it later. Several weeks after the convention, he resigned his chairmanship for reasons of "ill health." It was far more likely that he was sick at heart. Contact with Brophy could only bring offending miners retaliation from Lewis. And the course charted by Save the Union would only lead to more hardships, suffering, and misery.[22]

Despite a ragged appearance produced by collective destitution, the Save the Union conference did consider a serious agenda. Eleven hundred delegates, including more than four hundred from western Pennsylvania, elected Pat Toohey permanent secretary of the committee. Following pledges of racial equality, five blacks were elected to the national executive committee. William Boyce, a black miner from Indiana announced that for the first time in twenty-eight years he had been able to express himself at a union function. Isaiah Hawkins reminded his fellow delegates that they had come not to discuss the race problem, but to defeat Lewis. Brophy concurred and pushed for the adoption of the established agenda: creation of a labor party, nationalization of the mines, defeat of the Lewis machine and organization of the unorganized. But the convention went beyond what John Brophy liked to call "his program." The entire organization was mobilized for a strike in the coalfields. The date set for the walkout was 16 April. More than 250 delegates represented unorganized territory, and they pushed for a union drive in their regions. The convention agreed. In Pennsylvania, the Save the Union strike would focus on miners situated in Fayette, Westmoreland, Greene, and Somerset counties. Specific targets included Pittsburgh Coal Company mines in Delmont, Bethlehem mines in Washington County, and Carnegie Steel pits. Save the Union hoped to recoup the losses suffered by the UMWA in 1922 and 1925.[23]

Brophy's silence on this bold but futile strategy probably reflects his growing disillusionment with Save the Union. He resigned shortly after the strike began without comment. He must have known that a motley group of doctrinaire amateurs would not succeed where John L. Lewis had failed. Brophy understood that his adversary was neither a fool nor an incompetent. Lewis had not sold out in 1927; he had been beaten by superior forces. Save the Union seemed to offer movement—the UMWA strike was dead in the water by April 1928. For some angry, disaffected miners, movement and militance seemed to offer hope. By declaring their own strike, the Left hoped to steal the strike leadership from Lewis, and thereby control the hearts and minds of the UMWA rank and file. Brophy knew that the soft-coal miners' zeal was never too far removed from his common sense, and he surmised that the appeals of the left would fail.

The Communist party mobilized its forces and placed them at the disposal of the Save the Union Committee. The April strike was declared its first priority. Coupons were sold to raise money for relief efforts. After the strike was underway, the party hoped miners would be enrolled. On 16 April Save the Union picket lines appeared at scattered locations throughout western Pennsylvania, but the strikers numbered far fewer than the 100,000 predicted by some committee spokesmen. Reports in the press indicated that many of the picketers were women and children. Committee spokesmen claimed that 10,000 responded to the strike call, but probably only half were miners. On the second day of the strike, the *Pittsburgh Post-Gazette* surveyed twenty-two mines in western Pennsylvania. It counted 200 men, women, and children at the Pittsburgh Terminal mines at Avella; 250 marchers at Bethlehem's Acme Mine; 81 men, women, and children at Valley Camp's Kinloch Mine; and 400 pickets at the Pittsburgh Coal Company Mine in Delmont. The *Post-Gazette* reported that not a single miner in the old Frick Mines had left the pits—a major defeat for Save the Union in the coke fields, which were the prime target of Save the Union. The committee hoped to recruit those miners in Westmoreland, Fayette, and Washington counties who had been deserted by Lewis in 1922. Save the Union pickets appeared at Bethlehem's Acme Mine near Bentleyville on 2 April, two weeks before the strike officially began. One hundred twenty ragged men, women, and children appeared carrying banners: "Down with Charley Schwab and his open shop system." "Rid Bentleyville of all scabs." "To scab is to be a traitor." "Russia is progressing." "Down with all injunctions." "No wage cuts." On 16 April more than 500 Save the Union pickets staged two marches at Acme. Men, women, and children chanted, "Kill the yellow dogs and cossacks." A pitched battle ensued, and the pickets were easily driven off by the constabulary and industrial police. On the following day, 150 women fought the police at Acme; after that, relative calm was established. Production was not much affected by the work of the pickets. The chief of security at Bethlehem Mines believed that the Save the Union Committee was far less potent than earlier UMWA efforts had been. Sparsely attended meetings continued in the Bentleyville area until mid-August, but the industrial police did not regard them as particularly dangerous. Powers Hapgood and his wife, Pat Toohey, and Anthony Minerich attended rallies at Grant's Hall in Slickville, Westmoreland County, but the ever-present Coal and Iron police, in and out of uniform, kept those meetings under control. Bethlehem's superintendent of Security reported that Save the Union had largely spent itself by midsummer in his district.[24]

Save the Union enjoyed surprising success in the Kiskiminetas Valley, a region deserted by the UMWA in 1922. Lewis Hicks operated more than a dozen mines there, all of which were nonunion. Hicks's miners did not participate in the 1927 strike, and there was little reason to expect them to answer Save the Union's call. A representative of the Pennsylvania-Ohio Relief Committee had appeared at a miners' benefit in Apollo in mid-March. But spokesmen for Save the Union expressed surprise when more than 500 pickets appeared at mines near Apollo, Vandergrift, and Leechburg. Organizing in the Kiskiminetas Valley had been severely limited due to a shortage of funds. The *Daily Worker* reported that S. C. Nelson, a black organizer, had convinced black miners originally imported as scabs to answer the call of the rank and file in spite of past discrimination by the UMWA. Black organizer Frank J. Nelson (perhaps the same man) appeared at rallies with Minerich, Bloor, and Hapgood at Apollo's Lyric Theater on 25 April. The strikers in attendance represented more than a dozen mines, including the Vandergrift Mill Mine. The coal operators and local press were quick to label the strike a failure, nuisance, and inconvenience brought about by the "radical wing of the United Mine Workers." Unlike past strikes in the Kiskiminetas Valley, the Save the Union walkout was peaceful, and its participants took pains to point out that they were not "IWW's." The local press exhibited an unusual degree of sympathy for the miners, blaming the strike on the operators who had "brazenly violated both legally and morally, a pact which they had made with the union."[25]

At one point in the strike, three thousand of twelve thousand Kiskiminetas Valley miners were idled. The walkout, described by local miners as a "volunteer affair," did not blow over so quickly as predicted. The strikers managed to cling to their picket lines for nearly three weeks without an arrest or violent incident. On 1 May a Save the Union striker was involved in an altercation described as "a near shooting scrape" with a foreman at Vandergrift's Pine Run Mine. Less than a week later, a detail of state constabulary arrived in Vandergrift. They toured the mines in full battle dress and informed the strikers that Save the Union had no standing in Westmoreland County and that picketing would not be allowed to continue. They had come to enforce the order of Sheriff Ray Johnston forbidding picketing as dangerous to peace and order. News of Brophy's resignation sealed the fate of the strike, which collapsed in mid-May.[26]

The Save the Union strike was followed by a wave of UMWA reprisals. John L. Lewis correctly attributed the strike to four Communist dominated factions: the Save the Union Committee, the Pennsylvania-Ohio Relief Committee, the International Workers' Defense Association, and the Workers' Party. Locals that had done business with them were banished from the UMWA. Recalcitrant miners who would not recant were both ostracized and subjected to terrorism by Lewis's goons. Red Scare paranoia swept through the coal patches. Strangers who entered the coal camps were routinely asked, "Are you a Bolshy?" The wrong answer to that question might provoke a decisive response from deputy sheriffs, state police, and UMWA functionaries alike. At times, they seemed to be working in concert to defeat the "red menace."[27]

John Brophy could not in truth deny that Save the Union was dominated by Reds. The predominance of Communists may have been the chief reason he disassociated himself from the movement. The estrangement of Brophy from the radical Left proved to be ugly—and perma-

nent. In June 1928 Brophy heard that the Left was planning to bolt the
UMWA for another union. He told Hapgood that the leftist factions
were "creations of chance" who shifted so rapidly that "one had to be
pretty agile to keep up with them." He warned his friend that the
radicals had "definitely taken the road to dualism." Hapgood was no
more pleased with the prospect of a second miners' union than Brophy.
He dashed off a letter to his old friend Tony Minerich and posed three
questions: If the new union was to be composed mostly of strikers, on
what basis would they be put back to work, considering that there would
be both the old union and the coal operators fighting the new union?
Would there be any miners with jobs in the new union? Would revolutionary discipline permit one to sign a contract at a wage reduction to let
the new union get started, and if not, how would the members of the
new union live while they were getting control of the coal industry to
make the Jacksonville wage scale possible? Although a Socialist,
Hapgood was an experienced UMWA organizer. Like Brophy, he believed that organizing coal miners had to reflect the art of the possible.
Coal miners were practical men who often had large families to support.
Ideology alone did not put bread on their tables. Minerich's reply was of
small comfort to the skeptical Hapgood. Minerich expected to organize
miners with jobs in nonunion territories, particularly West Virginia and
Kentucky. (The UMWA had enjoyed little success in those states.)
Minerich's reply to Hapgood's first question was cryptic. According to
Minerich "some places went back to work [with an] open shop as a local
union." He did not think the "Lewis crowd" would do much infighting,
for Lewis supporters could get $25 a week. Minerich's reply to
Hapgood's third query was more precise: "Revolutionary [discipline] will
and must permit a movement to be defeated. . . . We fight as hard as we
can, but if we meet defeat we cannot help what we do. We will do the best
under the circumstances." As for wage scales, that question would be
dealt with as a matter of "realism."[28]

Minerich went on to become cofounder of the National Miners Union,
which was organized in Pittsburgh during September 1928. His in-
coherence on matters of organizational philosophy and strategy may
perhaps be attributed to excessive zeal or to an inability to be articulate in
English. The decision of the Communist party to abandon the reformist
Save the Union Committee for the creation of a rival coal miners' union
was not simply a knee-jerk response to failure. The Communists had
plunged into extensive self-analysis following their April strike. The
party acknowledged that its coal strike had faired badly, but claimed to
have organized dozens of units scattered throughout the Pennsylvania
coalfields. They asserted that those units averaged between fifteen and
thirty-five members, and that total membership exceeded four hundred

miners. Actually, many of the units represented mining communities in which the Progressive Bloc and the Pennsylvania-Ohio Relief Committee had long been established. Nevertheless, Save the Union accomplished something that had never been seen before in the coalfields of western Pennsylvania. The Left had managed to call soft-coal miners out on strike. The radicals hoped to build upon that limited success. Party functionaries believed the strike had gained their movement many sympathizers, but in the end it had not increased party membership in the coalfields. In fact, they eventually admitted that party membership in soft coal had suffered a sharp decline late in the strike. Party committees had become so involved in the strike action that the tasks of party building had been sorely neglected. An organization with tighter control and command might avoid such pitfalls in the future. In their quest for a well-coordinated, disciplined miners' union, the Communists made no effort to expel moderate Socialists such as Powers Hapgood and James Maurer, but were prepared to write them off if necessary. The National Miners Union was preeminently an organization of militant, revolutionary Socialists.[29]

The ideological gulf between John Brophy and the Communists continued to widen during the summer of 1928. The American Civil Liberties Union defended Brophy and Toohey against charges incurred in the Renton incident, but Brophy clearly continued to put distance between himself and the Left. Brophy told Hapgood that "boring from within" had failed, and the Communists had nothing left but to go down the dubious road of dual unionism:

If the UMWA was smashed there would be some chance for another union, but it is not in that condition. It is sadly weakened—very much so—but it can still carry on. Tony Minerich thinks of the new union as a propaganda affair rather than a working union. That will be all that it can amount to, I fear. It will provide a base of some kind for a few of the boys to work from. It will degenerate into another extra-communist organization. That may be all right for the communist miners, but it is not building a new union.[30]

John Brophy and Powers Hapgood did not join the National Miners Union. Hapgood remained on its fringes, as an interested observer, but Brophy condemned it publicly. He lamented the withdrawal of the Progressive miners from the UMWA, for their departure left the coal miners at the mercy of the "forces of reaction." Without the Progressive Bloc, Brophy warned, honest coal miners could expect nothing but terrorism from Lewis's "goons" and "paid gangsters." Mother Bloor snapped that a "traitor" like Brophy had no right to criticize those who chose to carry on the struggle, and likened him to the men who had signed the death warrants of Rosa Luxemburg and Karl Liebknecht. For Bloor, the line had been clearly drawn between those "who stood for the masters and those for the slaves." Powers Hapgood was appalled at Bloor's vindictiveness and rushed to defend his friend. "Brophy is not a traitor or coward," Hapgood scolded Bloor. "He believes as I do that what will be created is not a trade union, but a propaganda sect." He reminded Bloor that he had not joined the National Miners Union or the Communist party. The Socialist party might be slow and conservative, but its members were not required "to conform to orders from above." Despite Bloor's diatribe, Brophy had not gone soft on John L. Lewis. He continued to chastise the UMWA president as a "hypocrite and wrecker" whose "presence in the union [was] an insult to every honest man." These were harsh words from a man who would willingly return to the Lewis fold during the early days of the New Deal. But in September 1928, Brophy was out of the fight. Only the National Miners Union, perhaps the most radical union ever to function in western Pennsylvania, remained in the field to oppose Lewis and the coal operators.[31]

5

The National Miners Union, 1928–1933

THE SCENE WAS REMINISCENT OF A MEDIEVAL SEIGE. SEVERAL HUNDRED thugs, mustered by the UMWA, lined the streets and sidewalks outside Pittsburgh's Labor Lyceum on Miller Street. Bricks, bottles, clubs, truncheons, taped chains, and brass knuckles were much in evidence. Several attempts had been made to storm the entrance to the building, but they were repulsed by stout defenders within. The defiant occupants, midwestern delegates to the first National Miners Union Convention, had occupied the hall the night before. NMU delegates who arrived later were not so fortunate. They were beaten with impunity, for a UMWA badge exempted its wearer from arrest. Police were present from start to finish, and intervened only after the beatings had been administered. More than one hundred NMU delegates were arrested, but the UMWA goons spent not so much as a minute in jail. Delegates who escaped were followed to their lodgings at the Monongahela House and Home Hotel and beaten there.[1]

The leadership of the National Miners Union had reason to expect violence at their meeting. On 7 September, two days before the convention opened, violence erupted at a union meeting in Bentleyville. Louis Carbone, a Lewis loyalist, attempted to distribute UMWA fliers condemning both Save the Union and the NMU. Charles Glovak and George Moran objected, denouncing Lewis and his following "as a bunch of dirty thieves." A brawl soon followed. Carbone pulled a gun and began shooting, wounding Glovak and his son. Moran was killed. It was also common knowledge among miners that special "pickets" were being recruited at $25 a day by Pat Fagan. Their purpose was the disruption of radical locals. NMU miners were not inclined to turn the other cheek, but they were vastly outnumbered by UMWA men in the Pittsburgh district. A contingency plan was therefore prepared. While the attention of the UMWA focused on the Labor Lyceum, the NMU convened a second morning session at the Workers' House in nearby East Pittsburgh. That redoubt was situated high on a hill, and rocks and bottles were piled on the porch for use against intruders.[2]

By the time sheriff's deputies and UMWA pickets arrived at the second site, the work of the convention had been completed. Deputies kept the rival groups apart, and further violence was averted. John Watt, an Illinois miner, and William Boyce, a black Indiana miner, were elected NMU president and vice-president. Pat Toohey was designated secretary. *Coal Digger* became the official organ of the NMU. NMU districts were identical to existing UMWA jurisdictions. Powers Hapgood, in the company of John Brophy, had arrived by taxi at the Labor Lyceum just after the melee. Brophy was equally unpopular with both sides in the conflict, and he wisely chose not to remain. Hapgood lingered on the scene for several days, even though he admitted feeling "out of it." One "had to be a communist to be part of the decision-making process" in the NMU. Philip Murray justified UMWA violence against the NMU on the grounds of self-defense and anti-Communism— charges that Hapgood decried as "hypocrisy and lies." Hapgood's response to UMWA violence seems a bit pious, since he himself condemned the new miners' union as "dualist." Hapgood knew that the UMWA had never been tender when dealing with that heresy, but Hapgood's indignation concerning Murray's public explanations of the conflict was not unjustified. The UMWA vice-president claimed that the street violence was inspired by Coal and Iron police and coal company "hirelings" employed by the NMU. He attributed the founding of the NMU to "imported communist leaders" from Canada and the western United States. Murray argued that although 268 UMWA locals had chosen more than a thousand delegates to attend the NMU convention, he insisted that no Communist locals existed in western Pennsylvania. Murray knew better. According to the *National Labor Tribune,* more than eighty UMWA locals had been suspended in the wake of the Save the Union strike. If the NMU did not enjoy numerical majorities in locals at Renton, Avella, Harwick, and Bentleyville, they were nevertheless hotbeds of Communist activity. Small wonder, then, that Murray and his associates conducted a campaign of street violence in order to "impress upon the communists the grave injury they were attempting to do to the trade union movement of America, particularly to the U.M.W.A."[3]

The efforts of the UMWA to prevent the birth of the National Miners Union failed. Even if the Lewis forces had succeeded in smashing the NMU convention, it is unlikely that that sort of defeat would have discouraged the Communists. They were a tenacious, courageous lot. Recent scholarship has tended not to portray Communists associated with the labor movement as agents from Moscow. Rather, they are perceived as "typical members of a millenarian sect, ideologues and bickering zealots" who "naively worshipped at the Russian shrine." Those who directed the NMU in western Pennsylvania appear to fit that mold. Missionary zeal and creative energy enabled Pat Toohey, Vincent Kemenovich, Anthony Minerich, and Tom Myerscough to compensate for the meager resources available to them. The NMU was never much more than a skeleton union, and yet it was able to set strikes in motion in spite of seemingly overwhelming odds. More often than not, miners identified with the organization were blacklisted by the coal operators, and the NMU became what was essentially a union of unemployed miners, just as John Brophy had predicted. Destitute miners did not pay dues, and the union leadership was reduced to the status of beggars. Tag days and other fund-raising devices proved to be poor substitutes for a steady flow of union dues. Contributions from external sources were important to the organization, but the absence of financial records renders a precise analysis of their magnitude impossible. The NMU repudiated the checkoff, for it was a device employed by the "Lewis machine." The status of their membership made the use of the checkoff an irrelevant issue, and the NMU lost nothing by eschewing it. Impoverishment became a permanent state of affairs for the Communist miners, and they wore it like a badge of honor.[4]

NMU miners were, of course, denied access to UMWA relief. Such institutions as the Roman Catholic church, which aided the UMWA, were also loathe to support anyone identified with the Communists. The birth of the NMU occurred just before the Great Depression enveloped western Pennsylvania. As the Depression deepened during the early 1930s, Pittsburgh became a center of Catholic activism. The Reverend James Cox, "Pastor to the Poor," led hunger marches in order to bring attention to the plight of the region's industrial poor. Cox's activities rivaled those of the Communists, for hunger marches were a favorite tactic of the NMU. Later in the decade, the Reverend Charles Owen Rice emerged as the leading spokesman for Catholic trade unionism in the steel city. Rice admitted to being a "Catholic radical," and defended unionism as "a Christian thing." An ardent anti-Communist, Rice defended Brophy, Murray, and the CIO against charges of Communist subversion. Brophy and Murray later directed an anti-Communist purge within the CIO. It is, however, unclear whether their opposition was rooted in Catholicism, anti-dualism, or both. During the late 1920s and early 1930s, their condemnation of the NMU focused upon dualism rather than Communism. Brophy, like Murray, believed that the existence of the NMU damaged the cause of coal miners no less than the corrupt methods and "fascist terrorism" employed by the "Lewis gang."[5]

While in exile, Brophy warned NMU president John Watt that dualism would cause the "waste and diffusion of the all too meager numbers and resources of the progressives, leaving the reactionaries in unchallenged possession of the U.M.W.A." Brophy argued that there was no "mass demand" for a new union, and that NMU membership would never be large enough to force concessions from the operators. For Brophy, dualism was no solution for the failure of "boring from within." His objection to the NMU was not a matter of religious scruples, but reflected the practical outlook of coal miners. Rank-and-file miners who remained loyal to John L. Lewis even after the 1927 debacle dismissed the NMU organizers as "jackrabbits": men without a real program for miners who jumped from pit to pit spreading anti-Lewis propaganda. Such men looked upon NMU functionaries as "spoilers," who packed their thin picket lines with large groups of pitiful women and children in order to exaggerate their presence. The NMU was never able to overcome the image of "spoiler," and working miners did not flock to their banner in very great numbers.[6]

The decision to organize a rival Communist union was, according to Theodore Draper, a decision made by the upper echelons of the party. Field organizers in the Pittsburgh district enthusiastically accepted the new line and implemented it with missionary zeal. John Watt described the September convention that founded the NMU as a meeting of starving men. Destitution had no doubt been exacerbated by the Save the Union strike, which had been launched during the previous April. In the months preceding the formation of the NMU, party membership among miners in western Pennsylvania fell to fewer than two hundred. It was those members who constituted the dependable hard core of the NMU. Field organizers, such as Bill Dunne, Frank Borich, and Rebecca Grecht, were sent to Pittsburgh to organize the miners. But it is clear that Pat Toohey, Anthony Minerich, Vincent Kemenovich, and Tom Myerscough remained the heart of the NMU in western Pennsylvania. Without them, the NMU would have evaporated. Communist critics of the miners' organizing campaign attributed falling membership among miners to strikes that were conducted at the expense of "organizational tasks." In fact, party resources had been stretched to their limits, and many party organizers were forced to abandon the fight in a state of sheer exhaustion.[7]

Three weeks after the founding of the NMU, Pat Toohey informed Powers Hapgood that two hundred NMU locals functioned in the Central Competitive Field. The Communists viewed women and children as an integral part of their new organization, and auxiliaries and youth groups were included in their count. The number of miners actually enrolled is therefore virtually impossible to determine. It is probable that no more than two dozen of these amorphous locals existed in western Pennsylvania. NMU strength tended to remain in districts where Save the Union had been active: New Kensington, Renton, Harwick, Harmarville, Russellton, Avella, and Bentleyville. The NMU engaged in little overt activity in western Pennsylvania during the first two and a half years of its existence. In addition to organizing women's auxiliaries and youth groups, a Negro department was established. Hunger marches and demonstrations occurred, but strikes were rare. In March 1929 Mother Bloor was dispatched to Kinloch. An explosion, the second in thirteen months, had claimed the lives of fifty miners. The NMU claimed that three of the dead—black miners—were NMU members. The UMWA local at Kinloch had been embroiled in a ballot controversy during the Brophy-Lewis election in 1926. Save the Union had been active there in 1928, and the NMU no doubt enjoyed a measure of strength at Kinloch. Nevertheless, Bloor did little more than show the NMU colors.[8]

In 1931 the depression in coal reached its nadir. As operators slashed wages, strikes erupted throughout the coalfields. The Kinloch men struck the Paisley operations in January in what appeared to be a spontaneous work stoppage. Spontaneity characterized most of the miners' strikes that occurred during the early months of 1931, for both the UMWA and NMU were too weak to control events. Even as the Kinloch men left the pits, the NMU Pittsburgh district committee met and planned to exploit deteriorating conditions in the soft-coal fields. Western Pennsylvania and Ohio were targeted for a major NMU assault, dubbed the Two-Months Plan of Work by party officials. Shortly thereafter, a "party fraction" meeting attended by seventy-five delegates convened in Pittsburgh for the purposes of implementing the plan. A calendar was established, district representatives assigned, and "revolutionary competition" between districts adopted in order to build strike momentum. Hunger marches were also stepped up, and "Don't Starve—Fight" pamphlets were printed. All of this was approved by a District 5 convention, which opened in Pittsburgh on 23 May. The strike program was endorsed by 150 delegates, including 25 blacks, 15 women, and 40 "young workers" from locals purportedly representing 15,000 western Pennsylvania miners.[9]

The timing of the strike call was fortuitous, for work stoppages had erupted throughout western Pennsylvania's soft-coal fields. The "speed up" and wage cuts caused walkouts at Valley Camp, Hillman, Butler Consolidated, Bethlehem, and Pittsburgh Coal Company mines during the spring of 1931. Many miners worked fourteen hours a day at a rate of thirty cents a ton. Some were subjected to surveillance by efficiency experts as well as Coal and Iron police. The NMU convention had targeted the mines situated in Washington County for special attention. The operators in that district unwittingly aided their adversaries. On 25 May, the day after the Pittsburgh NMU convention, Carnegie Coal Company announced wage cuts, effective 1 June. Many NMU delegates had not yet left town, and upon hearing the news, they hastily arranged a series of meetings. On that very day, an NMU delegate rushed to the Carnegie mines in Atlasburg. After conferring with the miners, picket lines were thrown up around three Carnegie mines. Only one thousand Carnegie miners responded to the strike, but the great National Miners Union strike was underway.[10]

In spite of such perfunctory preparations, the NMU strike spread like wildfire. Before it had run its bitter, vicious, twelve-week course, an estimated forty thousand miners responded to its strike call at one time or another. The strike spread as far south as Uniontown and as far north as Sagamore and Yatesboro. Many miners who left the pits did so not as NMU members but as victims of impoverishment and repression. The NMU demands on behalf of the strikers included fifty-two cents a ton, a checkweighman at the tipple, recognition of the mine committees, and pay for dead work. The NMU agenda was in fact not much different from that put forth by the UMWA.[11]

At first blush, the strike appeared to be a modest success. Strike figures quoted in local newspapers were not nearly so optimistic as those supplied by the NMU. However, during the first week of June, the local press estimated that seven thousand, or 20 percent, of the employed miners in the Pittsburgh district had joined the strike. Statistical accuracy regarding the number of strikers remained elusive because strike discipline was weak. A man on the picket lines on a given day might be back in the pits on the next. Party field secretary Frank Borich complained that some party members on local mine committees opposed the strike. Perhaps their opposition was in part due to the fact that they were not directly involved in the decision to authorize the walkout, for the strike at many mines simply "happened" following the appearance of roving marchers and demonstrators. One result of this lack of coordination was internecine warfare between local and district committees, in which each attempted to expel and replace the membership of the other. The party rushed in Bill Foster, Bill Dunne, Jack Johnstone, and Alfred Wagenknecht in order to reorganize the strike, but they failed.[12]

The operators and the UMWA reacted sharply to the NMU strike. Carl Lesher, vice-president of Pittsburgh Coal, admitted publicly that production had been disrupted to the degree that state police and a force of special deputies were required to maintain security at his mines. Deputies also returned to the Valley Camp Mine at Kinloch. Truckloads of black strikebreakers imported from West Virginia had been driven away by pickets. Picket-line violence was, by that time, a tradition at Kinloch. The presence of the deputies only served to exacerbate tensions. When the deputies attempted to escort the vehicles bearing strikebreakers through the picket lines, they and their charges were stoned by the picketers. The deputies promptly retaliated by shooting three strikers. Some operators, such as Frick Coal in Fayette County, avoided conflict by simply shutting down. Confrontation on the picket lines was further inflamed by the presence of the UMWA. Pat Fagan and his associates had been badly mauled in 1927, but the UMWA had not been eliminated. Upon hearing of the NMU strike, the officials of District 5 flew to the coal patches and engaged in mortal combat with their rival. Their assault on the NMU led to a reconciliation of sorts between some of the operators and the UMWA.[13]

Mass picketing was prohibited by court order in Allegheny County. The sheriff also prohibited the presence of women and children in labor demonstrations. The NMU ignored those prohibitions. During the first week of June, the NMU established picket lines throughout Allegheny County. Demonstrators shut down the Creighton Fuel Company mine, situated south of Tarentum, on the west bank of the Allegheny River opposite Kinloch. Creighton Fuel was an interesting choice. It was a mine of intermediate size that employed approximately three hundred men. Labor relations at the mine seemed good. Superintendent V. L. Henry was burgess of nearby Tarentum, a community that had aided UMWA miners during the 1927 strike. Henry exhibited a conciliatory attitude toward unions, but he clearly preferred the UMWA. He attributed the walkout of his men to coercion and intimidation by "class struggle" pickets. A spokesman for the Creighton miners confirmed Henry's charges of coercion as well as the miners' preference for the UMWA. Creighton miners wanted no part of a union that had its "headquarters in Russia." The miner told the *Valley Daily News:* "While conditions were not as good as they would like them, they are much better than in other places. We have no reason to strike. The heads of the mine are very fair with us and always ready to talk over our problems."[14]

Three days later, Creighton Fuel signed an agreement with the UMWA. A wage scale of fifty-eight cents per ton was established. Superintendent Henry had, in effect, entered a closed-shop agreement with the UMWA, the first Allegheny Valley coal operator to do so since 1927. The NMU condemned the agreement as worthless UMWA newspaper propaganda. Picketing was intensified, and members of the local NMU women's auxiliary stoned UMWA miners on their way to work. Superintendent Henry had been content to close his mine during the conflict rather than hire guards. The violence did attract the attention of Sheriff Robert Cain, who arrested the picketers while threatening to institute deportation proceedings against the aliens among them. The confrontation at Creighton was also of interest to the *Valley Daily News.* The editors of that Tarentum newspaper professed little sympathy for the NMU-UMWA rivalry, and they noted that the NMU seemed to have more hatred for the UMWA than for the coal operators. *Valley Daily News* reporter Lem Schwartz decided to examine the strike from the bottom up. On the morning of 16 June, he put on some old work clothes, picked up a lunch pail, and assumed the identity of a miner for a day.[15]

Schwartz parked his automobile near the West Tarentum boundary, and then proceeded on foot south on the Pennsylvania Railroad tracks. He chose that route deliberately because a miner had told company officials that he had been turned back at gunpoint by four picketers at a place called Kier's Crossing. Schwartz encountered no one at that location. He left the tracks at that point, and proceeded down a highway toward the Creighton Fuel tipple. As he walked along the highway, Schwartz was approached by a group of twenty picketers, seven of whom were women and girls. A stocky Italian demanded to know where Schwartz was going. When he indicated that he was going to work (in feigned broken English), others addressed him in Italian and Polish. When Schwartz did not retreat, he was told in a nasty tone that he was about to "take the bread out of some loyal miner's mouth. Don't be a scab." Then, from the female contingent in chorus: "C'mon kid, don't go to work."[16]

Schwartz continued his journey. He left the highway and proceeded up Creighton Hollow Road and was directed by a watchman to take a little-used path to the mine. A small group of picketers exhorted him not to scab. As he crossed above the road, he was seen by a group of approximately forty picketers below. "Why don't you go out the road where you go in other times?" someone yelled. "You never went to work that way before." "That's no lie," Schwartz chuckled to himself. "C'mon down here, you yellow rat and you'll get the damndest beating you've ever had."[17] But Schwartz was not beaten on his way to or from work that day. He was subjected to verbal abuse and threats, but he was not touched.

The relative tranquillity experienced by Lem Schwartz at Creighton did not reflect the tone of the 1931 coal strike. As the conflict wore on, violence escalated and resulted in a tragic loss of life. Nor did the UMWA agreement with Creighton Fuel signify a revitalization of that organization. John L. Lewis did sign a contract with Pittsburgh Terminal Coal, the second largest coal producer in western Pennsylvania, shortly after the Creighton settlement. The Pittsburgh Terminal contract, secured through the intervention of Governor Gifford Pinchot, seemed to promise the return of the UMWA to the soft-coal fields. But that contract was not a breakthrough. Not even the presence of the Communist NMU was enough to drive most operators away from the open shop. The UMWA was less than candid about the provisions of its Pittsburgh Terminal contract. The *United Mine Workers Journal* reported only that that contract provided a "standard rate," for Pittsburgh Terminal miners. The *Journal* was far more specific in its denunciation of the NMU and pledged that nothing less than a total war would be waged against the red menace.[18]

The NMU was not impressed with UMWA bluster or "liberal" Governor Pinchot's intervention. The Communists sensed that the Creighton and Pittsburgh Terminal "contracts" were a defensive response by the UMWA, and the NMU intensified its strike activities. Creighton Fuel officials reported that more pickets patrolled their property than had been on duty before the UMWA contract was signed. Fewer than a dozen men were working at the Creighton Mine. Across the Allegheny River, three hundred NMU pickets stoned a train carrying sixty-one strikebreakers to the Kinloch Mine. The hapless pickets, more than half of them black, had not been told of the strike when they were hired in Cleveland. Six days later, the number of pickets at Kinloch had shrunk to fewer than forty, but new lines had been thrown up at nearby Renton. At Harmarville, officials of the Consumers Mining Company called a meeting of their miners and admonished them against fraternization with the NMU, a "Bolshevik organization." Three hundred of Consumers' miners walked out in defiance.[19] Each time an NMU strike flared up, UMWA representatives showed up to restore order. The NMU led the UMWA a merry chase throughout June and July 1931. Most NMU strikes lasted a few days or several weeks at most, and they rarely changed the status quo.

During the second week of June, unidentified NMU organizers from Kinloch entered the Black Diamond district and began to organize its miners. The Black Diamond fields straddled northern Armstrong and northwestern Indiana counties. Many mines in the region had operated under the open shop since 1925. UMWA miners in Indiana County had been effectively silenced by sweeping injunctions issued by Judge J. N. Langham in 1925 and 1927. Those injunctions were still in force in 1931. The Black Diamond region was administered by UMWA District 2, formerly governed by John Brophy. Brophy's defiance of John L. Lewis had split the district, and the morale of the rank and file was low. The new district president, James Mark, was a Lewis loyalist. Mark declared Brophy persona non grata, and district unity disappeared. Mark and his administration were unable to deal with court orders, layoffs, and wage cuts that sometimes exceeded 40 percent. The Black Diamond fields must have appeared ripe for the taking.

NMU organizers first appeared at the Buffalo and Susquehanna Mines situated near Sagamore, on the Armstrong-Indiana border. Only two hundred of seven hundred Buffalo and Susquehanna miners left the pits, but the strike spread quickly westward into northern Armstrong

County. Sheriff George W. Shaffer and a force of his Armstrong County deputies monitored marches from Sagamore to Nu Mine and Yatesboro, but failed to head off walkouts by miners in those communities. The UMWA reacted no less quickly than the sheriff. James Mark and district organizer John Ghizzoni arrived and drove the NMU men out. Mark and Ghizzoni announced that they had "restored peace." They had in fact been goaded into taking over a strike for which they had not prepared and which they could not possibly win.[20]

The UMWA was in charge, and it was compelled to do something. Mark and Ghizzoni staged mass marches, much in the manner employed by the NMU. One such affair, from Sagamore to the Sykesville Mines of Buffalo and Susquehanna Coal Company, spanned thirty-eight miles. Miners were recruited, and "locals" quickly organized. The strike message was also carried into the McIntyre district, in southern Indiana County. On 12 July Mark claimed that four thousand miners had joined the UMWA in a ten-day period. Union recognition and the election of checkweighmen, and not wages, were, according to Mark, the real issues in the conflict.[21] He never admitted publicly that the NMU had begun the strike.

The Black Diamond strike faded quickly. Armstrong County Judge J. Frank Graff issued an injunction that forbade all marches, demonstrations, and picketing. In neighboring Indiana County, Judge J. N. Langham issued yet another injunction on behalf of Rochester and Pittsburgh Mines in the McIntyre district. Under its provisions, the UMWA was forbidden to "annoy, hinder, unlawfully interfere or attempt by any scheme" to halt coal production at those works. Recalcitrant miners were subjected to mass evictions by the operators. No surety bonds were posted or barracks erected, for District 2 lacked the funds for such an undertaking. Displaced, destitute mining families were forced to take shelter in outbuildings provided by local farmers who took pity on them. Governor Pinchot condemned the evictions as "barbarous," and asked the operators to relent in the name of "ordinary humanity." B. M. Clark, president of Helvetia Coal Company, rebuked Pinchot, informing the governor that Helvetia paid forty-four cents a ton, a rate nine cents higher than that paid in Pittsburgh. The evictions had occurred because loyal employees had petitioned the company to protect their rights from invasion by men with whom they had nothing in common.[22]

The Black Diamond strike faded by the third week in July. Wage rates remained the same as they had been on 16 June, the day the Sagamore strike began. The strike's immediate result was the brutal impoverishment of already destitute mining families. The NMU returned to the scene briefly on 23 July. Field secretary Vincent Kemenovich spoke to the small groups of miners at Nu Mine and Yatesboro while the sheriff and state troopers looked on. An NMU rally called for 5 August drew fewer than a hundred miners. The NMU subsequently left Armstrong County, never to return. The operators refused to meet James Mark and John Ghizzoni, or to heed their pleas to rehire miners who had been prominent strike leaders. From start to finish, the Black Diamond strike was a fiasco for all who were touched by it.[23]

Pittsburgh was clearly the hub of the NMU strike. Armstrong and Indiana counties were simply too remote, and the limited resources of the NMU probably could not have been expended effectively there. On 13 June 250 delegates met in Pittsburgh. The delegates decided to press the attack in Allegheny and Washington counties. Less than a week after that meeting, Allegheny County Common Pleas Judge H. H. Rowand responded to an application presented by Butler Consolidated Coal Company for an injunction. Rowand issued a sweeping order that enjoined the NMU from "picketing, patrolling or gathering on the public highway" near that company's mine, located at Wildwood. Butler Consolidated's Wildwood mine had been a prime target of the NMU. It was situated near a major highway and was thus less than an hour due north of Pittsburgh. Butler Consolidated had installed new laborsaving equipment and also employed the speed up. The resentment of local miners was well known, and the opportunity for strike activity was too obvious to ignore. Shortly after Judge Rowand's order was issued, the central rank-and-file committee met in Pittsburgh, and drafted a resolution calling for mass picketing in defiance of the order.[24]

On the morning of 22 June, more than 150 NMU pickets walked down a public road toward the Butler Consolidated Coal Company Mine located in the tiny village of Wildwood in Hampton Township. The march was staged in direct violation of a court injunction issued in Pittsburgh a week earlier. The demonstration had been planned by the NMU rank-and-file committee at a picnic in nearby Acmetonia on 21 June. William Z. Foster had addressed a crowd of five thousand at that picnic, but it is not know whether he took part in planning the Wildwood march. He was not in Wildwood on 22 June. As the demonstrators approached the village, they were confronted by a force of deputies, commanded by Chief Deputy William ("Silver") Braun, a veteran of many strikes. Deputy Herbert Reel attempted to arrest a female picketer for stoning a passing automobile, and she retaliated by slapping his face. Reel unwisely drew his gun and fired into the ground behind the woman. Enraged picketers charged the deputy and pelted him with rocks. Reel was hit in the eye with a brick. Another deputy yelled, "If they want trouble, let's give it to them." The deputies were not given the order to fire, but they sent volley after volley into the scrambling pickets. Pistols, shotguns, and gas were brought into play. Nine strikers were shot, one fatally. No deputies other than Reel were injured.[25]

Newspaperman H. H. Harrison found himself on the wrong side of the road when the deputies opened fire. He fled in terror with the miners and radicals and took refuge behind a porch. (Harrison wondered out loud who or what the deputies were shooting at, for he counted five bullets in the wall behind which he had taken refuge.) The deputies later claimed that the radicals had returned volley for volley, but Harrison saw the entire battle and did not see a single striker in possession of a firearm of any kind. No guns were on the nineteen men and two women arrested by the deputies. The brutality of the deputies was compounded as they allowed the wounded to remain on the ground unattended for a half an hour as they made their arrests. The wounded were finally removed in coal trucks.[26]

The *Daily Worker* claimed that the unarmed picketers had been shot from "ambush" by the deputies. That was not true, but *Pittsburgh Post-Gazette* reporter Frank Butler and photographer Chester Brown confirmed Harrison's accounts of excessive deadly force used against picketers who were clearly fleeing the scene. The *Daily Worker* averred that the order "shoot to kill" was given all too frequently in labor confrontations in western Pennsylvania, particularly in those which involved NMU picketers. The *Daily Worker* believed it odd that the NMU would be held responsible for the loss of life, since only its members had been shot. Tom Myerscough and Deputy Herbert Reel were indicted for manslaughter. Myerscough, a native of Lancashire, England, had been among the first western Pennsylvania miners to join the Communists. He had once served as president of a UMWA local at a mine near Midland, Washington County. He had spent time in the Soviet Union and helped to found the Progressive Bloc in 1923. John L. Lewis ranked Myerscough chief among those who were "tools of Moscow, the enemies of God and constituted authority." Myerscough was the perfect scapegoat, and this "exceedingly dangerous character" would bear the full legal responsibility for Wildwood.[27]

On the day after the Wildwood melee, angry NMU miners regrouped at the Acmetonia picnic grounds. Shouts of "Get Reel" and the "Yellow-bellied leeches" filled the air, but cooler heads prevailed. The women on the rank-and-file committee presented a resolution that demanded the resignation of the sheriff, withdrawal of all deputies, and a suspension of injunctions. The committee adopted the resolution and promised to march whether the injunction was withdrawn or not. In the wake of the Wildwood incident, the adminstration of justice in Allegheny County assumed a character not unlike that which prevailed during the Sellins affair. Sheriff Robert S. Cain announced that he would seek deportation of all "aliens" arrested at Wildwood. Coroner W. J. McGregor was not particularly impressed with the testimony of the journalists who witnessed the events at Wildwood. McGregor seemed outraged that the press had been there. He questioned the credibility of the reporters and their editors because they had not forwarded the intentions of the NMU to the authorities. The antics of the coroner appeared to be a crude attempt to divert public attention away from excessive official violence at Wildwood. The wanton shooting of the pickets did not occur because Allegheny County was unprepared for the march. The NMU rarely relied upon stealth. Zealous proselytizing and participatory democracy made attempts at secrecy futile. It was widely assumed that the coal operators, UMWA, and government had planted spies within the NMU with a minimum of difficulty. The hostile tone of the official proceedings made it clear to all that Tom Myerscough alone would bear the legal opprobrium for the loss of life at Wildwood.[28]

Governor Gifford Pinchot dispatched a detachment of thirty state policemen to Wildwood. The NMU lashed Pinchot for sending troops to break the strike in order to restore the UMWA. Frank Borich led a delegation of black and white NMU miners to Harrisburg with the list of demands to present to Pinchot. The NMU demanded an open hearing in Pittsburgh, release of strike prisoners, removal of troops, the abolition of official terror, the elimination of company stores and scrip, unemployment insurance, relief, and the removal of prohibitive injunctions. Pinchot had done business with the UMWA since 1922, and attempts by the NMU to obtain equivalent status in Harrisburg failed. However, favorable publicity for the NMU was forthcoming from another quarter. On 24 June a committee of artists and writers, chaired by Theodore Dreiser, commenced "public hearings" at Pittsburgh's Seventh Avenue Hotel. Dreiser, John Dos Passos, Mary Heaton Vorse, Anna Rochester, and others solicited testimony from miners involved in the strike. A miner from Tarentum spoke of hunger and diets of "Italian Grass," composed solely of garden greens mixed with oil. A Kinloch miner testified that he had been paid only $5 in cash for six-months work. Wages of $1.80 per day came in the form of scrip. Wage rates were as low as thirty-six cents per ton, and the men were paid for only one of every three tons they mined. A black miner from Cedar Grove complained of racial discrimination by the UMWA and a company store debt that exceeded $200. The committee listened sympathetically for several days, and then issued its findings through a statement made by Dreiser. The AFL should be dissolved, for it was "a closed corporation of little groups." The NMU was preferable to the UMWA, because it opened its doors to all classes and conditions of labor, even the unskilled. The unrestrained violence sanctioned by Sheriff Cain was living proof that labor conflict should no longer be policed by deputy sheriffs.[29]

The NMU did not accept defeat at Wildwood, and the Communists were not cowed into abandoning their program of marches and picketing. It viewed the violence at Wildwood as just a typical example of the kind of skirmish produced by class warfare. The UMWA viewed Wildwood as a serious blow to the fortunes of its adversary and moved quickly to reestablish itself in northern Allegheny County. UMWA "truth squads" invaded Springdale, Russellton, Harwick, and Harmarville. The *United Mine Workers Journal* condemned the NMU campaign of class warfare that spawned hatred and violence. The *Journal* argued that well-meaning miners were pawns used by the Communists against "panicky mine deputies" who had guns "and [were] sure to use them." Weakened by the arrest of its leadership from the UMWA counterattack, the NMU withdrew its resources from Allegheny County and launched a last-ditch effort in nearby Washington County, which was the closest thing to a NMU stronghold. The strike had begun at the Carnegie coal mines there, and by mid-June NMU picket lines had closed eleven mines in Burgettstown, Atlasburg, Westland, Avella, Cokeburg, and Bentleyville. The UMWA challenged the NMU for control of this district, and a UMWA rally was scheduled for Canonsburg.[30]

On 19 July Pat Fagan mounted the speakers' platform at the Curry ball field. As the president of District 5 spoke to the UMWA faithful, a thousand NMU marchers appeared on the scene. Catcalls and curses filled the air, followed by bricks, rocks, and bottles. Fagan and his entourage were dragged off the speakers' platform and beaten. The Canonsburg riot was the first full-scale brawl between the rival miners' unions since the fight that occurred outside the NMU convention in Pittsburgh in September 1928. Canonsburg would be the last hurrah of the NMU in western Pennsylvania.

When the melee at Canonsburg ended, twelve men and two women—all NMU members—had been arrested for riot, conspiracy, and unlawful assembly. Free-lance writer Lauren Gilfillan covered the subsequent NMU trials in Washington, the county seat. Her autobiographical novel, *I Went to Pit College*,[31] provides the student of labor history with provocative impressions of the unique quality of what she termed "mining town justice." A recent college graduate, Gilfillan aspired to a literary career. She traveled to Avella and lived with miners' families during the strike. As an outsider, she was kept under surveillance by plainclothes police. Attempts were made to bar her from the courtroom. Note-taking during the trial was forbidden, a policy that she violated. During a break in the trial, her notes were seized by the county sheriff while she ate lunch in a nearby restaurant.

Gilfillan was present when the handcuffed defendants were led into the courtroom. The gallery was packed, and on a hot August day, the court reeked of whiskey and sweat. Several of the prisoners made a lasting impression on Gilfillan. Leo Thompson, an articulate nineteen-year-old Communist prodigy, with "thick black hair and deep set fanatical eyes," attempted to make the trial a forum for the NMU. Time and again, the prosecution cut off Thompson. "Communism as the rising political party will be the eventual salvation of—" (objection). "Communists are militant workers, fighting for their constitutional—" (objection). The district attorney and Thompson also sparred:

"Do you admit that the National Miners Union and the Communist Party are one and the same thing?"

"No, the National Miners Union and the Communist Party have nothing to do with each other."

"But the national miners are communist, just the same?"

"Not necessarily."

"Not necessarily! Then they are pretty apt to be communists! Their leaders are communists aren't they?"

"It is true that often the leaders belong to the Communist Party. The communists make the great leaders . . . are the most enterprising . . . and the most militant."[32]

Stella Rasefski, a young women with "Russian features" was known to be as militant as Thompson, but not so articulate. According to a prosecution witness (reputed to be a UMWA spy), Rasefski and Thompson planned the attack on Fagan. The witness also insisted that the riot was precipitated by a black NMU miner who pulled down and tore the American flag. Four of the defendants were black, three of whom, according to Gilfillan, bore the "map of Africa all over their brawny bodies." The blacks testified that Thompson had counseled against rioting, denied desecrating the flag, and claimed to be ignorant of Communism.

Pat Fagan was the prosecution's star witness. A small, wiry man with pinched features and a thin, perpetual smile, Fagan struck a dapper pose in the witness chair. Fagan had good reason not to forget July 1931. Less than a week after he had been driven from the field at Canonsburg, Fagan became the target of an assassination attempt. On the night of 26 July, "renegade miner" Pat Murphy appeared at Fagan's front door and asked the president of District 5 to identify himself. Fagan did, and Murphy pulled a gun. "I'm here from District 19, and I'm here to kill you." Fagan jumped Murphy, and the two men rolled in a deadly embrace down the steps of Fagan's front porch. The gun discharged, killing Murphy. The reasons for the attack on Fagan are not clear. Murphy and his accomplice, Fred Snyder, were not Pennsylvania miners. Indeed, press reports offered Texas, West Virginia, Tennessee, and Kentucky as possibilities for their homes. Snyder was reputed to be the cousin of Sid Hatfield, who was shot and killed by Baldwin-Felts detectives on the courthouse steps in Mingo City, West Virginia, in the early 1920s. The *United Mine Workers Journal* averred that Murphy had been identified by police as the leader of a Communist hunger parade, thus tying his assassination attempt to a NMU conspiracy to kill UMWA leaders. It is more likely that Murphy's attack was the act of what Appalachian miners refer to as a "gun thug." That tangled tradition of gunmanship existed in the shadow of the UMWA, and John L. Lewis did little to discourage it. Indeed, it is believed in some quarters that he employed this type of person from time to time. However, it would be a mistake to think of gun thugs simply as assassins in the employ of unions or coal operators. Gunmanship was an integral part of the code of honor of Appalachia, and it often served as the chief instrument of personal and family revenge.[33]

Fagan did not seem to be affected by his harrowing experience when he testified against the NMU in August. The role of innocent victim of a premeditated attack was new to him, but he played it to the hilt. Glib and confident, Fagan must have understood that the trial was a farce, or at best a mere formality. The NMU was now cast as the radical, disruptive intruder. The UMWA had become the defender of free enterprise, God, and the Republic itself. When the prosecutor asked Fagan what he was saying when the NMU raided his rally, Fagan replied, "Father, forgive them, for they know not what they do." Fagan's theatrics were unnecessary, for all associated with the trial knew that the Canonsburg rioters were on their way to jail. The Rasefski sisters—Anna and Stella— and Leo Thompson were sentenced to two years imprisonment in the Allegheny County Workhouse. The NMU was finished as an effective fighting industrial union in western Pennsylvania.

During the weeks following the Canonsburg riot, the NMU continued to hold conferences and committee meetings in Pittsburgh. Although the strike was collapsing on all fronts, union officials promoted "a second offensive" in central Pennsylvania and the anthracite region. The party continued to insist that the strike was not over, but by late August the leadership began to speak of "new tactics" and "organized retreat." The NMU also called for no discrimination against strikers who had returned to the pits—a sure sign that the strike was over. The Communists announced district elections in September, but no one paid much attention. NMU secretary Frank Borich announced in early October that only twenty functioning locals remained in western Pennsylvania. Communist organizers spoke of unemployed councils and a Metal Workers Industrial League. The party had apparently gone on to other things.[34]

The NMU strike divided the mining community much as the UMWA strike had in 1927. The UMWA was present in Avella, but that community was a NMU stronghold. Fred Siders, the first president of NMU District 5, was from Avella. The community had an active rank-and-file committee, a dedicated women's auxiliary, youth groups, a relief station, and it also served as a way station for International Labor Defense. Slogans and songs proclaimed class struggle, proletarian solidarity, racial equality, and hatred of the UMWA.

Down with capitalism.
Fight starvation.
Prevent the murder of the Scottsboro boys.
Down with lynching.
Down with Jim Crow.
Workers, white and negro, native and foreign born.

One, two, three,
Young Communists are we.
We're fighting for the working class,
Against the bourgeoisie.

Four, five six,
Happy Bolsheviks.
We go out on the picket line,
Despite the vicious dicks.

Pinchot's havin' a hell of a time.
Parlez-vous!
To break the strike in this ol' mine
Mussolini's went over the top,
He thought he heard a penny drop.

Fagan's havin' a hell of a time,
To get some scabs for this ol' mine.

Banker and boss hate the red Soviet Star,
Gladly they'd build a new throne for the Czar.
But from the steppe to the dark British Sea,
Lenin's red army wins victory.
So workers close your ranks.
Keep sharp and steady.
For Freedom's cause your bayonets bright.
For workers' Russia, the Soviet Union,
Get ready for the last fierce fight.

Long-haired preachers come out every night,
Try to tell us what's wrong and what's right.
But when asked about something to eat,
They answer in voices so sweet:
   You'll eat by and by,
   In that glorious land above the sky,
   Way up high,
   Work and Pray,
   Live on hay,
   You'll get pie in the sky when you die.

Working men of all countries unite,
Side by side we for freedom will fight.
When the world and its wealth we have gained,
To those grafters we'll say this refrain:
You'll eat by and by,
When you've learned how to cook and fry apple pie,
Chop some wood, twill do you good,
And you'll eat in the sweet by and by,
   (That's no lie).

The workers learned their lesson,
Now as everyone can see.
The workers know their bosses are,
The greatest enemy.
We'll fight and fight until we win,
The final victory.
Through the National Miners Union.

Solidarity forever!
Solidarity forever!
Solidarity forever!
For the Union makes us strong.

The men will stick together,
And the boys are fighting fine.
The women and the girls are all,
Right on the picket line!
So, scabs, no threats will stop us then,
We all march on time.
With one big National Miners Union.[35]

For Americans hardened by nearly four decades of cold war, NMU songwriting and sloganeering might seem naive and puerile. Yet, there is no doubt that Marxist ideology, though primitively expressed, was zealously expounded by a suffering, often isolated minority in the coal camps. But the NMU had little more to offer the miners than slogans, and disappointment was quickly followed by disillusionment. According to Gilfillan, paranoia also swept through NMU households much as it had in the UMWA camp. Suspicious NMU miners turned on their organizers, accusing them of being UMWA spies. Gilfillan's papers were searched by the Communists, and she was ostracized by the radical community without explanation. Strike unity did not flourish in such an atmosphere.[36]

The 1931 NMU strike failed, and would be the last walkout staged by the Communists in the coalfields of western Pennsylvania. During the months following the strike, the Communists conducted a postmortum. Organizer Jack Johnstone congratulated the NMU for arousing its miners to a "fighting pitch," but he complained that "no clear path of organization or continuity of tasks performed" existed during the conflict. Johnstone acknowledged that the rank-and-file participation was essential to the successful conduct of the strike, but he was clearly distressed that the miners had "taken charge." From the beginning the NMU leadership argued that the miners' strike was not a spontaneous work stoppage, but a planned revolutionary act. Johnstone believed that "fighting enthusiasm" was no substitute for organization. Spontaneity was a sometime thing, and the kind of ardor it spawned was bound to dissipate in time unless nurtured by revolutionary ideology. For the NMU leadership, that point was critical. Such NMU officers as Borich, Myerscough, and Kemenovich were party members, but many strikers were not. The union and party were perceived as separate entities, and the Communists firmly believed that the former would not survive without the latter.[37]

The party therefore recommended a standard procedure for organizing miners. The organizers' first duty was to establish a strike committee and picket line. Thereafter, the strike committee was to be used as a vehicle for the establishment of a local union. The membership of that local was supposed to select delegates to district strike committees. Party organizers were expected to provide guidance and leadership in strikes carried on by the rank and file in the NMU locals. Party organizers were also expected to recruit party members from the union rank and file. The NMU was reasonably successful in organizing picket lines and committees; but by their own admission party recruiting was a miserable failure. The ranks of party regulars were thin, and much of their time was spent jumping from picket line to picket line. In their absence the fledgling strike committees foundered, and strike discipline disappeared. Party regulars complained that in their absence miners picketed when they wished, and that internecine warfare stripped strike committees of authority and continuity of membership. In the wake of the strike, the party admitted that serious ideological instruction had been virtually nonexistent in the coalfields and that party building did not enjoy a status equal to that of strike duty. If the NMU was to survive, the party nucleus would have to be "one of the strong pillars" of the union. Experienced organizers warned their colleagues that in the future, if new party cadres were to be created, changes in tactics would be necessary. Organizers were warned to "guard against formalism" and to use "simple language" in explaining the meaning of class struggle to coal miners. Theoretical training would, by necessity, go slowly.[38]

A more deliberate approach to ideological training would probably not have changed the outcome of the 1931 strike. Angry, destitute miners were not likely to be enthralled by the joys of ideological discovery while their families were denied the necessities of life. The NMU believed that the question of relief was a "matter of life and death," and yet it was woefully unprepared to deal with the problem. On a strike front that sometimes exceeded seventy miles, twenty relief tents distributed three meals a week to striking families. The party concluded that weak relief was primarily responsible for the miners return to work. Legal aid was no more forthcoming. The NMU had no money to post bond for miners facing eviction as the UMWA had done during the 1927 strike. The party activated the International Labor Defense, but its purpose and capabilities were widely misunderstood by the strikers. The ILD had no regular staff or officers. Occasional, professional legal advice was provided by sympathetic lawyers who volunteered their services. Some miners expected ILD to provide them with a legal defense and to pay their fines. The ILD was prepared only to provide "legal education" to miners ignorant of the law and the courts. But mass arrests made even that limited service tenuous. The expectations of striking miners had been raised once again, only to be dashed again upon the hard rocks of economic reality.[39]

The eradication of jim crow in the coalfields was a cherished goal of the NMU. A Negro department, headed by black organizers, was established to recruit black miners and to spread the credo of interracial solidarity in the coalfields. The resentment of white miners for their black counterparts ran deep in western Pennsylvania, for many blacks had entered the region as strikebreakers during the decade after World War I. Such organizers as Fannie Sellins had successfully recruited black miners for the UMWA long before the NMU had come into being. One scholar insists, however, that the NMU succeeded where the UMWA had failed by "fighting racism within its own ranks and by organizing black and white miners on an equal basis." During the strike, NMU organizers found the absence of racial chauvinism and prejudice gratifying. They reported that "negroes were among the first to strike, and among the militant on the picket lines." Black miners were also active on strike committees. NMU sources reported that the radical activism of the blacks was enthusiastically received by white miners. Lauren Gilfillan was not so sure. Signs that declared "We don't want no black meat" were clearly posted in communities known to be sympathetic to the NMU. Communist sources later admitted that the failure to mount an effective campaign against jim crow was a major shortcoming in the 1931 strike.[40]

That the NMU was unsuccessful in its assault on racism does not diminish or obscure the noble quality of its ideals. No miners' union had ever made such a forthright declaration damning institutional racism. Despite decades of humanitarian rhetoric, the UMWA had never made the elimination of jim crow a priority. Historian Linda Nyden suggests that the NMU campaign to organize the unorganized—black and white—later influenced John L. Lewis and the recruiting strategy of the CIO. Lewis did employ Communist and black organizers in 1936, and blacks poured into the CIO. Nyden believes that the NMU campaign forced Lewis's hand on race. Nyden's thesis is provocative, but important questions remain unanswered. It is clear that Lewis's UMWA was guilty of racial discrimination, a reality decried by black miners throughout the 1920s. But it is equally apparent that blacks were not excluded from his union. No historian has yet pinpointed Lewis's attitudes on race. Did he pander to the racial prejudice of his rank and file, or was Lewis a racist bigot? For all Philip Murray's racial slurs during the 1927 strike, there is nothing in his early career that marked him as a race-baiter. Lewis and his chief lieutenant were pragmatists, interested primarily in building and securing their power base among the miners. Lewis opposed the Progressive miners not on ideological grounds but because they challenged his right to rule. He had been forced to wrestle with the Progressive Bloc and its program for nearly a decade. The Progressive miners had advocated racial equality since 1923, so it is unlikely that Lewis was surprised or cowed by that issue in 1936. The CIO needed dues-paying recruits, and it is far more likely that Lewis responded to that need rather than to lessons learned from the NMU.[41]

The egalitarian ideals espoused by the NMU did not appear to make much of an impression on the press in western Pennsylvania. Communist organs complained bitterly that the *Pittsburgh Press* and *Post-Gazette* were in league with the UMWA, and that their reporting of strike violence was distorted. In an alleged interview, Vincent Kemenovich was widely quoted as saying that "unless the coal company officials changed their attitude, there will be another Herrin here. I don't have to tell you that all miners are armed." An outraged NMU claimed that the "interview" was faked by the Hearst syndicate and consituted a serious breach of journalistic integrity. Editorial bias became the subject of lively discussions in the *Daily Worker*. It reported that the editors of the *Post-Gazette* supported the UMWA as the best means of "combating the radicalism which would go to the point of violence." Those very editors characterized the local UMWA leadership as "men who have been known for years to the miners . . . and the fact that they have held their offices through many trials speaks for itself of their trustworthiness." John L. Lewis could not have said it better if he had written those editorials himself. The UMWA leadership, no stranger to violence, had been cast as the apostles of peace. Lewis and associates must have snickered when the *Post-Gazette* condemned the Canonsburg riot as "pure hooliganism," and the *Pittsburgh Press* characterized the NMU as the "common enemy" of the coal operators, UMWA, coal miners, as well as the general public. Had the editorial tone of western Pennsylvania's press equaled its even-handed reporting of the Wildwood massacre, the public interest would have been far better served. Editorial preoccupation with "violence and hatred" attributed solely to "class warfare" did little to enlighten anyone about the issues that separated the contending miners' unions. Clearly, editorial red-baiting had not died in 1919.[42]

The NMU called off the western Pennsylvania strike in early August and devoted what was left of its meager resources to a ferocious strike being conducted in Harlan County, Kentucky. The NMU had reached its zenith in June 1931, and thereafter its fortunes declined. NMU strikes were defeated on all fronts. Tom Myerscough was in jail. Deportation proceedings had been begun against secretary Frank Borich and others. Since most NMU miners had been blacklisted by the operators, the union had become an organization of the unemployed. Spies in the employ of Bethlehem Mines continued to monitor NMU meetings in Bentleyville and Marianna as late as March 1933. Strikes were planned but did not come to pass until the UMWA uprising in the coke fields later that year. The reports by industrial police to Bethlehem Mines management reflect no sense of imminent danger. Apparently, the peril posed by the "red menace" had passed, and security police did not feel compelled to respond with measures other than surveillance.[43]

In March 1932 the third annual NMU convention was held in Pittsburgh's Pythian Hall. Two hundred twenty-five black and white delegates were addressed by Jack Stachel, Ben Bernard, and Frank Borich. Stachel, assistant national secretary for the Trade Union Unity League, admitted that the majority of miners on strike in 1931 were not actually led by the NMU. Those who did become associated with the NMU were blacklisted. Unemployed miners could not pay dues or strike. Ben Bernard, organizational secretary of the NMU, concurred. The NMU secretary ticked off the reasons for the failure of the 1931 strike: weak recruiting, organizational looseness, failure clearly to articulate demands, absence of dialogue with miners, and an unorganized return to work by miners who did not understand the meaning of "organized retreat." Borich announced that less than 25 percent of NMU miners were employed in the mines, and that the NMU was "completely isolated" from those working in the pits. Borich as much as admitted defeat when he called for a "real united front" with the UMWA on the basis of "common struggle" against the coal operators. Two months later, he appeared at the TUUL meeting in New York and admitted that the NMU had "underestimated the U.M.W.A.," and that the radical union had succumbed to internal pressures generated by "white chauvinism."[44]

In June 1932 twenty-five hundred Pittsburgh Terminal Coal miners walked out in protest over wage cuts that reduced earnings to thirty-five cents a ton. The UMWA had signed a "contract" with that company in June 1931. Pat Fagan and Father Cox urged the miners to return to work. The NMU was too feeble to take advantage of the walkout, and its response was limited to accusations of "betrayal" aimed at the UMWA leadership. Tom Myerscough was paroled in September, after serving eleven months of a two-year sentence for manslaughter. Myerscough spearheaded a hunger march in Pittsburgh, but did nothing in the name of the moribund NMU. Party observers reported that the NMU was facing "tremendous difficulties" that would be overcome only by the "most determined struggle" and "real revolutionary sacrifice." Its leading organizers were asking for leaves of absence or were staying home in order to recover from exhaustion. The NMU no longer distributed so much as a pamphlet. In March 1933 Frank Borich and Vincent Kemenovich were ordered to appear before immigration authorities in Pittsburgh. In April the Department of Labor ordered the deportation of Borich and Morgan Davis, a local organizer active in Washington County.[45]

In mid-March the NMU convened its fourth and final convention in Pittsburgh. Three hundred delegates, one third of whom were employed, discussed a "United Front" strike effort with the UMWA, scheduled for 1 April. The NMU proposed an alliance of the NMU, UMWA, Progressive Miners Union, and the West Virginia Miners Federation. According to NMU spokesmen, "lower functionaries" in the UMWA were ready to take up the United Front struggle. However, John L. Lewis would not meet with radicals and schismatics in the coalfields, and in a matter of days, the failure to establish a United Front was being attributed to the "treachery of top U.M.W.A. officials."[46] In fact, Lewis was entirely consistent. He had never been willing to cooperate with insurgent elements that threatened his authority. Lewis would finally bury his radical adversaries in the spring and summer of 1933.

The New Deal, and more specifically the provisions of the National
Recovery Act, took the coalfields by storm. As NMU influence waned in
the coalfields, John L. Lewis apparently decided to revive and rebuild
the UMWA. During the months following Roosevelt's landslide, Lewis
and his associates met and planned a recruiting campaign. A strike was
scheduled for 1 April. Lewis's timing was fortuitous, but the reasons for
it are anything but clear. Perhaps the election of a "softer" Democratic
administration encouraged him. The presence of a sympathetic Gifford
Pinchot in the governor's mansion must surely have influenced his decision to make western Pennsylvania the fulcrum of the organizing campaign and walkout. Lewis must have known the NMU was finished, and
he simply brushed aside its call for a United Front. But neither Lewis nor
the coal operators were prepared for the spontaneous mass miners'
rising that erupted in the spring and summer of 1933. The reason for
the UMWA resurgence was not so much due to Lewis's charisma and
planning as it was to the passage of the National Recovery Act. Western
Pennsylvania miners revere the memory of John L. Lewis only slightly
less than that of Franklin Delano Roosevelt. Union organizers invoked
the name of Roosevelt while recruiting, but that probably was not necessary. According to John Brophy, the UMWA did not have to work at
organizing. The men simply left the pits, formed picket lines, and signed
union cards. The miners simply returned to familiar moorings. The
UMWA had survived the 1920s, a decade-long test of faith for its rank
and file.[47]

Anti-union bastions fell quickly. In Indiana County, Judge J. N. Langham still presided "like a mighty emperor of old" in the Court of
Common Pleas. Most of Langham's injunctions, issued in 1927 and
1931, were still in force. Organizer John Ghizzoni informed John L.
Lewis that the miners had simply ignored the court orders and that most
of the Indiana and Armstrong mines had been won without incident.
The operators had not requested restraining orders, and no contempt
citations had been issued. The UMWA had been driven from the
Kiskiminetas Valley in 1922. With the exception of the brief Save the
Union strike in 1927, its miners had been quiescent for more than a
decade. On 3 June more than a thousand men left the pits. Lewis Hicks
responded with a 10 percent wage increase, but the men were not
moved. Black miners, led by Charles Hales of Kiskimere, and white
miners, directed by Sam Cook of Vandergrift, stood shoulder to shoulder in an unprecedented demonstration of solidarity. Pat Fagan appeared at mass meetings at Indian Diamond, near Vandergrift, and later
at Gosser Hill, near Leechburg. Fagan assured his miners that "Roosevelt
and Pinchot were sympathetic," and that the NRA would be the "salvation of the coal industry." The UMWA had, according to Fagan, em-

barked upon a "rehabilitation program" on 1 January. The NRA guaranteed its right to exist. Miners, some of whom had drawn less than $35 in cash for three-years' work, would never again be forced to endure conditions that had been "worse than slavery." Lewis Hicks held out against union recognition until mid-July. His position was made untenable when the Graff coal interests, second largest in the Kiskiminetas Valley, surrendered to the union and the NRA in June. The stubborn Hicks capitulated on 18 July. With the signing of a union contract, the open shop, the company store, and all their contingent evils passed into history in the Kiskiminetas Valley.[48]

The situation was much the same in the Allegheny Valley. Fred Broad, an old friend of the UMWA, presided at union rallies in New Kensington. By late June, most of the commercial mines in New Kensington, Renton, Harwick, Harmarville, and Russellton had fallen to the UMWA. The National Miners Union was nowhere in evidence. The isolation of the coal patches, which had been enforced by company guards for more than half a decade, disappeared overnight. Schoolteacher Elizabeth Wright moved through the coal camps at Kinloch, Renton, Harwick, and Harmarville unmolested. A critic of company towns, she inspected housing facilities and distributed *Black News*, a publication of the Pennsylvania Security League. She was welcomed by company officials at Renton and shown company cost records. At Harwick, she was invited to go anywhere she wanted, for "there [was no such thing] as trespassing" there. Throughout her travels, miners and operators alike sang the praises of the NRA.[49]

It is impossible to exaggerate the importance of the National Recovery Act to the UMWA renaissance. The NRA permeated communities throughout western Pennsylvania. The blue eagle, the official symbol of the NRA and the New Deal, was displayed in shops and storefronts, large and small, in communities that had once been conservative Republican strongholds. Coal operators, who had been no more prepared for the NRA than for the union onslaught, embraced the coal codes. Without the apparent promise of stability that the codes seemed to offer, it is unlikely that the commercial coal operators would have surrendered so easily. An anonymous Allegheny Valley operator was certain that the codes would eliminate cut-throat competition and stabilize prices as well as wages. If that were done, he had no objection to the union or a return to the Jacksonville scale. Some Pittsburgh operators, led by Frank Taplin, principal owner of Pittsburgh Terminal Coal, formed a Coal Code Association of Western Pennsylvania. Pittsburgh Terminal Coal had broken with the open-shop operators in June 1931 and had signed a contract with the UMWA. More than forty other operators joined Pittsburgh Terminal, vowing to adopt a coal code acceptable to all. Mellon con-

trolled Pittsburgh Coal Company, and the Rockefeller interests refused
to accept the code accords reached by the Taplin group and the UMWA.
They decided to formulate their own rates. The open-shop bloc in soft
coal was nevertheless shattered beyond repair. Eventually, even the
recalcitrant Mellon and Rockefeller interests were forced to come to
terms with unionization and the National Recovery Administration.[50]

The United Mine Workers' rapprochement with the commercial coal
producers was not duplicated in the coalfields dominated by "captive
mines" operated by big steel. No doubt the steelmakers understood that
unionization of their mines might well mean organization of their mills.
Led by Henry Clay Frick Coke Company, a subsidiary of U.S. Steel, the
"captives" employed an army of detectives, deputy sheriffs, and industrial police to defeat the UMWA. A company union was also organized.
The UMWA miners led by firebrand Martin Ryan established picket
lines in Fayette and Greene counties. Pitched battles erupted throughout
those counties, and Governor Pinchot sent in the National Guard.
Pinchot engaged in a running feud with the sheriffs in the coke fields
and refused to use state police to quell the strikers. Pinchot also suspended the issuing of industrial police commissions. The sheriffs responded by hiring more deputies, which exacerbated the violence.[51]

On 4 August NRA Administrator General Hugh Johnson arranged a
truce between the contending parties. A temporary agreement guaranteed a checkweighman and required all future disputes to be placed
before a National Labor Board. But union recognition was not forthcoming, and the truce collapsed. Fayette miners remembered the 1922
strike, in which they were abandoned without recognition or a contract.
Bands of roving pickets composed of Frick miners appeared at UMWA
mines in Armstrong, Allegheny, and Westmoreland counties in August.
Union miners left the pits. Not even the signing of the coal codes by the
commercial operators in September halted the unauthorized walkouts.
Pat Fagan attributed the wildcats to "strike fever," and admitted that he
had issued no strike call. Although Fagan was clearly not in control, he
attempted to put the best face on the situation. He claimed that the "aim
of the union was to shut down the industry until an agreement was
reached on the codes." But an unauthorized "holiday" shut down commercial mines from Pittsburgh to Blairsville. Spokesmen for the rank
and file indicated that the walkout was inspired by the Fayette pickets,
and not dissatisfaction with local operators. Kiskiminetas miners balked
at the wage scales set forth in the codes, but full recognition of the union
remained their chief priority. The wildcats dragged on into October, and
the men even refused an order by Philip Murray to return to work. It
appeared that the old nightmare of 1922 had returned.[52]

The intransigence of the "captives" brought the UMWA to the brink of anarchy. Only the presence of the Reverend Casimir Orlemanski, Natrona's labor priest, averted a riot at a mass meeting of 2,500 miners at the Indiana County Fairgrounds. Union officers attempted to coax the men back to work, only to be shouted down by agitators in the crowd. Orlemanski took control and told the men they were welcome to stay out "until hell freezes over," But, he added, "you've been fighting for years for the right of free speech and assembly. If you don't care to hear these men, why did you come here?" After peace was restored to the proceedings, it was learned that fifteen of eighteen locals present had voted to return to work—only the presence of coke county pickets, Fayette and Westmoreland county miners, perpetuated the walkout. In late October, men who worked at the commercial mines began to return to work. The resumption of mining at the commercial mines was hastened by the action of Roosevelt. In late October, he convinced the steel magnates to allow the National Labor board to hold representation elections at the captive mines. The elections were held on 23 and 24 November and produced a mixed result. The UMWA won elections at Inland, Allegheny, and Jones and Laughlin Mines, but carried only seven of sixteen Frick camps. The Miners Independent Brotherhood, a Frick company union, remained in control. Lewis had failed to win the "captives," but the elections justified the return of his miners to the commercial pits.[53]

Throughout the great events of 1933, the National Miners Union was relegated to the position of spectator. Tom Myerscough, newly elected president of the NMU, simply did not have the resources with which to challenge the UMWA resurgence. Vincent Kemenovich and Frank Borich, two NMU stalwarts, faced deportation. The NMU had no funds, official organ, or program. It sensed that the captive-mines controversy was the issue it needed, but was powerless to exploit that breech in the UMWA ranks. Martin Ryan was viewed as a potential ally, a "progressive," but inexperienced, a man afraid of John L. Lewis. Predictably, Lewis was accused of selling out to his old associate Al Hamilton, "fiscal agent for U.S. Steel." The Fayette fiasco of 1933 was a repeat of Lewis's performance there in 1922.[54]

The Communist party condemned the New Deal, the NRA, and its "slave codes." Nevertheless, a small band of NMU representatives appeared at the NRA hearings in Washington and presented its own codes. With the exception of a higher wage scale, and the termination of regional wage differentials, the NMU and UMWA codes were virtually identical. Delegate Margaret Snear did present proposals for maternity care and playgrounds, purporting to speak for women connected to the mining industry. But the old revolutionary fire was gone. New Deal reform, and not the radical ideology of class conflict, had captured the hearts and minds of western Pennsylvania miners. The company store, scrip, and the short tally had all been swept away. William Z. Foster later admitted that NMU had failed, but he claimed that it threw a scare into the operators and weakened their resistance to the NRA and the UMWA resurgence. Mother Bloor was convinced that NMU "strength" aided the establishment of the UMWA. In fact, neither of those observations have much validity. The 1931 strike did not stampede most western Pennsylvania coal operators into the arms of the UMWA. And it was more probable that the promise of stability and prosperity rather than the threat of Communism paved the way for the NRA. As for NMU "strength," it had none to give in 1933.[55]

The failure of the National Miners Union to take hold and grow in western Pennsylvania was not merely a matter of insufficient resources and defective strategy. Two decades before the founding of the NMU, organizers for the IWW sensed that Pittsburgh and its environs harbored a working-class conservatism that was particularly strong. The Wobblies assumed that that brand of proletarian conservatism reflected the power and influence of the industrial giants that dominated the region. The overwhelming power of the Republican party in western Pennsylvania must also have influenced the perceptions of workers. The presence of conservative religious groups, including Roman Catholics, Greek Orthodox, Free Methodists, and Presbyterians, may well have influenced the behavior of workers. The pervasive presence of Masonry, especially among skilled workmen, must have reinforced a conservative outlook. One cannot converse with miners who experienced the rigors of the pre–New Deal era without confronting their commitment and adherence to traditions and institutions. Their very survival underground discouraged deviations from established patterns. In an industry racked by depression, survival depended upon self-help that could only be delivered by the family and the community. Many coal miners regarded the UMWA as third in importance only after family and church. For all its corruption and incompetence, the UMWA was a revered institution that had given the coal miner dignity, or hope of it, and released him from serfdom. Those feelings of allegiance sometimes withered, but rarely died. The National Miners Union stood in the tradition of schism. Like the Progressive Bloc, Save the Union, and even the contemporary Miners for Democracy, the NMU had its day, but not much more. The coal miner of western Pennsylvania rarely divided his loyalties, and the United Mine Workers—*the* Union—was seldom far from his mind.

6

The Arbiters: Law Enforcement and the Picket Line

THE ERRATIC PERFORMANCE OF PENNSYLVANIA'S POLICE FORCES DURING THE Great Coal Strike suggests that the quality of law enforcement in labor disputes had not advanced much beyond that of the Molly Maguire era. Although the commonwealth had experienced more than half a century of pervasive industrial conflict, coherent, consistent, impartial law enforcement remained in short supply. Policing labor disputes was a thankless and difficult task. Parties to strikes often engaged in violence and other lawless acts, but their motives clearly differed from those of the traditional criminal classes with whom the police most often had to deal. Strikes often involved entire communities and frequently assumed the characteristics of guerrilla war. Separating combatants from non-combatants was sometimes impossible. Mass picketing often resulted in mass arrests. The subsequent burden on the courts often meant that justice was dispensed with callous disregard for individual rights. Strike activities were carried out without regard for political and judicial boundaries. Jurisdictional disputes therefore complicated the strike problem for prosecutors and especially police. Businessmen, particularly coal operators, responded by relying more upon their own industrial police, whose jurisdictional authority was legally vague and therefore flexible.

Pennsylvania did little to correct the inconsistencies in the policing of its labor conflicts. A plausible strategy or policy was not forthcoming from Harrisburg. More often than not, violence on the picket lines was followed by clumsy, ill-conceived, knee-jerk reactions by a patchwork of local, county, state, and private authorities. At times, the antipathy that existed between police forces rivaled that which existed between labor and management. Local police often resented the intrusion of state forces and sheriffs into their jurisdictions. The state constabulary, local constables, and municipal police considered industrial police and deputy sheriffs to be little more than hired gunmen. Industrial police complained that local officers and magistrates were too sympathetic to strikers. Governor Gifford Pinchot charged that coke district sheriffs in southwestern Pennsylvania were subservient to big steel and used the state police as a wedge against their authority. This muddle persisted well into the New Deal era.

The maintenance of public order in strikebound areas fell to four types of police: local police and constables, county sheriffs and their deputies, the state constabulary, and company security forces. Of the four, local police were the least consequential in large industrial strikes. Municipal officers were generally employed full time in cities and large boroughs. Constables were predominately part-time officers hired by small boroughs and sparsely populated townships. The jurisdiction of municipal police and constables was limited to the geographic confines of the polity that they served. Municipal officers worked closely with locally elected justices of the peace, or "squires." Jeremiah Shalloo, a graduate student in sociology at the University of Pennsylvania, interviewed local squires and constables in the coalfields immediately following the Great Coal Strike. Shalloo concluded that judicial neutrality was in short supply. Constables and squires often favored the miners, and "nigger scabs" had no legal rights in their jurisdictions. Industrial police and sheriffs' deputies did not expect convictions by local authorities, and preferred higher courts to handle their cases. The Coal and Iron police did, of course, have "company squires" at their disposal—their antidote to the "red neck" justices who protected the union miners. Coal and Iron police did arrest constables "doing their duty" on coal company property. At Moon Run, near Crafton, one constable was arrested in excess of a dozen times, but he was never convicted.[1]

Captain Jacob Mauk of the state constabulary concluded that Justice J. M. O'Rourke of the Bruceton-Broughton district, a prominent "redneck squire," had collaborated with a local constable in forcing a confession from a black nonunion miner. Mauk's findings overturned the conviction of the strikebreaker, but served only to strengthen O'Rourke's ties with the UMWA. In the Bentleyville district, Bethlehem Mines attempted unsuccessfully to register its black strikebreakers in order to break the union hold on the local ballot. The union defeated that company's candidate for local constable, an industrial policeman once in Bethlehem's employ. Local law enforcement was not always biased or venal. In June 1931 New Kensington police chief, Daniel Zeloyle, armed with a Thompson submachine gun and accompanied by an officer carrying a riot gun, arrested two deputy sheriffs for felonious assault. The deputies were on duty at Valley Camp's Kinloch Mine just south of New Kensington, and had shot several union miners. Violence at Kinloch had sporadically spilled over into New Kensington since 1927. The citizens of the community had petitioned Governor Fisher that year, and a force of state police had been dispatched. However, the constabulary eventually departed, leaving a force of company-paid deputies behind. The presence of UMWA miners, NMU marchers, and trigger-happy deputies virtually guaranteed a renewal of violence. Zeloyle intervened in an earnest attempt to avert the kind of violence that New Kensington had experienced all too often. His arrest of the deputies had been the first in the district since Allegheny Coal and Coke deputies had been charged with murder in the Fannie Sellins killing. The chief also warned the miners that his department would show "no side any quarter in maintaining peace."[2]

Two nights prior to the arrest of the deputies, Zeloyle locked up eight armed miners who had stopped and searched automobiles while "looking for scabs." The terrified motorists, confronted by clubs and flashlights in the dead of night, demanded protection. The Kinloch Mine was situated outside New Kensington borough, but was adjacent to the main highway that connected New Kensington and Greensburg, the county seat. Motorists were also harassed by armed deputies on duty along the highway. The shootings on 10 June gave Zeloyle all the justification he needed to deal with what many believed to be rogue law enforcement officers.[3]

Both Zeloyle and the citizens of New Kensington were acutely aware of the shortcomings of deputy sheriffs on strike duty. In 1928 Chief Deputy E. M. Kepple, in charge at Kinloch, testified before the U.S. Senate investigating committee that Valley Camp Coal Company paid the Westmoreland County sheriff $7.50 per day for each deputy that he supplied. The deputies were in turn paid $5.00 per day for their work. The sheriff presumably pocketed the remaining $2.50, an act considered by many residents to be little more than racketeering. A store proprietor in nearby Braeburn reported that deputies on duty at a small mine there fired shots and used physical coercion to force strikebreakers to work in a local mine.[4]

The editors of the *Valley Daily News* were prompted to observe:

The charge that the Westmoreland County sheriff is more interested in protecting the property of companies where coal strikes are in progress than in guarding the lives and safety of the public had been heard before. This time the allegation is made by chief of police Dan J. Zeloyle of New Kensington, that the Westmoreland County sheriff has neglected to take steps against riotous miners who invaded New Kensington.

At the average strike, it usually happens that deputies and state police are hurried to the premises of the company. They are required to devote their full attention to protecting the company property.

Little, if any regard is paid to disorders which spring up on the outside. And it usually happens that the effect of the police activity is to aid the company break the strike. Officers of the law assigned to a strike zone are supposed to be impartial between the company and the men. But it rarely happens that the officers act in the interest of the men and the general public. And this condition is only too true in case of privately paid coal and iron policemen.

The law, too often, has been arrayed upon the side of companies in labor disputes. And it must not be forgotten that not all strikes are unjust and unfair. Many of them are the result of unfair treatment of workers who have no other means of fighting for their rights. Disorder, of course, is not to be tolerated. Life and property must be guarded. Too often, however, the police are used to intimidate strikers who are conducting themselves in an orderly manner and within the rights guaranteed them by law.[5]

The press was on hand two weeks later as Allegheny County deputy sheriffs fired volley after volley into NMU pickets near Wildwood, in Hampton Township, north of Pittsburgh. The miners marched in violation of court orders, but were not, according to witnesses, armed. According to reporters, the deputies, led by William ("Silver") Braun, "lost their heads," firing into the men long after they had begun to flee the field of battle. The deputies, "gone wild with excitement," were in no hurry to quit the bloodletting, and were slow to bring relief to the men who were wounded. Local residents also agreed that the deputies had been "too quick with their guns." The local press professed no sympathy for the miners and particularly their "red" leadership, but regretted that the men had been "mowed down like animals." That sort of thing, the *Valley Daily News* averred, would continue so long as "hoodlums are given clubs and revolvers and made deputies."[6]

Jeremiah Shalloo discovered that deputy sheriffs were much used but not highly regarded in western Pennsylvania. Businessmen and public officials alike characterized them as "riff-raff, bums, ward healers and city hall loafers" employed by the sheriff in payment for political favors. Appointment and dismissal of deputies was the exclusive prerogative of county sheriffs. Indiana County employed 104 deputy sheriffs in 1928, but the number exceeded 6,000 in Fayette County during the 1922 strike. Critics charged that deputies sometimes held Coal and Iron police commissions concurrently and were on two payrolls. The use of aliases and meager record keeping makes precise verification impossible, but it nevertheless appears that in some cases local deputies and industrial police were one and the same. On 30 June 1931, Gifford Pinchot revoked the commissions of all industrial police, thereby depriving the Frick Coal Company of the use of its force of sixty-one Coal and Iron police. Frick Coal applied to Fayette County Sheriff Henry Hackney for deputies. Hackney deputized many of Frick's former industrial police and the Coal and Iron police continued to operate under sponsors independent of Harrisburg. A commission on industrial police appointed by Pinchot found that Frick's force of deputies had grown to over 300 men by April 1934. UMWA efforts to organize the captive mines in the coal district induced Frick Coal, which employed more than 50 percent of Fayette County's miners, to recruit many experienced Coal and Iron officers, former state police, and men with military experience. These men were actually selected by the company, subject to the sheriff's veto. Hackney was nominally in command of this force, but actual control was exercised by the chief of security of Frick Coal, H. A. Chambers. According to Pinchot's commission, Sheriff Hackney also employed a force of 146 "roving deputies," responsible directly to him. These deputies wore no uniforms but were armed. For $5 a day they patrolled the county's roads and kept union miners under surveillance. They were not, according to the commission, chosen with great care.[7]

Although deputy sheriffs played the most prominent role in policing the industrial strike zone in Pennsylvania, it was the Coal and Iron police who elicited the greatest condemnation. Deputy sheriffs were a shambling, sloppy, inefficient, often unpredictably dangerous lot. But industrial police were perceived quite differently by their critics. These men were not viewed as trigger-happy courthouse toughs. The Coal and Iron police seemed to be a well-organized, disciplined force of mercenaries. They were employees of corporations, yet were also agents of the commonwealth. Their depredations, which allegedly ranged from simple assault to kidnapping, rape, and murder, appeared to be sanctioned by the state.

The commonwealth empowered its railroads to organize private police forces in 1865. A year later that privilege was extended to coal and steel companies. Businessmen who petitioned the governor for industrial police commissions received them upon payment of one dollar for each document issued by the secretary of state. Commissions were kept on file by that office, but Harrisburg did not investigate, regulate, or supervise those who held them. For more than forty years, the Commonwealth of Pennsylvania assumed virtually no responsibility for the conduct of the industrial police it licensed. In 1923 Gifford Pinchot directed Sergeant George W. Freeman of the state constabulary to investigate the backgrounds of those who held industrial police commissions. Subsequent to Freeman's inquiries, Pinchot revoked the commissions of 4,000 officers; however, the completion of Pinchot's term brought an end to the process of review. In 1927 *Pittsburgh Press* reporter Mark Shields found that the administration of industrial police had fallen into a state of chaos. Despite a questionnaire sent by Governor John Fisher to eighty-seven coal companies that used industrial police, more than 2,300 of 3,982 commissions in effect could not be accounted for. William Warden, board chairman of Pittsburgh Coal, indicated that his company had abandoned deputy sheriffs for a more "reliable" force of company police. Nevertheless, Pittsburgh Coal, which spent $472,220 on its industrial police in 1927, could not account for 135 of 255 commissions charged to that company. Officials of Pittsburgh Terminal Coal admitted that their officers signed a resignation form on the day they were hired to facilitate their release. President Horace Baker acknowledged that his company had spent $200,000 for private police, but Pittsburgh Terminal could not account for 102 of 156 commissions still in force. Industrial police may have been more "reliable," but they were clearly no less transient than deputy sheriffs.[8]

The failure of the commonwealth to define precisely the jurisdiction of industrial police added to the storm of controversy concerning their activities. Captain John Searsch, organizer of the Coal and Iron police at Pittsburgh Coal, asserted that the duties of an industrial policeman were the same as those of a constable. They were empowered to arrest for all crimes committed within their view. Searsch's assertion was supported by Major Lynn Adams, superintendent of the state constabulary. Adams believed that industrial police enjoyed the same authority as municipal officers, even though they were not accountable to local civil authorities. The officers themselves believed that they possessed broad powers. Sergeant W. M. Akers, a former state police officer in the employ of Pittsburgh Coal, told a Senate committee that he was empowered to make arrests for any offense committed within the county in which he held his commission. Critics protested this assumption of broad police powers and argued that the work of private police was confined to the property of those who employed them. But that was clearly not the case. UMWA official Pat Fagan was arrested by Coal and Iron police outside the Wabash Building in downtown Pittsburgh and taken before a magistrate in Mt. Lebanon, in the southern part of Allegheny County. And the Coal and Iron police did far more than protect strikebreakers and defend company property against union violence and sabotage.[9]

In 1926 UMWA activists generated a good deal of work for the police employed by Bethlehem Mines. O. R. Check, superintendent for security, reported more than twelve hundred shootings and forty dynamitings during a five-month union campaign. Check attributed the violence to the company's decision to resume operations on a nonunion basis. He believed that Bethlehem's victory resulted from the "eternal vigilance" and hard work of fifty-two Coal and Iron police. Four hundred thirty-eight arrests were punctuated by a gun battle with bootleggers and the fatal shooting of a black strikebreaker who drew a gun on Check's officers. Most of the arrests were of the expected variety; disorderly union marchers and pickets, saboteurs, and trespassers. However, 1927 brought a virtual end to UMWA activity at Bethlehem's mining operations. The resumption of the "normal routine" enabled Bethlehem to reduce its force, but arrests more than doubled. Of 965 persons arrested by Bethlehem's police in 1927, 724 were company employees. Summary convictions were given to 452, and 44 were held for court. There were 626 arrested for disorderly conduct. Other charges included assault and battery, violations of the motor vehicle code and liquor laws, rape, robbery, desertion, nonsupport, bastardy, fornication, and riot. Bethlehem Mines clearly assigned the broadest kind of jurisdictional authority to its officers.[10]

Most industrial police forces were organized on a paramilitary basis. A typical chain of command included privates, corporals, sergeants, lieutenants, and captains. At Pittsburgh Coal, privates earned $160 per month, corporals $190 and sergeants $200. The men supplied their own uniforms, but the companies provided weapons and equipment, as well as room and board. In the period from 1925 to 1930, Pennsylvania coal companies employed an average 2,000 officers a year. According to Jeremiah Shalloo, salaries averaged $150 a month, and payrolls were approximately $300,000 per month. The companies involved had an average annual aggregate payroll of $3,600,000. The chief of security at Pittsburgh Terminal Coal testified that his company spent $150,000 per month for security forces during the height of the UMWA strike in 1927. In 1925, before its decision to operate under an open shop, Pittsburgh Coal spent $22,882 for industrial police. When the UMWA strike began, expenditures leaped to $199,500 in 1926, and $472,200 in 1927. Following the defeat of the union, costs fell to $12,000 in 1928.[11]

INDUSTRIAL POLICE COMMISSIONS ON FILE IN HARRISBURG[12]

	18 January 1927	12 November 1927	1 March 1928
Bethlehem Mines	78	88	64
Pittsburgh Coal	75	260	106
Pittsburgh Terminal Coal	0	156	82

Uniformed officers, normally armed with handguns, nightsticks and shotguns, patrolled Bethlehem Mines' three divisions in western Pennsylvania. The Ellsworth division, which encompassed most of Washington County, involved an area of forty-five square miles and a population of 8,500. The Heilwood division, situated in Indiana County, included three mines and 2,600 people. The Johnstown division, included a third of a square mile at Slickville, Westmoreland County, and two-thirds of a square mile at Wehrum, Indiana County. The combined population of this last division was 3,000. In 1926, 131 Coal and Iron police patrolled those sites. In 1927, when strike activity subsided, the force was reduced to 38 men, and in 1928 to 19 full–time men. The officers normally patrolled in twelve-hour shifts, although twenty-four-hour tours were not uncommon. These men had thirty-seven riot guns, twenty-two rifles, thirty-nine revolvers, two Thompson submachine guns, and sixty tear-gas grenades at their disposal. The machine guns excited public controversy, but like those owned by Pittsburgh Terminal Coal, they were never actually used by Bethlehem.[13]

Bethlehem claimed that the officers in its employ were "gentlemen of the higher type." The chief of security assured his superiors that his men had been selected with the greatest care and in cooperation with other police authorities. Employment required a personal interview, a common-school education or better, and good physical stature and appearance. References were investigated. John Searsch of Pittsburgh Coal claimed that he required five letters of recommendation for employment on his force. His recruits came from city police, state police, and members of the Governor's Troops. He claimed that his successor at Pittsburgh Coal, Estey Jim Couskey, was a retired state police officer. According to Shalloo, former state police became prime candidates for the industrial police because they were forced to resign from the constabulary when they married. Of 104 Coal and Iron police employed by Pittsburgh Coal in 1928, 66 had military service, 19 were former state police, 6 had served in the highway patrol, 7 had been municipal police, 4 had been railroad police, and 9 had been deputy sheriffs and border patrol officers. Management asserted that Captain E. R. Sourbeer had been a captain in the state cavalry assigned to the governor's office. Lieutenant W. J. Lyster, later tried in connection with the death of miner John Barcoski, was said to have served in the state constabulary.[14]

The Pennsylvania Constabulary, or state police, had been regularly involved in industrial strife since its inception in 1905. In 1927 Philip Murray publicly complimented the constabulary for its neutrality and professionalism on the picket lines. Murray's comments were exceptional, because for more than two decades the constabulary had been condemned as a "strike-breaking institution." The constabulary was particularly detested and feared by the state's immigrant population. Among the Slavs, the gray-uniformed officers mounted on horseback were known as the cossacks, which was clearly no term of endearment. For many, the constabulary represented the very antithesis of what it was intended to be: an orderly and effective alternative to the Coal and Iron police.

When Governor Samuel Pennypacker signed the legislation that created the constabulary in 1905, many believed that the Coal and Iron police would pass into history. But that did not happen. The constabulary became just one more police force to patrol the strike zones. In some cases the uniforms of the constabulary and industrial police were so similar that the constabulary was often mistaken for the Coal and Iron police. It was of course, a very different entity. The original force of 232 men was divided into four troops. Two such troops, composed of 55 men each, were stationed permanently at Butler and Greensburg. The men were housed in barracks and subject to strict discipline. The commonwealth attempted to attract, and largely succeeded in recruiting, dedicated, courageous young men to the force. Many a coal miner has expressed a grudging but sincere admiration for the gray-clad troopers on horseback who were sent alone into remote coal patches to restore order. Less endearing memoirs were generated by the mounted-phalanx tactics employed by troopers riding shoulder to shoulder into crowds of strikers. The unrestrained use of truncheons by troopers did not enhance their image.[15]

James Maurer, a machinist from Reading and president of the Pennsylvania State Federation of Labor, became an implacable enemy of the constabulary. A socialist, he was elected to the state legislature. He observed a phalanx drill at a barracks and learned that its purpose was to "stampede a mob." When Maurer inquired about what was meant by a "mob", he was allegedly told, "a riot of assembled men or a strike." For several years, Maurer compiled a record of the constabulary and its work, subsequently producing an indictment entitled the *American Cossack*. Coal miners involved in the 1910 Westmoreland County strike accused the constabulary of riding into pickets, of beating miners and their families, and of disrupting peaceful meetings. In Tarentum, on the west bank of the Allegheny River twenty-five miles north of Pittsburgh, a transit strike against West Penn Traction Company raged for more than two years. The company discharged striking motormen and threatened to operate with strikebreakers. A public boycott and street violence ensued, followed by an occupation by twenty-eight state police. According to Maurer, local merchants and elected officials were harassed and arrested by the zealous troopers. Tarentum was a union stronghold, and the presence of the constabulary was widely resented. The troopers were, in a sense, uninvited guests, for their presence had been requested by the Allegheny County sheriff, not the town fathers. The troopers were no more welcome in Tarentum than the sheriff's deputies, for their presence implied that local officials had lost control of their communities. Tarentum's burgess and council asserted that such was not the case, and demanded that the sheriff rescind his request for the troopers. The practice of dispatching troopers to strike areas upon the request of the sheriff continued until 1931, when Gifford Pinchot made such action subject to the direct approval of the governor's office. Pinchot was all too aware of charges made by organized labor that county sheriffs, particularly those in the coke district of southwestern Pennsylvania, were simply agents of the coal operators and steel magnates. Pinchot was determined to protect the separate identity of the state police while repudiating the charge that the constabulary was an instrument of corporate repression.[16]

Pinchot's modest change of policy would probably not have satisfied Maurer. In a speech given in Harrisburg on 16 March 1911, Maurer charged that the constabulary was created "for the purpose of aiding the great combinations of capitalists." Its method was "intimidation." Maurer led the political opposition to legislation that expanded the constabulary, and on several occasions introduced bills that would have disbanded it. He also testified before a federal commission on industrial relations that the constabulary was specially trained as a strikebreaking tool. Maurer ultimately failed in his attempts to destroy the state police, and his efforts evoked a chorus of protests from its defenders.[17]

On two different occasions, widely separated by time, two embattled Westmoreland County sheriffs defended the state police. In 1933, during the UMWA drive to organize the coke fields, Sheriff William Humes lauded the state police for their superior training and tight discipline during labor conflicts. Almost twenty years earlier, Sheriff Ben Steele had rushed to defend the constabulary against charges of official repression. Steele averred that strikers in his county favored the presence of the constabulary over deputies or Coal and Iron police. Untrained deputies and Coal and Iron police were frequently charged with fomenting disturbances and causing trouble. The constabulary was experienced, tactful, and impartial in dealing with labor disputes. Furthermore, sixty unincorporated mining towns existed in Westmoreland County. According to Steele, those towns were populated with foreigners, many of whom were "vicious fugitives from justice in other lands." "Farmers were [their] natural prey." In Westmoreland County, farmers constituted the largest support for the state police. The *Kittanning Daily Times* also defended the state police, arguing that "only longhaired fanatics" opposed the constabulary. The implication was clear. The state police offered protection against radical and foreign elements. Captain John C. Groome, first commandant of the constabulary, gathered these sentiments of support and published a rebuttal to Maurer. In *A Reply to the American Cossack*, Groome argued that "farmers," "genuine workingmen," and other "law abiding citizens" strongly favored his force. Only "labor agitators," who made their living by "fomenting trouble between the employers and the employed," did not.[18]

Groome's comments were hardly those of an unbiased arbiter of industrial conflict. Groome considered Maurer to be little more than a self-serving political opportunist. In order to refute his charges, Groome also testified before the federal Commission on Industrial Relations. He apparently did not impress the panel with his defense of the constabulary, for the commission concluded that it was an

> extremely efficient force for crushing strikes, but it is not successful in preventing violence in connection with strikes, maintaining the legal and civil rights of the parties to the dispute, nor in protecting the public. On the contrary, violence seems to increase rather than diminish when the constabulary is brought into an industrial dispute; the legal and civil rights of the workers have been on numerous occasions violated by the constabulary; and citizens not in any way connected with the dispute and innocent of any interference have been brutally treated and in one case shot down . . . Organized upon a strictly military basis it appears to assume in taking the field . . . that strikers are its enemies and the enemies of the state, and that a campaign should be waged against them as such.[19]

The controversy concerning the role of the state police in industrial disputes continued to simmer through the 1920s. The dispersal of demonstrators at a Sacco and Vanzetti rally near Cheswick, Allegheny County, in 1927 raised new questions about tactics employed by the constabulary as well as the professional objectivity of the troopers. The crowd was composed largely of people of Italian extraction. Many of the protestors were miners who used the occasion to circumvent a sheriff's order against mass demonstrations. The UMWA officially disavowed the gathering, but representatives of Save the Union and the Workers' Party were clearly involved in organizing the rally. According to participants, the events of 22 August were entirely peaceful until a detachment of mounted constabulary arrived. The demonstrators apparently did not disperse quickly enough to suit the troopers, and the latter rode into the crowd swinging clubs. Protestors were allegedly subjected to ethnic slurs such as "dirty wop son of a bitch," "hunky," and "dago bastard." As the troopers pursued the fleeing crowd, one officer was shot and killed.

Afterward, according to the American Civil Liberties Union, the UMWA and the Communist press, a police riot and reign of terror ensued. Residents of nearby Harwick and other communities claimed state police invaded private property and beat residents in their search for the murderer. Murray wrote to Governor Fisher and complained that John Rodko, a Russellton-area miner, was arrested and interrogated in a basement cell at the Greensburg barracks for three days. Rodko insisted that he was forced to endure physical abuse as well as death threats while being held incommunicado. The senseless arrest of John

Brophy and the assault upon Pat Toohey at Renton a few months later did little to enhance the reputation of the constabulary. However, so long as the Coal and Iron police were in the field, the alleged misdeeds of the state police would remain of secondary interest.[20]

Despite his best attempts to remain aloof from the conflict in the soft-coal fields, Governor John Fisher was forced by the alleged depredations of the industrial police to evaluate their activities. Gifford Pinchot, who had revoked many industrial police commissions during his term, accused Fisher of allowing the coal operators to revive the "thug system" in the commonwealth. Congressman John Carey insinuated that the governor was merely a pawn of the Mellon interests. An "armed force of private gunmen" was allowed to run amok throughout the state. "No matter from what angle one approached the situation, one sooner or later arrived at the doorstep of Pittsburgh Coal, a Mellon Company," In February 1928 Fisher seemed to be on the brink of making some changes in the industrial police system. Acting on orders from Fisher, Deputy Attorney General Philip Moyer sent questionnaires to eighty-seven coal companies that employed commissioned industrial police. The results of that survey revealed a serious administrative muddle. The Fisher administration simply did not know precisely how many Coal and Iron police were employed in Pennsylvania. Just as the results of that survey were released, the Senate committee swept into the commonwealth. Fisher became locked in a war of words with that body, and he stonewalled on all issues connected to the coal strike. A siege mentality enveloped official Harrisburg, and Fisher apparently eschewed any action that might have been construed as knuckling under to outside political pressure. The industrial police system was not reformed. Pennsylvania's uninvited political guests soon departed. Summer came, and the UMWA strike collapsed. The coal operators reduced their police forces, and violent incidents virtually ceased. The Fisher administration had seemingly weathered the storm of controversy generated by the Coal and Iron police.[21]

Tragically, that tranquillity would not long endure. In February 1929 the Coal and Iron police were again front-page news. On 10 February John Barcoski, a farmer and miner from Tyre, Allegheny County, was arrested by Coal and Iron police employed by the Pittsburgh Coal Company. While in their custody, he was apparently interrogated with a poker. His skull, spinal cord, rib cage and pelvis were crushed, suggesting that he had been the victim of a systematic beating. The incident seemed to substantiate charges that the Coal and Iron police were devoid of humanity, and that they exercised the authority of "judge, jury, and executioner." When news of the incident reached Fisher, he suspended the commissions of the three officers and demanded an explanation of the episode. Three officers—Lieutenant W. J. Lyster, and officers Harold Watts, and Frank Slapaki—were arrested by Allegheny County authorities and indicted for murder. The Barcoski killing was followed by the expected condemnations by civil libertarians and the UMWA. However, conservative opinion was also inflamed by the incident. Editorials in the *Vandergrift News,* a paper that served a conservative Republican steel-trust town, typified conservative outrage throughout the commonwealth.

> Primitive savagery displayed by Coal and Iron Police who stomped and beat an unresisting farmer to death is but a natural outgrowth of a system that has become fastened upon Pittsburgh like a virulent cancer.
> The members of the Coal and Iron Police are, for the most part, people who are no better than the most ruffianly among those whom they guard. The only difference is that the law stands behind the Coal and Iron Police. The coal companies wanted men to enforce by brutality and savagery, the laws which they passed to apply to miners. They got such men in Pennsylvania, asleep as the state usually is, investing hired ruffians with the majesty and power of the law.[22]

In March Representative Michael Musmanno and Senator W. D. Mansfield, both of Pittsburgh, each introduced industrial-police reform bills in their respective houses of the state legislature. Their bills were similar, but there were areas of conflict. Neither bill called for the abolition of industrial police. Each called for a thorough investigation of applicants, the wearing of uniforms and badges, the posting of bonds, letters of recommendation, and state residence. The Musmanno bill would have confined the jurisdiction of industrial police to 1,000 feet from company property. The Mansfield bill was more flexible on that issue. Both pieces of legislation were showered with amendments. The amended bill that emerged from committee resembled the Mansfield rather than the Musmanno version. The notion that industrial police should be confined to within 1,000 feet of company property was rejected, for if that was done, they could not guard payrolls, water lines, or other isolated properties. The bill, in fact, vested in private police the authority enjoyed by police in cities of the first class. Fisher signed the legislation on 18 April, amid charges that the Coal and Iron police now enjoyed greater powers than they had before.[23]

The "weak and silly" Mansfield bill was condemned by critics of the Right and Left alike. For some, only the total abolition of private police forces constituted meaningful reform. The acquittal of Lyster and Watts in September by a jury characterized by the presiding trial judge as "incompetent and without moral stamina" heightened fears that the Coal and Iron police were ready for yet another rampage. A month after the Barcoski murder trial, the *Pittsburgh Courier* complained that a black miner, or "race miner," William Young, had been another victim of the "cold brutality and careless gunplay" of the Coal and Iron police employed in Allegheny County. With the Not Guilty verdict of Lyster and Watts still ringing in their ears, Coal and Iron police at Montour No. 1 Mine murdered William Young because he refused to adhere to a "Move on" order from Private James Lucas. Residents of the coalfields could expect more of the same because, according to the *Vandergrift News,* "Pennsylvanians could expect no decent government decision from those in power" in Harrisburg.[24]

Stung by both the venom and the persistence of his critics, Governor Fisher moved decisively on two fronts. Shortly after signing the Mansfield bill, he appointed George Lumb, a former officer in the constabulary, to the post of superintendent of industrial police. Lumb was charged with drafting a set of regulations that would govern the activities of industrial police throughout the commonwealth. Fisher also ordered Major Lynn Adams of the constabulary to conduct a clandestine investigation of the American Civil Liberties Union. The latter order, no doubt the product of petulance rather than common sense, demonstrates just how deeply Fisher was annoyed by the press and leftist civil libertarians. Judge Langham wrote his old friend and confessed that he "loved [Fisher] for the enemies [he] had made." The "enemies" to whom Langham referred were the editors of the *Pittsburgh Post-Gazette,* who attacked Fisher while "knowing nothing of the real facts." Fisher replied that the Pittsburgh newspapers were "foreign controlled," but he must have known there was little that he could do to silence them. The ACLU was another matter.[25]

Fisher believed that the American Civil Liberties Union was "hostile to the execution of the law, especially where the police power was concerned." He ordered Adams to ferret out the facts about the organization and to present his findings to him directly. Adams dutifully complied, but his findings did little more than fortify Fisher's prejudices and assuage his frustrations. Adams reported that the purpose of the ACLU "seemed fair," but it had "as its moving spirits those that are always found present when things communistic are being advocated." Its activities in the Sacco and Vanzetti case, "giving out false information concerning that case throughout the world, amounted to treason." According to Adams, the ACLU "never defended the constitutional rights of anyone that had been threatened by a mob of strikers." Adams also dredged up the IWW and tied it to the ACLU. An old adversary, the IWW was in fact no more active in the coalfields in 1929 than it had been when Adams patrolled the Turtle Creek Valley fifteen years earlier.

Fisher thanked the major for his succinct report on the ACLU and opined that "they are known by their works, and the membership of such persons as Foster, Nearing, and Elizabeth Gurley Flynn. They will be found promoting disorder and lawlessness, condemning the courts and police departments in maintaining law and order, and by silence, at least, approving the murder of police officials." Having thus exorcised a personal political demon, Fisher dropped the investigation of the ACLU and never raised it again.[26]

George Lumb implemented his Regulations and Code of Conduct for Industrial Police on 1 June 1929. The regulations conformed to the provisions of the Mansfield bill. Officers were required to wear numbered badges and uniforms of forest green. Patrols were restricted to company property, and officers were forbidden to use "undue violence." Monthly reports were to be submitted by every company employing industrial police, a policy that Lumb believed "had good moral effect upon the conduct of the men." Lumb suggested that the industrial police problem was solving itself, for on 1 October 1929, fewer than a thousand commissions were in force in the commonwealth. According to Lumb, sixty-two companies had discontinued the employment of industrial police. During his first six months as superintendent, Lumb investigated twenty-one companies employing Coal and Iron police in order to determine whether there was any criticism of their conduct. Lumb polled neighboring businessmen, public officials, bankers, and local justices. No complaints were made to them by "representative citizens" in residence near those companies, and none was recorded by Lumb's office. The termination of the UMWA strike had reduced conflict in the mining camps, and the relaxed atmosphere enabled the operators to reduce or eliminate their forces. As the Fisher administration prepared to leave Harrisburg, in 1931, it appeared that the commonwealth had turned the corner on the industrial police controversy.[27]

Gifford Pinchot campaigned in behalf of industrial police reform in 1930, but it is clear that it was not a burning issue in that Depression year. Representative Michael Musmanno introduced a second industrial police bill in January 1931, but that bill died in the state senate. Senator William Rial of Westmoreland County, a defender of the industrial police system, commented that Musmanno had "gone insane" in his attempts to eliminate the Coal and Iron police. Musmanno's failure to compromise, Rial averred, accounted for the defeat of his legislation. Besides, the people of Westmoreland County did not "give a hoot" about the issue of industrial police. Public indifference to the industrial police issue no doubt prevailed throughout the commonwealth, for only an emasculated UMWA offered supportive testimony during hearings held in Harrisburg. Gifford Pinchot introduced a third bill that would have placed industrial police directly under the control of the constabulary, but that, too, was defeated in the legislature. The UMWA supported the Musmanno bill, and Pat Fagan accused Pinchot of reneging on a campaign promise to eliminate the Coal and Iron police. Pinchot's bill would simply make industrial police an auxiliary of the constabulary, a move that would strengthen rather than weaken private police forces. In the end, neither the Musmanno nor the Pinchot legislation was adopted. A frustrated Gifford Pinchot finally cut the Gordian knot by revoking all industrial police commissions by executive order on 30 June 1931. The Coal and Iron police would not function again while Pinchot resided in the governor's mansion.[28]

Pinchot had rid the commonwealth of its "bad rubbish" on the eve of the National Miners Union strike. No doubt many Coal and Iron police found employment as deputy sheriffs during that conflict, for Pinchot had no control over the hiring practices of county sheriffs. Two months before his revocation of all industrial police commissions, Pinchot ordered the state police to observe strict neutrality toward all parties involved in strikes. On 4 March 1931, Major Lynn Adams issued General Order No. 17, which embodied the principle of state neutrality in industrial disputes. Two months later, a violent strike raged along a two-hundred-mile front in southwestern Pennsylvania. Pinchot attributed the troubles to Communists transporting truckloads of troublemakers from mine to mine. The Communists retorted that Pinchot was conspiring with the operators and the UMWA to crush their union. Deputy sheriffs gunned down union demonstrators at Wildwood. The NMU broke up an UMWA rally at Canonsburg. Ironically, the constabulary and Coal and Iron police largely escaped public notice during the 1931 NMU strikes, although both participated in the conflict.[29]

Private police had their last fling during the UMWA strikes in the coke district. During the summer of 1933, John L. Lewis attempted to organize men employed in the "captive mines" owned by the nation's steel companies. According to Pinchot, the miners were "simply wonderful," but the tactics employed by the "Swine of the Steel Trust" had forced them to desperate measures. Subservient sheriffs in Westmoreland and Fayette counties hired former industrial police as deputies. Their salaries were paid by the steel companies. Pinchot refused to cooperate, and he judiciously deployed the National Guard throughout the coke district in order to weaken the authority of the sheriffs who openly defied him. A curious state of martial law prevailed in Fayette County, in which the police power of the state was pitted against that which served corporate America. The UMWA ultimately lost the coke district struggle, and Pinchot, stymied by the steel trust, was denied his party's senatorial nomination and subsequently left politics forever. The steel industry had won the struggle in the coke fields, but the concept of private police suffered irreparable damage. Pinchot's successor, George Earle, made abolition of the industrial police system and elimination of privately paid deputy sheriffs major priorities on the agenda of the Little New Deal. When the legislative session in Harrisburg closed in 1937, both had passed into history. Henceforth, private and public police authority would not conflict on the picket lines in the commonwealth.[30]

7

Last Chance: The Amalgamated in Apollo and Vandergrift, 1933–1937

WHATEVER HAPPENED TO THE MILITANT STEELWORKERS AND THEIR union—the Amalgamated—during the decade and a half that followed the collapse of the Great Steel Strike of 1919? Industrial relations in steel during the 1920s are generally discussed in terms of abject submission. Company unions, the open shop, and the American plan are frequently used to characterize the industry during that decade. Industrial warfare seemed to be the exclusive province of the miners, and the seemingly docile mill towns appeared to be untouched by the strife. When labor historians discuss the ultimate unionization of steel during the 1930s, it is often presented as a rescue mission carried out by John L. Lewis, the Steel Workers Organizing Committee, and the CIO. But were the mill towns of western Pennsylvania mired in defeat and resignation? Had the proud old Amalgamated Association of Iron, Steel and Tin Workers, become, as its critics suggested, a union dominated by a self-serving elite, "content to cultivate its little garden of dues-payers without worrying about the masses outside its fold?"[1] After decades of failure, were the steelworkers of western Pennsylvania ready to give up on the Amalgamated?

Until recently, historical literature exaggerated the homogeneity of western Pennsylvania mill towns. The very term *mill town* carried with it a pejorative connotation: grime, ugliness, cultural deprivation, political repression, and economic dependence. Contemporary historiography has begun to break through those community stereotypes, exploring important differences generated by race, religion, ethnicity, local politics, company policy, and a host of other factors. Those forces produced community personality, or temperament. Industrial communities, whether coal patch or steel town, each possessed a unique social chemistry and often responded very differently to crisis.

For all his political acumen, charisma, and ruthlessness, John L. Lewis was constantly bedeviled by the inconsistent behavior of his locals. In coal, the interests of union local and coal patch were often synonymous. Most locals and patches were compliant, if not loyal to Lewis. Others were defiant and ever rebellious. Lewis usually offered the carrot, and if that failed, wielded the stick. Mike Tighe, the eighty-year-old president of the Amalgamated, faced similar pockets of resistance during the early 1930s. But the question of community temperament went far beyond the problems of union administration. Local municipalities, their power structures and inhabitants, responded in very different ways to industrial crises. Tarentum, in northern Allegheny County, was a union town. It permitted organizing activities by coal miners and steelworkers, even during the Red Scare. Tarentum was known for its relief activities, especially in behalf of striking miners. Town fathers resented the imposition of outside police forces by the county and state. On a number of occasions, particularly during the Great Steel Strike, they demanded the withdrawal of the constabulary and deputy sheriffs from their community.[2]

In New Kensington, directly opposite Tarentum on the eastern bank of the Allegheny River, hospitality for organized labor was in short supply. Labor had its benefactors, such as Fred Broad, but aid from the community at large was less forthcoming. New Kensington was a Mellon town, created to serve a growing aluminum industry. Town fathers were much more likely to call in county and state police forces, decisions that were more often than not counterproductive. In 1919 the burgess, ostensibly acting as a peacemaker, called a meeting of striking steelworkers. Following opening amenities, he revealed his real intentions. He told the strikers that most of the men employed by two local American Sheet and Tin plants were "Americans" and desired to return to work. He planned to guarantee their safe return. If the strikers who remained out started trouble, the burgess vowed that the "authorities would finish it." Two days later, fifty deputies stood by as a fewer than a hundred men reentered the mill.[3]

Historian Herbert Gutman argues that as industrialism swept late-nineteenth-century America, organized labor was not alone in opposing its power. According to Gutman, labor found friends and allies, particularly at the local level. Although labor and its friends were largely swept aside by the industrial tide, pockets of resistance appeared to linger in western Pennsylvania well into the twentieth century. Gutman also suggests that much of the resistance to industrial hegemony was not due to the work of outside agitators; it was generated by a local, home-grown leadership. The Amalgamated's experiences in Apollo and Vandergrift offer an opportunity to examine labor unrest and its roots in the

community. The Amalgamated attempted to organize Apollo and Vandergrift in 1901, 1909, and 1919. Its fourth and final attempt occurred
during the New Deal.[4]

Nestled on opposite banks of the Kiskiminetas River, Apollo and
Vandergrift were mill towns marked by sharp contrasts that masked a
common heritage. Apollo was first prominent as a stop on the Pennsylvania Mainline Canal. Steel production began during the 1880s. George
McMurtry, a native of Belfast, Northern Ireland, emerged as the most
prominent steelmaker in the Kiskiminetas Valley during that decade.
Apollo Iron and Steel flourished under his direction, but McMurtry's
plans were disrupted by a strike in 1893 and by the inability to purchase
nearby land necessary for expansion. Amid much bitterness generated
by the strike, McMurtry announced that he was moving his operation to
a new site located on the Westmoreland County side of the Kiskiminetas,
two miles downriver. The construction of McMurtry's new mill was to be
accompanied by the erection of a new town, named Vandergrift.

McMurtry intended to build a model industrial town. Determined to
avoid the ravages of waterborne disease so prevalent in western Pennsylvania mill towns, McMurtry took steps to insure an adequate supply of
fresh water and the efficient removal of sewage. Renowned landscape
architect Frederick Law Olmsted was engaged to design the community.
Broad streets conformed to the contours of the hilly terrain and expedited the removal of rainwater and sewage. Parcels of land were surveyed and sold to workers by an improvement company closely
associated with the mill. Land speculators, like dispensers of alcohol,
were not welcome in Vandergrift.[5]

Many Apollo people who had helped McMurtry break the strike
followed him to Vandergrift. It was widely believed that the purchase of
a lot in Vandergrift was a prerequisite to employment in the new mill. It
is clear that the early Vandergrift mill was dominated by a hard-core
anti-union labor force from southern Armstrong County. Attempts by
the Amalgamated to penetrate Vandergrift in 1901 were easily defeated.
Vandergrift flourished under the McMurtry regime. Benevolent paternalism yielded explosive growth. In less than two decades, the mill
became an important part of American Sheet and Tin Plate, employing
3,400 men.[6]

No less a personage than Ida Tarbell visited Vandergrift in 1914, a
year before McMurtry died. Tarbell characterized Vandergrift as "probably the most successful workingmen's town in the country." The community was virtually crime free and temperate. Four of seven
councilmen worked in the mill, and the burgess was a roller. Absent
were the grime, filth, and disease associated with most mill towns. Lawns,
trees, and flower gardens were much in evidence. It was "a site of natural

health and beauty." Vandergrift was a success because it was not the product of a huge, insensitive corporation. It was a small town that had been built upon the ideals of one strong man, George McMurtry. Tarbell believed McMurtry to be progressive, a man who advocated the eight-hour-day for steelworkers, as well as no work on the Sabbath. She acknowledged that Vandergrift was an American town, no place for the thousands of unskilled workers confined to East Vandergrift, North Vandergrift, and Vandergrift Heights. Indeed, she implied that their absence enabled Vandergrift's founders to establish temperance and order in their community.[7]

Tarbell might well have authored George McMurtry's laudatory obituaries. McMurtry, those writers averred, had grasped the truth that in interested, homeowning, loyal workmen lay the secret of industrial success. He made a cult of tin-mill workers, he dignified labor, giving to his employees the best schools, the finest living conditions, and the lowest death rate of any city in this territory. McMurtry accomplished all of this, but "avoided paternalism."[8]

For all its material progress, Vandergrift remained in fact a flawed and troubled paradise. The great bulk of the unskilled foreign labor was excluded from the political and cultural life of the community. Across the river in Armstrong County, bitterness and resentment remained among those who were left behind. And Vandergrift, for all its prosperity, was a community closed to dissent, particularly to that brought in from the outside. In the view of the Amalgamated, Vandergrift was little more than a nest of strikebreakers. Its mill remained a prime target of the union for more than thirty years. In 1909 the Amalgamated once again attempted to penetrate Vandergrift. The management of the mill, aided by the local government, was determined to resist. In the struggle that ensued, the divergent paths taken by Apollo and Vandergrift would play significant roles.

In the decade that followed McMurtry's departure, Apollo languished. Local businessmen referred to the period as Apollo's Dark Ages, a condition what was remedied only when Apolloites raised the money for a new mill of their own in 1912. Prior to that time, some Apollo steelworkers enjoyed employment in McMurtry's mill. The arrival of Amalgamated organizers in the Kiskiminetas Valley in 1909 put that tenuous privilege in jeopardy. A mob assaulted the Amalgamated vice-president, Llewellyn Lewis, and a squad of organizers in Vandergrift and Vandergrift Heights on 12 July. Some of the men were so hard pressed that they were forced to take to the Kiskiminetas River to escape. The beleaguered party took refuge in Apollo, where they were not entirely welcome.[9]

The organizers found lodgings at the Parks Hotel, but no one would rent a meeting hall to them. They subsequently established headquarters at the Uncapher poolroom and were able to rent a vacant lot for meetings. The pressure against the unionists was great, however, and the owner of the lot attempted to return the rent fee and rescind their right to use his lot. Apollo burgess George W. Steele and several prominent local businessmen convened a meeting and asked the organizers to leave. They refused. Local newspapers refused to print union handbills. The local press admitted that the Amalgamated had a following among the younger steelworkers in the borough, but that the older men employed at the Vandergrift mill feared that the union presence would cost them their jobs. The editor of the *Apollo News-Record* invited the "unwelcome guests" to leave. Vandergrift men had once been given preference for employment at American Sheet and Tin Plate if they bought property, but Apollo men now enjoyed an equal share of the work there. The presence of the Amalgamated placed Apollo "in a false light," and might mean the loss of jobs.[10]

Undaunted, the Amalgamated held its meeting at the rented vacant lot on the last Saturday night in July. After the meeting the organizers returned to the Parks Hotel. Soon after, a mob from Vandergrift, led by mill superintendent Oscar Lindquist, marched to the Parks Hotel and demanded that the proprietor turn over the union organizers. The proprietor refused, and extra constables, placed on duty by the burgess, were able to prevent a riot. Lindquist was well known in the Kiskiminetas Valley. He had served on the Vandergrift town council, as well as a term as burgess. Lindquist proclaimed that he was the "Scottish chief" of the Kiskiminetas Valley, and that all there were obliged to obey him. But he did not have his way in Apollo. The Amalgamated remained in Apollo several more months before the organizing drive collapsed. The town had become a beachhead for union activists in Black Valley, and the Amalgamated would launch organizing campaigns from Apollo in 1919 and 1933. Vandergrift's local government closed the community to organized labor. During the weeks following the episode in Apollo, Vandergrift's burgess and council issued a proclamation and an ordinance against the activities of "outside influences" that threatened the "peace and harmony" of the community. Parades, meetings, and demonstrations were banned on both public and private property. The distribution or posting of handbills and circulars was banned unless a permit was issued by the burgess. In Vandergrift, permission for union activity was not likely to be forthcoming.[11]

Apollo and Vandergrift differed in other important ways as well. Apollo was a typical western Pennsylvania town. Unplanned, its narrow streets and alleys were simply superimposed on a rough terrain consisting of hills, ridges, and hollows. Its horse-and-buggy vintage was further reflected in the lack of sewers before the WPA projects of the New Deal. Many homes clung to steep hillsides, while others squatted on the Kiskiminetas floodplain. If Apollo was the typical unplanned river town, it was not a "company town" in the classic sense. In 1912 a local syndicate spearheaded by twelve prominent citizens procured a site for a new mill in Apollo. Working capital was provided by local subscribers and by the Oppenheimer family of Pittsburgh. Steelmaker Robert Lock opened the mill for production on 16 June 1913. A. M. Oppenheimer managed the mill, and his brother Oscar served as secretary-treasurer. Apollo Steel began slowly, but its fortunes prospered as the war in Europe brought an increased demand for steel. After the war, Apollo Steel continued to be the chief employer in Apollo, but it never cast quite the shadow that American Sheet and Tin Plate did in Vandergrift. During the 1919 strike, Apollo men seemed far less intimidated by the management of the small independent mill than their counterparts on the opposite banks of the Kiskiminetas. Local steelworkers regarded Vandergrift as a community dominated by the so-called steel trust. American Sheet and Tin Plate manipulated the political climate there in ways not possible in Apollo.[12]

In 1919, strike fever and the Red Scare swept into Apollo and Vandergrift. The Amalgamated quickly established locals in both towns, and in early September both mills were closed due to the strike. Public officials and businessmen on both sides of the Kiskiminetas condemned the walkout, but anti-union activity was subtle. The heavy-handed repression of civil liberties such as occurred in Allegheny County did not happen in the Kiskiminetas Valley. Strikers were labeled Bolshevik dupes, and a few black and Mexican strikebreakers were imported to frighten the men. Mounted state constables and deputy sheriffs escorted a few men to work, while union organizers bravely proclaimed that "Black Valley" had become "White Valley."[13]

In both communities, commitment to the strike was weakest among the native-born American steelworkers. In Apollo, Americans dominated the work force; there were few ethnics and no blacks employed in the mill. In Vandergrift, skilled heaters and rollers stayed on the job. They were virtually all native-born Americans. The strikers were Poles and Lithuanians from East Vandergrift, a town known locally as Morning Sun. North Vandergrift, a Slovak village, and Vandergrift Heights, an Italian community, supplied the rest. The fact that the "foreign element" constituted the bulk of the strikers made it that much easier for anti-union forces to cast opprobrium on them. The *Vandergrift News* warned that there was "an intense feeling . . . against . . . radical troublemakers and if they started anything there was no telling what might happen. The American people in this community would not stand for any Bolshevism."[14]

As the play *Red Viper* revealed the horrors of Bolshevism at Vandergrift's Kiski Theater, men fortunate enough to reclaim their jobs struggled back to work. In Vandergrift, the strike ended without a whimper. In Apollo, organizers complained about defections, newspapers that were "scab to the core," and falling attendance at union meetings. Businessmen who had financial interests in Apollo Steel withheld credit, while the town fathers questioned their patriotism. Yet for all of that, a tenuous tradition of militance begun in 1893, and nourished in 1909, continued to linger in Apollo. A numerically small but dedicated group of diehards held out to the bitter end. Their poet laureate, A. G. Shupe, articulated both a sense of history and a spirit of defiance:

There'll be no black valley in the USA,
There'll be no black valley in the USA,
There'll be no black valley in the USA,
When Union Labor wins the day.

Trace its history back to 1893,
Scabs sent out o'er the land of the free.
Wherever white men struck, they always have tough luck,
Scabs from Kiski Valley they always had to buck,
But there'll be no black valley in the USA,
When Union Labor wins the day.

Kiski Valley, known far and wide in every countryside,
"Black Valley," they chide, "have no industrial pride?"
Go back home and be a man and stand up for the right.
Organize your mills and make your valley white.
Then there'll be no black valley in the USA,
When Union Labor wins the day.

With a Union of States the question should appeal:
Why shouldn't we have a union in the U.S. Steel?
Why shouldn't we have a union in the Independent Mills?
then we wouldn't have to swallow those autocratic pills.
Then we'll work with our might to make this valley white,
And there'll be no black valley in the USA,
When Union Labor wins the day.

Union Labor has been true to the old Red, White, and Blue,
Worked and fought and saw the world war thru,

Worked and fought for Democracy,
Worked and fought that the world might be free,
Let these promises be fulfilled and let labor have some say.
Then there'll be no black valley in the USA,
When Union Labor wins the day.

We've worked and saved, bought bonds and stamps to help foot the
    bills,
There's yet one task that's left till last, important tho' it be:
Call Gary's bluff, convert his scabs, and organize his mills,
Bring all the black sheep to the fold and make this valley free.
Then there'll be no black valley in the USA,
When Union Labor wins the day.[15]

Millworkers on both banks of the Kiskiminetas enjoyed the "high prosperity" brought by the 1920s. Beyond that, the experience of Apollo and Vandergrift steelworkers diverged. In 1927 half of the thousand-man work force at Apollo Steel walked out in protest against a 5 percent wage cut. No union was involved. The Apollo men walked out again in April 1930, in the teeth of the Depression. But not even the hardships wrought by the Depression disrupted more than a decade of labor peace at American Sheet and Tin Plate. No doubt the work of the Steel Workers Relief Association alleviated some of the hardships in Vandergrift, although some of its critics regarded it as simply another device that served management. Survivors of that era attribute the pugnacity of the Apollo men and the docility of those employed in Vandergrift to tradition and local conditions. The Apollo millworkers did not face an all-powerful industrial titan. The Oppenheimers were tough managers, but direct and reasonably accessible. According to the recollections of Apollo steelworkers, less than 10 percent of the men employed there were of foreign birth. No blacks or Hispanics were employed in the Apollo mill. Solidarity was more easily achieved in Apollo, since the men were regarded as fellow citizens by their community. In Vandergrift, the great bulk of the laborers were Slavic and Italian immigrants imported through the local padrone system. They lived in geographically divided communities on the periphery of Vandergrift. In the wake of the Great Steel Strike, mutually suspicious Slavs and Italians blamed one another for going back to work first, and each nervously eyed the black and Hispanic strikebreakers imported by the management. Labor solidarity was not easily achieved in such an atmosphere. American Sheet and Tin Plate reputedly had a network of informants at work both within and without the English-speaking community. Foremen chosen from the ranks of ethnic labor maintained cliques in the mill that stifled dissent.

Local government in Vandergrift remained under the domination of American Sheet and Tin Plate, as management personnel and skilled steelworkers were elected burgesses and councilmen.[16]

The Depression brought not only suffering but also rebellion to Apollo, unlike Vandergrift. On 1 March 1930, the Apollo mill opened after a three-month shutdown. Apollo steel earned profits that exceeded $340,000 in 1929, and the mill averaged 866 employees for that year. But the company would pay a fifteen-cent dividend in 1931, an act that it would not repeat until July of 1935. Apollo Steel would remain in the red for six consecutive years, reaching its nadir with a deficit of nearly $80,000 in 1934. Management tried a work-sharing program that featured four six-hour shifts rather than the three eight-hour shifts. With the mill operating at just 70 percent of capacity in April 1930, management announced a 10 percent wage cut for men on the sheet floor. Superintendent H. H. Holloway offered the 10 percent cut or a new double mill shift, which would feature half as much manual labor as before. The installation of automatic heat-control equipment at a cost of $800,000 had also eliminated the need for many heaters, pair heaters, and helpers. Fears were raised by reductions in labor force, but were exacerbated by charges that men long employed by the mill were being moved aside in favor of the relatives of mill management and other lackeys brought in from outside the valley. The sheet-floor men moved quickly and decisively. They met as a body and refused to accept the cuts. Moved by that act of defiance, more than 500 men joined a general walkout the following day.[17]

On Monday, 7 April, the strikers chose a committee of twelve to draft resolutions to be presented to Apollo Steel. That committee met at the home of millworker Jess McIllwain and drafted nineteen resolutions, including a demand for the resignation of mill superintendents Holloway and D. H. Benbow. On Wednesday, 9 April, the committee met with Apollo Steel president A. M. Oppenheimer, but failed to reach an accord. Oppenheimer threatened to operate the mill with men brought in from other towns. Unmoved, the committee recommended continuation of the strike and threatened the establishment of a "permanent organization." The following evening, the strikers joined a public meeting with the burgess, borough council, and local businessmen. The men agreed to withdraw their demand for resignations at the mill and urged the burgess and local businessmen to intercede. On Friday, 12 April, Apollo Steel opened its books to Burgess S. S. Baldridge and businessmen George Wallace, T. F. Tucker, and W. W. Fiscus, who had helped to raise $15,000 in 1912 for the purchase of the Apollo Steel mill site. None was particularly critical of the strikers, but all feared that a prolonged work stoppage might lead to a loss of the mill and a return to the "Dark Ages." After inspecting the company books, the businessmen urged the men to accept the cuts and return to work. The company, in turn, guaranteed 75 percent mill operation. Reprisals against the strike leaders were never discussed. On Monday, 14 April, the men returned to work.[18]

The 1930 Apollo strike was an ephemeral but notable event. Strikes by steelworkers were rare during the early years of the Great Depression. Discontent was manifest in the mill towns, but few dared risk the loss of already meager employment opportunities. The Amalgamated was nowhere in evidence during the week-long Apollo strike. Mike Tighe had promised a membership drive in 1929, but that had withered with the crash. The threats of the Apollo men to form a permanent union came to nothing, and working conditions at the mill continued to deteriorate. Men were called to work and were paid nothing. They often reported with only the hope of being paid. To refuse such an offer meant the loss of any opportunity to work. Paychecks ranged from as much as $11 for two-weeks' work to as little as one cent for a day's labor. Management continued to hire relatives and to play favorites in their choice of who was called back to work. Local merchants, some of whom had supported the termination of the strike, extended credit to the beleaguered steelworkers. The extension of credit did assuage some of the bitterness many steelworkers felt, believing that the merchants were "under Oppenheimer's thumb."[19] But the condition of most workers in Apollo remained so desperate that neither the benevolence of local businessmen nor the hard-line tactics of mill management could prevent another rebellion.

The New Deal, and more specifically the National Recovery Act, changed the mood of Apollo. The NRA blue eagle was displayed in storefronts throughout the community that had once been staunchly Republican. The dramatic success of the UMWA in organizing local mines operated by the anti-union Hicks interests seemed to indicate that organized labor enjoyed both protection and sanction under the law. Amalgamated president Mike Tighe, sensing that the political winds had shifted in favor of labor, announced a major organizing drive in late June 1933. Amalgamated organizer James Eakin was assigned to the Kiskiminetas Valley. He conducted his first rally in Apollo on 15 July. Four hundred steelworkers responded to his call for an end to "industrial slavery." Thereafter, events moved swiftly in Apollo. Apollo Steel president A. M. Oppenheimer announced the "election" of delegates for an Employee Representation Plan three days later. A 15 percent wage increase was also initiated to bring Apollo Steel's salaries into line with the NRA steel codes. But the men were not taking their lead from management. They proclaimed their determination to establish "their own codes," and condemned the ERP as an "insult to intelligence."[20]

Proclaiming an end to life "under the Czar," five hundred Apollo steelworkers met at their municipal building on 28 July and formed Amalgamated Lodge 159. The fact that meetings were moved from secret proceedings in private homes and barns to a public building is a testimony both to the unity of the men and to their confidence that "the New Deal [gave] a man the right to join the Amalgamated."[21] A full slate of officers was elected, making Lodge 159 the first functioning steel-workers' local in the Kiskiminetas Valley. The Amalgamated provided an established parent body for membership purposes, but it is clear that its agents did not actually organize the Apollo men. Collective action was not new to the labor force at Apollo Steel. They had walked out in 1927 and in 1930, in both good and bad times. In 1933 a tenacious leadership emerged from the mill rank and file that channeled their discontent into coherent action as never before. Roller Hugh McIllwain, a sober Free Methodist widely respected for his integrity, was elected financial secre-tary. Not only did McIllwain put his lodge on firm financial footing, he added a fearlessness to the proceedings that made a repetition of earlier collapses unlikely. Equally militant were catcher Ira Hancock, a lay preacher, and heater George Aytha, an outspoken Scot. The former spoke for the more conservative element in the mill. Aytha, in sharp contrast, emerged as a radical industrial unionist, and was a party to the schism that later developed within the Amalgamated. The younger ele-ment among the men was typified by Preston Busch, who volunteered his automobile for union business and helped to expand the Amalga-mated into Vandergrift. Busch later became chairman of the Democratic party in Armstrong County.[22]

The leadership of the Apollo lodge was diverse, but cohesive and unyielding. Despite the intransigence of Apollo Steel president A. M. Oppenheimer, the union could not be dislodged. Oppenheimer argued that Lodge 159 had no special authority and refused to negotiate. (Col-lective bargaining did not become a reality in Apollo until the CIO appeared at the mill.) Oppenheimer threatened plant closings and the importation of strikebreakers, but employed those tactics in a half-hearted fashion. With the blue eagle on display throughout the com-munity, militant coal miners on the march, the Pinchot administration championing the cause of industrial labor, Oppenheimer adopted a course of action best described as stubborn but cautious. In effect, he stalled by attempting to use his company union against the Amalga-mated. Apollo's town fathers were equally circumspect. The borough hall was made available for union meetings, and no anti-union statements emanated from the burgess or borough council. Public officials and local businessmen maintained, at least publicly, a scrupulous neutrality during the struggle between the mill and the union.

Events would take a much different course in Vandergrift. Like Apollo Steel and the Hicks coal interests, American Sheet and Tin Plate ostensibly embraced the NRA codes. A 15 percent wage increase and the formation of an Employee Representation Plan were announced in June. To qualify for membership in the latter, a worker had to be an American citizen, twenty-one years of age, and an employee for at least one year. Representatives were to be elected for one-year terms. "More effective communication" was the desired goal. The Amalgamated and its agents were clearly not welcome in Vandergrift. The union managed to rent office space, but was unable to hire a hall for mass meetings. Attempts to use the Vandergrift High School auditorium were denied, despite a petition signed by 130 local citizens. In September AFL spokesman John Arnold reported that Apollo and West Leechburg were in the Amalgamated camp and that Vandergrift, "the toughest spot in the United States," soon would be.[23]

Arnold's optimism was misplaced. As Amalgamated lodges appeared in Leechburg, Natrona, and New Kensington, Vandergrift stood as an anti-union Gibraltar. In Leechburg, six miles downriver from Vandergrift, Catholic and Protestant clergymen aided in the formation of Kiski Valley Lodge 177. Methodist minister F. A. Edmonds told a group of assembled steelworkers that they had a right to a living wage and a decent home, and a "lack of fair play" made the union necessary. The Reverend John Liska of Saint Martha's told the same audience that the Roosevelt administration was a godsend, and that the NRA would "bring labor and capital together." The New Deal provided an opportunity to eliminate labor strife and offered unionists "intelligent leadership [without] radicalism." In the nearby Allegheny Valley, the Reverend Casimir Orlemanski, pastor of Our Lady of Perpetual Help Church, West Natrona, told six hundred steelworkers meeting at Natrona town hall that they "must fight and organize to win [their] rights and union, for organization [is] the remedy for industry." Soon after, on 14 September, borough councilmen addressed a meeting of the Straight Forward Lodge, which met at Tarentum High School. A month later, the union announced that Cornelia Bryce Pinchot, wife of Governor Gifford Pinchot, would speak to their membership in New Kensington and Tarentum. Mrs. Pinchot arrived in those communities on 19 October and shared the speakers' platform with Father Orlemanski, Philip Murray, local union officials, and the burgesses of New Kensington and Tarentum. After flaying the "steel trust" and its company unions, Mrs. Pinchot noted that attempts by steelworkers to find a place for her to speak in Vandergrift had failed because the local government and school board there were "subservient to steel."[24]

All connected with the union movement in the Kiskiminetas Valley expected Vandergrift to be a tough nut to crack, but the exclusion of the governor's wife seemed extreme, even when judged by the harsh standards of Black Valley. Union organizers from Apollo found some tenuous support for their cause among the men who resided in the Slavic and Italian neighborhoods. However, the old American stock of Vandergrift proper remained anti-union to the core. In early October, their tactics took an ugly turn. More than a hundred members of American Legion Post 114 stepped forward and offered their services as a "vigilance committee." Their announced objective was to protect the community from "outsiders" suspected of having "Communist leanings." The Tarentum legion post had threatened to maintain law and order in their town against "wandering pickets," but their threats had not received much local support. The action of the Vandergrift legion was supported by the burgess, council, and mill management. Spokesman H. Ross Belding professed that his organization was "fighting outside radical agitators, not organized labor unions." One hundred sixteen men had volunteered to serve a tour of duty against the "Reds." Burgess William Dick swore the men in with the approval of the town council. Wages, expenses, and supplies for the "vigilantes were to be paid for by American Sheet and Tin Plate."[25]

Except for a handful of Amalgamated organizers, the only "outside" agitators in the Alle-Kiski Valley at the time were roving pickets from the coke district of southwestern Pennsylvania. And they appeared to present no direct menace to Vandergrift or its mill. Westmoreland County Sheriff William H. Humes had been present at the swearing in of the legionnaires. In an interview published in the *Greensburg Morning Review,* he attributed the mobilization in Vandergrift to fears that demonstrations might jeopardize the operations at the mill. "They think up there (in Vandergrift) that since Mrs. Pinchot is going to speak for the Amalgamated Iron and Steelworkers, the same outfit that was in the Old Homestead Strike, they might have trouble and they don't intend to stand for it. They are not going to allow any parading or picketing at their works." The following day, the sheriff attempted to retract that statement, claiming that he had been misquoted. The vigilante movement was "wholly spontaneous" and was simply a community response to the threat of invasion by "outside radical agitators." The enemy at hand was not union men, but "roving communist pickets." Amalgamated organizer James C. Eakin later quipped that "Adolf Hitler ought to send a representative to [Vandergrift]. The ox-cart methods he is using are not nearly as efficient as the up-to-date and un-American methods used to deceive the steel-workers in the United States."[26]

When it became apparent that Mrs. Pinchot would not be permitted access to Vandergrift, the Amalgamated requested permission for her to speak in Apollo. The Pinchots were not universally popular in the commonwealth. Ralph Turner, professor of history at the University of Pittsburgh, denounced Gifford Pinchot as a "political opportunist" who sent his wife campaigning all over the state in the name of "social legislation." Turner, chairman of the Pennsylvania Security League, accused Pinchot of exploiting labor unrest in order to take the Republican nomination for United States senator away from incumbent David Reed, a conservative enemy of the New Deal. Pinchot, of course, wanted that nomination, and the charge of political expediency was not without foundation. In her speeches in behalf of labor, Mrs. Pinchot attacked Reed as an anti-Progressive tool of the Mellons and the steel trust. The Pinchots employed the rhetoric of old-line Bull Moose Progressives, citing unions as the best way to free western Pennsylvania mill towns from industrial "autocracy."[27] However, Pinchot's campaign was not merely politics as usual. The governor had supported the UMWA in 1922 and had curtailed the coal industry's use of the Coal and Iron Police. Pinchot had spoken out against abuses perpetrated by private police again in 1928 and had withdrawn industrial police commissions during his second term as governor. As he campaigned against the steel trust in 1933, he was engaged in a running battle with county sheriffs, including Sheriff Humes, who policed the picket lines in the coke district. Political ambition notwithstanding, Pinchot was in his own way responsive to the needs of industrial labor.

Apollo Burgess S. S. Baldridge granted permission to the Amalgamated to hold a rally at the Apollo borough building. The date set was 11 October. It was understood by all concerned that Cornelia Bryce Pinchot would be the featured speaker. The Amalgamated made no secret of the fact that Apollo was its second choice for this Pinchot rally. Organizer Eakin had tried to rent five sites in Vandergrift and had failed. An Amalgamated lodge had not yet been established in that trust town. Two days before the scheduled rally, Baldridge withdrew his permit. The burgess claimed that Eakin had invited the valley's coal miners, and that the municipal facility could not accommodate a crowd of miners, steel-workers, and their families. Baldridge was probably correct, for the borough hall could not safely accommodate a crowd that would exceed five hundred persons. The building itself was situated in a confined residential area, whose narrow streets would have faced severe traffic and crowd-control problems. Eakin politely extended thanks to the town fathers for the courtesies they had shown the union in the past and moved the rally to Griftlo Park. The new site was two miles downriver from Apollo, spacious, and within view of Vandergrift.[28]

The governor's surrogate did not receive the news from Apollo gracefully. "The truth is Apollo is a steel town, controlled by the steel operators and the burgess has been given orders to stop the steelworkers meeting—whatever the constitution may say about the rights of free assembly. Mr. Baldridge's action insures an extra large attendance at the meeting tomorrow in the park outside of Apollo. Its only significance is that it serves as one more illustration of the brutal and un-American methods used by the steel magnates in their attempt to control and enslave their workers." That prerally hyperbole set the stage for an enthusiastic reception at Griftlo Park. On 11 October Mrs. Pinchot arrived at the rally site in the company of gray-clad state troopers. Impeccably dressed, her presence accentuated by bright red hair, Cornelia Pinchot did not disappoint a crowd estimated at more than five thousand men, women and children. "They tried to keep me from speaking to you." Alluding to Sheriff Humes and Burgess Dick, Mrs. Pinchot confessed that "this is the first time I have ever been considered a dangerous person." Mindful of her audience, she assailed the state's coal operators who continued to "hire gunmen to cause trouble." She then turned her attention to the steel industry. First, she charged, the steel trust "flooded the state with the lowest grade of labor, men of many nationalities who couldn't speak English." Afterward, "terrorism, intimidation and violence" were employed by the industry in order to keep its workers subservient.[29]

Mrs. Pinchot urged the workers to organize unions of their own choice, treat their employers fairly, and obey the law. "I hope to see the day when every man who works in steel is a member of a union. Six months ago such a wish was absurd and fantastic. Now the picture has changed. It is no longer a dream.[30]

Cornelia Bryce Pinchot continued to stump western Pennsylvania for more than a month after she appeared at Griftlo Park. On 22 November she actually made an appearance in Vandergrift in the company of uniformed state police and spoke to a crowd from a second-story window of a deserted bank building. How she managed to penetrate Vandergrift may never be fully explained. The Amalgamated admitted that her appearance was never authorized by borough officials, but they never explained precisely how they managed to stage that meeting at which thousands gathered on Grant Avenue, a major thoroughfare. Pennsylvania's first lady, characterized by the unions as a "splendid personification of good American womanhood," departed very little from her Apollo script. She castigated the steel trust, praised the NRA and unionization, and advised that Vandergrift's burgess be sent back to school to learn about constitutional free speech and right of assembly. The only new item to appear in her presentation was an attack on the state supreme court. That body had struck down as unconstitutional an old-age-pension law that had been inspired by her husband. She attributed the court's decision to five justices whom she alleged were in the employ of J. P. Morgan.[31]

The governor's wife made one last swing through the Kiskiminetas Valley in May 1934. By this time her speechmaking had reached a point of diminishing returns, as fewer than a thousand persons attended a rally at Griftlo Park sponsored by the Amalgamated. The union had clearly overplayed its trump card in using her so often. And as the primary election approached, her increasing attacks upon Reed made it clear that she was on the campaign trail. Gifford Pinchot, forever the Progressive maverick and new found friend of the New Deal, lost the nomination to Reed in May. With that defeat, labor temporarily lost its leverage in Harrisburg, and the Amalgamated its most prestigious spokesman. The Amalgamated had, however, relied too much upon public relations. Cornelia Bryce Pinchot and Father Orlemanski, for all their activism in behalf of the Amalgamated, could not actually organize steelworkers. That mundane task fell to the union itself and to its all-too-thin squad of organizers.[32]

Amalgamated President Mike Tighe seemed committed to an all-out recruiting campaign, particularly in western Pennsylvania. The drive, which began in late June 1933, had yielded (according to the Amalgamated) 28 new western Pennsylvania lodges by mid-August and 125 new locals nationally. The union claimed that a membership of 3,000 had climbed to over 60,000 in four months. The Amalgamated even succeeded in establishing a lodge, No. 197, albeit on paper, in Vandergrift during February 1934. "Everything was," in the words of the *Amalgamated Journal,* "going fine." Indeed, burgeoning membership rolls seemed to indicate that all was well with the Amalgamated. In the Kiskiminetas Valley, the union had reached its zenith at the time of the first visit by Mrs. Pinchot in October. Shortly thereafter, Tighe began to close the regional Amalgamated offices in districts that had just been organized. Since local lodges were functioning there, he believed that there was no reason for those regional offices to remain. Incredibly, Tighe chose to withdraw his forces at a time that would prove to be most critical to his union.[33]

Vandergrift's hostility toward the Amalgamated remained unchanged after Mrs. Pinchot's visit. The only labor organization that actually functioned was the company ERP. Despite calls for a boycott by the Amalgamated, an ERP "election" was conducted by American Sheet and Tin

Plate in February. The ERP got the votes of 1,464 men, 660 voted against, and 556 ballots were unmarked. That tally was hardly a ringing endorsement of the company plan, but the Amalgamated was unable to exploit that weakness. Lodge 197 was able to conduct regular meetings at the local Italian hall despite harassment by "company agitators." Lodge elections were conducted following a visit by Father Orlemanski in November 1934, but the local did little else but survive. American Sheet and Tin Plate simply would not deal with Lodge 197, and Tighe all but deserted it. The Vandergrift lodge was probably typical of most new Amalgamated locals being all but orphaned except for the payment of dues. The union movement in Vandergrift would languish until the arrival of the CIO, and Lodge 197 would play no role in an internal struggle that would rock the Amalgamated.[34]

The situation in Apollo was quite different. The Apollo men had elected a mill committee in November 1933, and that body engaged in a running battle with Apollo Steel for more than a year. A. M. Oppenheimer refused to recognize the union, but his obstinacy incited rather than discouraged the union men. The Apollo local received no more help from Tighe than the Vandergrift lodge had, but its mill committee was directed by militants George Aytha and Hugh McIllwain. Impatience with Tighe's caution was growing in Apollo, and a strike was the frequent subject of heated debate at lodge meetings. In March 1934 someone sent an unsigned letter to the National Recovery Administration complaining that Apollo Steel violated the steel codes by its refusal to recognize Lodge 159. A few weeks later, fifty employees at Pittsburgh's Steel Drum Company (owned and operated in Apollo by the Oppenheimer family) went out on strike. The workers, members of Local 18972, United Steel Drum Workers, an AFL affiliate organized in October 1933, demanded a 40 percent wage increase and union recognition. Pittsburgh Steel Drum offered a 5 percent increase, which the union refused. The strike lasted eleven days, until a settlement was reached with the aid of mediation supplied by the Pittsburgh Regional Labor Board. The steel drum workers received a 15 percent wage increase, but the Oppenheimers steadfastly refused to recognize their union.[35]

The strike at Pittsburgh Steel Drum left the union men at Apollo Steel straining at the bit. A militant faction had developed that demanded that Mike Tighe shut down all steel plants that refused to recognize their Amalgamated lodges. Lodge 159 elected Aytha as their chief delegate to the Amalgamated convention, due to convene in April. Tighe was clearly reluctant to take on the steel industry, but he had come under increasing public criticism from Aytha, Earle Forbeck, and Bill Spang, Forbeck and Spang representing Monongahela Valley lodges. Tighe stalled, threatening a "holiday" for the steel industry, while demanding written recognition by the companies. His deadlines, set for 21 May and again for 10 June, passed without action by management. Tighe continued to stall. Spang and Forbeck had formed their own "executive committee" in May and had stormed Tighe's Pittsburgh office, charging the elderly president with betrayal of a strike "pledge" that he had appeared to make at the Amalgamated's 21 April meeting. George Aytha had gravitated to the Monongahela insurgents, apparently without official authorization by his lodge. The growing militance of the Apollo men was punctuated by a week-long walkout in early May. Elmer Sowers, president of the Apollo lodge, was a close friend of Tighe. Their relationship probably prevented an unauthorized strike to gain recognition. Lodge 159 had grown increasingly defiant of both management and Tighe, and its membership warned both that it "had one more weapon and [was] about to use it."[36]

Tighe was compelled to schedule another meeting on 14 June in Pittsburgh for the purpose of discussing the strike. The local press attributed Tighe's "recognition or strike" position to pressure exerted by "left-winger" Earle Forbeck. But Forbeck was a problem for Tighe only because of rank-and-file impatience with his cautious policy. A beleaguered Tighe blamed the problems facing the Amalgamated on the inaction of the National Recovery Administration. General Hugh Johnson, Tighe asserted, was enforcing all sections of the National Recovery Act except 7(a)—that provision which was intended to protect and foster organized labor. Johnson's implementation of the codes enabled industry to reap huge profits by exploiting labor. Tighe warned that a national steel strike was inevitable unless President Roosevelt took "immediate and forceful action."[37]

The Amalgamated gathered in Pittsburgh on 14 and 15 June. Tighe was barely able to keep the militants at bay. On 15 June AFL President William Green appeared (presumably at the request of Roosevelt) and lobbied against a steel strike. Green asked the assembled delegates to support the creation of a regional Steel Labor Board. The board, staffed by three presidential appointees, would hear complaints and grievances, offer mediation and conciliation services, and supervise union elections. Since Green had made the proposal in the name of President Roosevelt, the steelworkers agreed to go along. Within weeks after the delegates dispersed, the Steel Labor Board was created by executive order. Green's appearance had spared Mike Tighe much grief, or so it seemed. The creation of the Steel Labor Board had seemingly defused a rank-and-file rebellion. In July Tighe defeated insurgent candidate George Williams for the presidency of the Amalgamated, and his position seemed secure. Tighe faded temporarily into the background as the attention of western

Pennsylvania's steelworkers focused upon the work of the Steel Labor Board that convened in Pittsburgh.[38]

Apollo Lodge 159 supported the creation of a labor board as an alternative to strike action. Indeed, the Apollo local would be among the first to test the new board's effectiveness. The labor board appeared to many to be an arm of presidential authority. It also enjoyed the endorsement of AFL President William Green. That organization continued to enjoy considerable prestige in Apollo, in spite of its president's conciliatory posture at the Amalgamated convention. On 11 July the Apollo local presented a contract proposal to Apollo Steel that the company promptly rejected. Local unionists remained determined to move A. M. Oppenheimer in spite of the faltering leadership of Tighe. Lodge 159 claimed 614 of 1,150 Apollo Steel employees, and it would easily carry a fairly administered representation election. A Kiski Valley Central Labor Union had been formed in February, and its founders expected an eventual membership of 25,000. Dominated by militant coal miners, the central labor body maintained unionist momentum as disillusionment with the Amalgamated continued to mount. The Central Labor Union, denied access to Vandergrift's picnic grounds by Burgess J. A. Grimm on the premise that it had been reserved by the American Legion, met in Griftlo Park in late July. The members of thirty local unions and their families celebrated and pledged support for the Apollo Steel workers and their cause.[39]

Lodge 159 took its case before the Steel Labor Board as soon as that commission convened in Pittsburgh in late July. It charged that the company violated the NRA codes by demanding longer hours of its men and enforcing its demands through the use of arbitrary firings. But the failure of Apollo Steel to recognize the union was the paramount issue. At one point, the Amalgamated claimed the allegiance of 900 men at the mill, but the figure was later reduced to 614. Both figures constituted a majority, but Apollo Steel disputed both. The board ordered a representation election for 27 August. No one expected the board to act so quickly and decisively, for its duties were ill-defined, and in the opinion of some observers its findings were not legally binding. The attention of the steel industry was focused upon the Apollo Steel case, for its outcome might have well set a precedent for labor relations in the industry. Apollo Steel had established a company union to forestall the work of the Amalgamated, a policy cited by Lodge 159 as a violation of Section 7(a). Company officials were aware that their union did not have the votes to win an open election. The proposed election was to be supervised by two company union men, two Amalgamated representatives, and an impartial observer chosen by the Steel Labor Board. George Aytha, spokesman for the Apollo mill committee, applauded the proposed election but admitted that he had difficulty keeping his rank-and-file militants on the job. Aytha and the Amalgamated were confident of victory in the election, and they had every reason to be. But would an election victory be meaningful? No one was sure. Aytha's lodge members had high expectations, however, and told him "not to come back until [the union received] what they were entitled to" under Section 7(a).[40]

The representation election was a can of worms that Apollo Steel did not wish to open. Company vice-president and counsel W. H. Guthrie wrote to the Steel Labor Board and admitted that the Amalgamated represented a majority of his company's workers. Guthrie indicated that Apollo Steel agreed to receive the bargaining committee of the Amalgamated, but reserved the right to meet with other organizations. Guthrie petitioned the board to cancel the election and to make provision for "a minority position." The latter point was of importance, for virtually every steel company had a company union or Employee Representation Plan. Amalgamated attorney Charlton Ogborn opposed the petition, for his union demanded nothing less than exclusive bargaining rights with Apollo Steel. The Steel Labor Board canceled the election, but backed away from the issue of minority representation. A board spokesman explained obliquely that it acted as a mediator in the controversy and that its role in such disputes was not defined.[41]

It soon became apparent that Apollo Steel's "recognition" was simply a ploy to deflect government intervention. Subsequent events would prove that the steel industry had little to fear from Roosevelt's labor board, and that it would have minimal impact upon labor relations in the mill towns. The board's failure to render any meaningful decision in the Apollo Steel case left several important questions unanswered. First, did company recognition of a union obligate it to bargain collectively? Second, did meeting with union representatives satisfy a collective bargaining requirement? Third, what was the role of company unions in the process, particularly if they did not represent the will of the majority in a given mill? Subsequent rulings by the Steel Labor Board implied that a union that represented the majority of workers in a mill constituted a bargaining agent. But answers about the nature of collective bargaining were not forthcoming. In fact, very little that the Steel Labor Board did or said meant anything in Apollo or any other mill town. Spokesmen for Lodge 159 had no doubts about Apollo Steel's obligations. Company unions and other minorities were of "no importance" to the collective bargaining process. Minorities might meet and confer with company representatives, but the Amalgamated was the "sole collective bargaining agency representing employees of the plant."[42]

In the weeks that followed the Labor Board's withdrawal from the Apollo Steel dispute, rumors abounded in the Kiskiminetas Valley that big steel had placed its considerable legal resources at the disposal of A. M. Oppenheimer. It is not known how much, if any, aid the crusty president of Apollo Steel received, but it is clear that the steel industry had a vested interest in destroying government-sanctioned collective bargaining on this beachhead. Rumors of aid from outside the Kiskiminetas Valley may well have stiffened the old man's resolve. For more than a year Oppenheimer had threatened to close his plant rather than recognize the Amalgamated. In August and September he met with the local mill committee, without result. In September Oppenheimer proposed a further reduction of the labor gangs in the mill. The men demanded the restoration of fifty jobs lost more than year earlier. Oppenheimer refused, and a work stoppage, described by Lodge 159 president Elmer Sowers as a "lockout," ensued. Neither Tighe nor the Steel Labor Board intervened, and the beaten men straggled back to work in less than a week.[43]

The failure of the Steel Labor Board to support union recognition and collective bargaining was decisive for Tighe and the Amalgamated. The insurgent spirit was rekindled throughout western Pennsylvania. Militants within the Apollo lodge clamored anew for a strike, with or without the leadership of Mike Tighe. On 30 December 1934, rank-and-file delegates met in Pittsburgh and planned their own convention, which was scheduled for 3 February. Lodge 159 was thoroughly identified with the insurgents, even though its president enjoyed a warm personal relationship with Tighe. A report sent by an anonymous corresponding secretary (the regular correspondent had left for parts unknown) to the *Amalgamated Journal* reflected a new brand of radicalism present in the Apollo lodge. "We are facing a breakdown of the capitalist system," the writer averred. "Unemployment and poverty are inevitable products of the present system. Capitalism spells not only widespread economic disaster, but class strife [and] the ever-present threat of international war." Warfare was the result of a struggle by the capitalist class "to find world markets and investment areas for their surplus goods and capital." Their search was a "prime cause of the World War," and also "fostered militarism and imperialism." The Republican and Democratic parties, the correspondent continued, were both controlled by great financiers and industrialists. In this crisis, their chief purpose and desire had been to help the railroads, banks, insurance companies, and other capitalist interests. We, the workers, ought to have a party of workers. A labor party would mean the transfer of ownership of principal industries to "social ownership and democratic control."[44]

The above leftist manifesto, probably written by George Aytha, did not represent the political climate in Lodge 159. Apollo steelworkers exhibited little interest in the creation of a labor party or Socialist state.

What they desired was action on a nationwide steel strike. Apollo's insurgents chose Aytha to represent their interests in Pittsburgh on 3 February. Aytha did not speak officially for his lodge, but he might as well have. The Tighe administration had a few defenders in Apollo, but their credibility would be swept away by the actions of the Amalgamated president. Tighe warned the membership that any lodge that sent delegates to the "outlaw convention" would be suspended. He characterized the 400 men in attendance as "militants, reds, and pinks," unworthy of membership in the Amalgamated. The delegates devoted their energies to dumping Tighe and taking direct action against the steel industry. George Aytha returned from Pittsburgh an acknowledged "rebel leader" in the Amalgamated's "civil war." Aytha defended the insurgents against the charge of Communism, agreeing that the younger, energetic militants represented the most "progressive" element in the union. "Our purpose," Aytha protested, "is to build up the Amalgamated, not to break away."[45]

Lodge President Elmer Sowers complained that Aytha had acted without the authority of his local. But Lodge 159 did not repudiate Aytha or the "rump convention" that he had attended. Shortly after his return, the local passed a resolution that supported Aytha and the Progressives while taking note of Tighe and his failure. The membership was not going to "stand idly by and let the organization go down as it did in 1919." "Nothing is being done," the resolution added, "undercover or in any way that could lead to communism, but on the contrary it looks to us as though we were under Hitlerism when the membership [is] barred from holding meetings and taking progressive action." Tighe was not impressed with any of this. On the front page of the 14 February issue of the *Amalgamated Journal,* Lodge 159 headed a list of thirteen locals suspended by Tighe. Apollo's tenuous, sometime relationship with the Amalgamated, which had spanned four decades, ended forever.[46]

Tighe had repelled the "borers from within," rivals for his power, but in doing so, he had sacrificed his most vigorous membership. Stripped of its Amalgamated charter, and threatened by Tighe with lawsuit for the recovery of membership dues, the Apollo lodge continued to function. Loosely affiliated with the Kiski Valley Central Labor Union, the defiant Apolloites struck Apollo Steel in February 1935. A. M. Oppenheimer remained as adamant as ever. Company posters were distributed throughout Apollo, warning the men to return to work or face a plant closing. The strike collapsed in less than a week. In April the employees at Pittsburgh Steel Drum walked off their jobs, demanding a 35 percent wage increase. President O. W. Oppenheimer threatened to move the plant to a site in Butler if the strikers did not return to work. The workers retorted that management was "bluffing." Less than a week later, trucks arrived, and the plant equipment was moved to Butler. Oppenheimer confirmed the move, explaining that the Butler site offered larger quarters and better railroad facilities. He made no mention of his company's labor problems. In a last-ditch effort to save their jobs, some workers tried to block the entrance to the plant, and were promptly arrested by Armstrong County Sheriff I. D. Doverspike. With union fortunes in Apollo at a low ebb, the Central Labor Union held a rally at the municipal building. Speakers railed against the "old fogies in swivel chairs" who ran the AFL, but the militant rhetoric could not hide the fact that the union movement appeared to be dead in the water.[47]

If the union cause had reached its nadir in Apollo, the situation in Vandergrift was no better. American Sheet and Tin Plate was absorbed by Carnegie-Illinois in 1936, but the company Employee Representation Plan remained intact. The company policy of promoting men who had demonstrated their loyalty while serving as ERP representatives to managerial posts also continued. An effective challenge to flagrant company unionism seemed beyond hope, for only the UMWA functioned on the west bank of the Kiskiminetas. The sudden emergence of the CIO offered a fresh and unexpected challenge to company domination in Vandergrift. CIO agents had attended the 1936 Amalgamated Convention in Canonsburg as uninvited guests. Only a hundred delegates were present at Tighe's gathering, and it required little persuasion by Pat Fagan and John Brophy to convince him to join the new movement. Tighe would issue charters to new locals, but the Steel Workers Organizing Committee collected the dues. Officially the bargain was a merger, but in reality SWOC swallowed up the Amalgamated. In December 1936 SWOC announced its intention to "bore from within" all the ERP bodies in the mill towns. ERP spokesmen denounced SWOC as Lewis "racketeers" and formed a "defense committee" to fight it. William B. Hadden, chairman of the Carnegie-Illinois ERP, and recently named director of personnel and welfare in Vandergrift, was called before the National Labor Relations Board to answer allegations of company "domination." Elmer Maloy, a Lewis ally, was ousted from the ERP because he had subjected Hadden to a verbal attack. Maloy had called for Hadden's resignation, accusing him of being a management pawn. Amid its attempts to sabotage and disrupt the work of the ERP, SWOC entered Vandergrift for the first time on 22 January 1937.[48]

SWOC agents distributed copies of *Steel Labor,* the CIO newspaper, and denounced Vandergrift's company union. The ERP fought back, calling for a $5 a day minimum wage, time and a half for overtime, and increased pension benefits. SWOC arranged a public debate between Maloy and ERP representatives at the Silver Garden Skating Rink. The subject at hand was "outside union vs. company union." When the CIO men arrived at the skating rink on 17 February, they found it padlocked, with ERP spokesmen nowhere in evidence. SWOC indicated a readiness to "do what Mrs. Pinchot did three years ago." Four days later a sound truck appeared on the streets of Vandergrift proclaiming the union cause. Spokesman for the Kiski Valley Central Labor Union also announced their readiness to jump to the CIO. A major confrontation seemed to be in the offing, when news reached Vandergrift that Myron Taylor, chairman of U.S. Steel, and John L. Lewis had reached an accord. ERP spokesman Thomas A. Grogan confessed that he was "unable to grasp fully" the turn of events that had brought recognition to the CIO.[49]

The Taylor-Lewis negotiations were a well-kept secret, and the announcement of U.S. Steel's recognition of the CIO shocked everyone connected to the steel industry in the Kiskiminetas Valley. CIO sympathizers had every reason to expect another long, bitter fight with their antagonists. But the Taylor-Lewis negotiations preempted that struggle, and accomplished what the Amalgamated had not been able to achieve in four decades of trying. On 3 March Philip Murray announced in Pittsburgh that SWOC and its Amalgamated locals constituted the bargaining agent for employees at U.S. Steel and its subsidiaries. The ERP collapsed rapidly in the wake of that announcement. In Vandergrift, several ERP defectors were actually elected officers in the newly formed CIO local. CIO organizer Phil Clowes commented that the company union was "dying a natural death, flopping around like a chicken with its head cut off."[50]

On 7 March Allegheny County Court Judge Michael Musmanno addressed a CIO rally in Vandergrift, the first union meeting ever held there that was without visible opposition. Long a champion of industrial labor, Musmanno addressed a crowd estimated to be 2,000 strong at the intersection of Grant and Farragut avenues. "Craft unions" were good for the building trades, Musmanno assured his listeners, but an "utter failure in mass production industries." The CIO was the obvious choice for steelworkers in Vandergrift, and the nation.[51]

Ironically, union recognition was achieved in Vandergrift before Apollo. Carnegie-Illinois was a subsidiary of U.S. Steel, and Taylor's agreement was binding on its Vandergrift operation. But Apollo Steel was a small independent company, and it was far from certain whether A. M. Oppenheimer would sign a union contract. On 14 March Oppenheimer spoke to his work force from the stage in Apollo's municipal building. He announced that the union scale would be paid and a forty-hour work week observed at his mill regardless of whether he signed a contract with the Amalgamated effective 1 April. He then issued his final warning as president of Apollo Steel, which he assured the men was "no bluff, no threat." "If work is stopped by a walkout or by the management for any reason, notices will be posted on the bulletin boards saying, 'This plant will be closed indefinitely.' We will not attempt to operate. There will be no state police, no sheriffs' deputies, no militia—only a watchman at the gates." The old man, obviously wearied by four years of labor strife, complained that his company suffered from a shortage of steel—particularly bars that had to be obtained from larger rivals. Oppenheimer hoped his willingness to sign a contract with the CIO would make labor and management "partners in business." On 31 March Oppenheimer signed a contract with the CIO that was ratified by the men on 10 April.[52]

The Amalgamated faded rapidly into obscurity during the halycon days of the CIO. To those who remembered the old union, its demise did not seem to be due to philosophical or structural defects. The fact that the Amalgamated was steeped in the tradition of craft unionism did not appear to matter much to the rank and file in the Kiskiminetas Valley. It was a failure to act boldly in the interest of desperate and militant steelworkers that brought the Amalgamated down. Apollo's depression-bound millworkers yearned for the kind of leadership that the valley's coal miners enjoyed.[53] The CIO did not organize the Kiskiminetas Valley steelworkers in the traditional sense, but took them by default whether they had been previously recruited by the Amalgamated or not. Twenty miles downriver, Allegheny Valley aluminum workers endured similar difficulties as an AFL affiliate. Their struggle delineates structural deficiencies within the AFL as well as a failure of leadership. It is to their story that I now turn.

8
CIO Victory: The Aluminum Workers of the Allegheny Valley

THE UNIONIZATION OF NEW DEAL–ERA ALUMINUM WORKERS IN THE ALLE-gheny Valley offers an uncommon opportunity to examine collectively the salient issues that confronted industrial labor. Never were questions of ideology, organization and structure, the uses of power, and sources of authority brought more clearly into focus than in New Kensington. Though the town possessed a diverse economic base, it was largely dominated by Alcoa. Industrial workers found jobs in glass, steel, coal, and heavy machinery, but employment in aluminum was preeminent.

Remarkably well preserved and complete records make an accurate, detailed analysis of industrial unionism in aluminum possible. Competing ideologies, organizational philosophies, power struggles, and sources of authority are all reflected in the official record. Unlike that of miners, the solidarity of aluminum workers was put in jeopardy, not by Communists or insurgents, but by established trade unionism. Since no local equivalent to John L. Lewis emerged in New Kensington, ideological conflict became entwined with, rather than subordinated to, the needs of structure and organization. The aluminum workers happily accepted the aid of the miners, but did not emulate their submission to an administrative despotism. Like the steelworkers of Apollo, the aluminum workers were homegrown rebels who schooled themselves in the art of participatory union democracy. Unlike their contemporaries in steel and coal, the aluminum workers sought far more than benevolent neutrality from the local power structure. For a short time, the union hall captured city hall. Aluminum workers briefly became policy and opinion makers. Their newfound authority seemed to justify the logic of industrial democracy on the march, but in less than a decade all of that would come tumbling down. Much of my telling of the aluminum workers' story will be devoted to an assessment of the meteoric rise and fall of an industrial union movement that for a short time appeared to have fulfilled its destiny.

The decision by the Aluminum Workers to abandon the AFL despite a thirty-year association with that body provides an opportunity to examine the inadequacy of craft unionism in an industrial setting. Unlike their brethren employed by the steel mills in Apollo and Vandergrift, the aluminum workers were not orphaned by their parent AFL affiliate. Mike Tighe, president of the Amalgamated, signed up the militant Kiskiminetas Valley steelworkers and then seemingly set them adrift upon a sea of indifference. David Williams, sent personally by AFL President William Green to organize and direct the Aluminum Workers Union, was not an old man bereft of vigor. However, the AFL was not prepared to offer the aluminum workers a union that was on equal footing with its other craft affiliates. It was not official lassitude or neglect but conscious policy choices by Green that alienated the rank and file and accounted for the defection of the Alcoa workers to the CIO in 1937.

The association of the AFL and the aluminum workers began on a militant note. On 27 March 1900, thirty-seven workers in the wire mill department of the Pittsburgh Reduction Company's New Kensington Works went out on strike. The men presented petitions to company management demanding wage increases from $1.50 to $1.75 for ten hours' work. A company counterproposal of ten cents was rejected. Men in other departments joined the walkout, and a strike committee was formed. Workers imported by management to fill vacancies were intercepted at the local railroad station and persuaded to leave town. One hundred men joined a "permanent union," and solicited support from local craft unions, boardinghouses, and hotels.[1]

A settlement was reached on 4 April. The strikers received a 12 percent increase and a reduction in Sunday work. AFL Local 8261, Aluminum Workers Union, was apparently recognized by the company. The local press applauded the absence of violence and "intense feeling" during the conflict. Local 8261 passed a resolution thanking the local burgess and the police committee of the town council for their assistance in bringing about a swift end to the conflict.[2]

The deceptively easy victory of the aluminum workers seemed initially to sustain the belief of local craft unionists that New Kensington was one of the strongest union towns in the nation. Events subsequent to the strike would quickly discredit that assumption. In September 1900 members of the Glass Cutters League attempted to organize American Window Glass plants located in Arnold, a small community pinned against the Allegheny River by New Kensington. That strike was ruthlessly broken. Members of the Cutters League were fired and blacklisted. Employees who were allowed to return to work in December were forced to join a company union. Local steelworkers fared no better. In

1901 the Amalgamated Association of Iron, Steel and Tin Workers attempted to unionize two American Sheet and Tin Plate plants in New Kensington. Scabs and the threat of plant removal quickly brought that conflict to an end.[3]

The long-term survival of the Aluminum Workers Union was an unlikely probability in such an antilabor environment. The Aluminum Company of America moved against its unions by replacing machinists with nonunion labor during a brief strike in 1907.[4] In the midst of a major production slowdown in 1908, a depression year, the company issued an ultimatum. Members of the Aluminum Workers Union were ordered to rescind their charter, disband their organization, and accept an open-shop plan, or face the loss of their jobs. The union men complied quickly, "voting unanimously" to give up their AFL charter.[5]

The destruction of the Aluminum Workers Union was a manifestation of Alcoa's growing power and presence in New Kensington. The Pittsburgh Reduction Company had moved from its Smallman Street location in Pittsburgh's strip district seventeen miles upriver to New Kensington in 1891. The efforts of the Burrell Improvement Company, real estate developers associated with Thomas Mellon and Sons, paved the way. According to Charles Martin Hall, the site's chief attractions were free land, cheap coal, $10,000 in cash for moving, and no taxes.[6] Alcoa's expansion was an integral part of an industrial boom that occurred in New Kensington. In 1891 not a single heavy industry existed in that community. A decade later Pittsburgh Reduction, two American Sheet and Tin Plate mills, and numerous glass manufacturing plants employed thousands of workers in New Kensington and nearby Arnold.[7]

During the first decade of the twentieth century, Alcoa's fabricating and processing operations (including cooking utensils, wire drawing, cable making, bronze powder, and extrusion departments) were established in New Kensington. The boom continued as Alcoa's operations expanded into adjacent Arnold in 1913. Two new Arnold plants, employing 2,500 workers, generated a payroll that rivaled the $1 million a year carried home in paychecks by Alcoa workers in New Kensington.[8] Real estate situated near the new plants was developed and sold by Thomas Mellon.

The ethnic composition of New Kensington and Arnold changed abruptly during those boom years. A Polish Falcon Hall was founded in New Kensington in 1911, and Young Italy was established there in 1913. When plans for a sanitary sewer system for Arnold were published in 1913, lot ownership by persons of Italian and Slavic origin had risen to nearly half the population in Arnold's new neighborhoods.[9] It was that "foreign element" which had, according to the local press, succumbed to the solicitations of an IWW organizer in 1913.[10] He allegedly promoted a strike in Alcoa's polishing department that led to a walkout of one hundred men. The organizer was arrested and fined. The strike collapsed within a week.[11]

Three years later Alcoa machinists, apparently unaffiliated with any labor organization, walked out on a spontaneous strike. Nearly three thousand men and women joined them several days later. The strikers met at the Polish Falcon Hall and formed a strike committee that presented their grievances to management. The workers demanded an eight-hour day with pay for ten, time and a half for overtime, double pay for Sunday work, an end of the bonus system, and better ventilation in company shops. Management responded that the market for fabricated aluminum products was poor and announced that the company had only remained open in order to provide employment for its workers. Alcoa politely rejected the demands of its workers and waited for the strike to collapse. The burgess of New Kensington interceded, assuring the strikers fair treatment. He also announced that Alcoa would continue its policy of "frequent adjustment of hourly wages just as if the strike had not occurred."[12] The strikers returned to work two weeks after they had walked out.

The walkout of 1916 was followed by nearly two decades of labor peace at Alcoa's New Kensington Works. Aluminum workers were not drawn into the bitter steel and coal strikes that raged throughout the Allegheny Valley in 1919. Alcoa's management began an Americanization program for its workers consisting of films, lectures, and classroom instruction, but did not participate in the virulent Bolshevik-baiting campaign generated by management in local steel mills.[13] In the four strikes that occurred at Alcoa's New Kensington Works prior to World War I, management did not emulate the strikebreaking techniques utilized by steelmakers and mine operators. Scabs and hired thugs were not imported by the trainload. Company-inspired industrial violence was not a weapon of choice. Alcoa apparently preferred a measured policy of economic coercion, attrition, selective dismissals, and watchful waiting in labor conflicts. By the standards of the Allegheny Valley, Alcoa's approach to the resolution of industrial conflict was moderate, persisting even after serious unionization campaigns resumed in New Kensington in 1933.

Hard times brought on by the Depression and renewed hope inspired by the National Recovery Act rekindled union activity throughout the Allegheny Valley during the spring and summer of 1933. The UMWA, which had been driven from the valley in 1927, returned in 1933 and signed a union contract with Lewis Hicks, the most recalcitrant anti-union coal operator in the region. By March 1934 organizers of the Glass

Cutters League had signed up 3,000 workers for their union. Howard Crowe and Edward Croghan, organizers for the Allegheny Valley Central Labor Union, appeared at the gates of Alcoa's New Kensington Works in July 1933.[14] They made speeches and distributed literature exhorting aluminum workers to take advantage of the protections offered by Section 7(a) of the National Recovery Act. Fred Broad, a local entrepreneur active in promoting the UMWA, donated office space to the fledgling Aluminum Workers Union.[15] On 1 August 1933, Aluminum Workers Union Local 18356 was chartered by the AFL. On 25 August 1933, a representation election was conducted in New Kensington. Of the votes, 2,897 were cast for Local 18356, 831 for Alcoa's Employee Representation Plan.[16]

Nick Zonarich, a disciple of Socialist Norman Thomas, reluctantly joined and promoted the Aluminum Workers Union. Although he would eventually rise to the union presidency, Zonarich would have preferred the creation of an international metalworkers' union strong enough to take on Alcoa. Union activist John Haser recognized that the activities of Thomas, Zonarich, and others had nurtured rebellion in New Kensington. However, Haser believed that hard times rather than ideology was responsible for pushing most aluminum workers into the union camp. Few workers shared Nick Zonarich's well-defined organizational goals. Most signed union cards in order to strike back against a company policy of low wages, preferential hiring, and selective layoffs.[17]

Mary Peli, a storeroom clerk, was moved to action by intolerable working conditions imposed by Alcoa's management. In many of the Alcoa's shops, female employees constituted the majority. Each day thousands of women would appear at the plant and were forced to endure the company's version of the shape-up. The women were lined up and inspected in military fashion. Those who were hired were admitted to the shops and were subjected to harassment and intimidation. Personal insults, demeaning rest room policies, and a "bonus system" that deprived workers of their just wages incensed Mary Peli. After conferring with her family and co-workers, she and forty-two female Alcoa employees marched in a group to the Broad Building and signed union cards. Shortly thereafter she was called into the shop superintendent's office and fired for "unsatisfactory work."[18]

The decision to fire Mary Peli proved to be a serious miscalculation. A coal miner's daughter, she was at home with adversity. Recognizing her courage and leadership qualities, the AFL organizers hired her to do clerical work and spot organizing for them. She emerged as an important spokeswoman for Italian-American workers, who constituted more than 60 percent of Alcoa's labor force.[19] An Alcoa plant superintendent appeared at her home in Logans Ferry and offered her family financial security if she would give up her union activities. When that offer was rebuffed, she was called in by her parish priest. He had already denounced the union from his pulpit and was reputed to be closely associated with the Mellons. As an Alcoa representative looked on from a darkened anteroom nearby, the priest offered Mary Peli a job at the Italian consulate in Pittsburgh. She politely refused the position and indicated her intention to remain actively involved in the union movement in New Kensington.[20]

Nick Zonarich, John Haser, and Mary Peli were the cutting edge of a union movement that was sorely tested in the months following the creation of Local 18356. Company tactics, government policy, defections, abortive strikes, and internecine strife rapidly eroded its membership. Initial recruiting efforts that had yielded 3,300 members in August 1933 proved ephemeral as the union was reduced to 17 active members in January 1935. Mary Peli ran a penny bingo game in order to sustain the operations of the local, which received little financial assistance from the parent AFL. The existence of the local was made even more precarious by the mysterious disappearance of $400 from the union safe. Union officers were suspected of making private arrangements with management. The first elected president of Local 18356 accepted a managerial position with Alcoa amid accusations of "treason."[21]

Alcoa lost no time in exerting its power in the community. Its Employee Representation Plan was promoted throughout New Kensington. Workers who subscribed to the plan were given preferential treatment by local merchants and company foremen. Retail credit dried up for Alcoa employees who supported the union. Union committees were received politely by management, for Alcoa publicly adhered to the union representation provisions of the National Recovery Act. However, Roy Hunt, president of Alcoa, made it clear that compliance with the act in no way obligated the company to accept specific union demands. Local 18356 received nominal recognition, but demands for a union contract and checkoff were refused.[22]

The National Recovery Act, which seemed to offer so much promise to unorganized aluminum workers, actually undermined their cause. Alcoa played the dominant role in drafting the NRA codes for the aluminum industry. On 14 October 1933, a basic wage scale consisting of forty cents per hour for male aluminum workers and thirty-five cents for females was presented to the National Recovery Administration.[23] Local 18356 protested that the codes caused a reduction in real wages for many workers and thereby eroded their faith in the National Recovery Administration. Condemning the codes as "an elaborate collection of superfluous verbiage to bring about the enslavement of workers in the aluminum industry," Local 18356 advised the AFL that its membership had repudiated the codes in a vote of 2,757 to 14.[24] The AFL seemed indifferent to their dissatisfaction and moved very slowly to address the conflict.

The relationship of Local 18356 and the AFL was uneasy from the start. AFL representatives who were sent to New Kensington appeared to be comfortable with the provisions of the NRA codes and the local status quo. Attempts by Local 18356 to negotiate directly on its own behalf were given little encouragement. AFL representatives did not hesitate to bargain without the authorization of the local rank and file. After one such incident members threatened to throw AFL representative William Swift off New Kensington's Ninth Street Bridge. Swift had been sent in to help the inexperienced negotiating committee selected by Local 18356, but his penchant for intrigue turned local meetings into angry shouting matches. Swift had helped to organize Local 18356 and should have understood the temper of the local. But his clandestine tactics generated distrust and encouraged the growth of anti-AFL sentiment. On 1 March 1934, two months after Swift's arrival, Local President Karl Burke Guiney resigned, ostensibly because of his "inability to conduct the business of the local."[25] On that same day 3,800 aluminum workers walked out on a job "holiday." While workers stood picket duty in ten inches of snow, union militants demanded a minimum $1.00 per hour wage rate, a checkoff, and a five-day workweek. Alcoa responded immediately with an offer of an across-the-board wage increase of 11 percent retroactive to the first day of the strike. Management also offered to negotiate all other issues following the return of its employees to their jobs.[26]

The strike produced a mixed result, for it was the product of anger and frustration rather than coherent planning. The union reluctantly accepted the company wage offer but a union contract and checkoff were not forthcoming. Swift proved true to form by passing up Local 18356 negotiators in favor of direct but unauthorized meetings with management. The strike was never endorsed by the AFL, and Swift treated it as a wildcat. Local militants John Haser and Nick Zonarich responded by sponsoring a resolution condemning Swift for undermining the "moral confidence" of their union.[27] Alcoa was well aware of the factions within the union camp and had little difficulty exploiting their differences during the muddled bargaining sessions. The walkout ended in defeat less than two weeks after it had begun.

The March strike opened a breach between Local 18356 and the AFL that was never closed. The failure of the AFL to provide strike benefits or any other tangible support for the strike was condemned as a "sellout." Swift was thoroughly discredited. He was replaced by David Williams, who was to direct Local 18356 from the AFL district office in Pittsburgh. Apparently Williams's chief function was to keep the rebellious New Kensington local in line. Local 18356 sensed this and accused their new adversary of usurping executive authority for the purpose of establishing a personal dictatorship.[28]

The appearance of Williams evoked a new and more significant response by Local 18356. In a direct appeal to AFL President William Green, the local demanded an international charter for all aluminum workers. What Local 18356 had in mind was nothing less than the creation of an industrial union such as those proposed for auto and rubber workers. Green parried that demand, arguing that the time was not opportune. Green questioned the financial viability of an Aluminum Workers International Union, insisting that member locals were not yet established on a "firm and permanent basis." President Paul Howlett of Local 18356 countered that if an international charter was not granted, aluminum workers would refuse to pay dues.[29] Green avoided a confrontation by founding an Aluminum Workers Council in June 1934.

The Aluminum Workers Council was an administrative device designed to placate those who demanded an industrial union. It was also an instrument of control that director David Williams might use to master such hard-line locals as 18356. Most aluminum worker locals, particularly in the South and Midwest, were not nearly so militant as their New Kensington brethren. By manipulating votes and resolutions in the plenary sessions of the council, Williams hoped to isolate and control troublemakers. Local 18356 recognized the council for what it was and subverted its cautious and conservative purpose at every opportunity. Pleas that the local quietly cooperate with Williams were ignored. Local 18356 continued to lobby for an industrial union. In that spirit, it courted dissident machinist Mark Robb. New Kensington machinists' Local 541 eventually defected to the Aluminum Workers in spite of Williams's assertion that AFL rules superseded the NRA principle of right of choice.[30]

William Green's ploy failed to silence the militants. When the council he conceived met, dissidents used the opportunity to goad Williams and more conservative locals, such as Alcoa, Tennessee, into action. In July 1934 a beleaguered Williams and his allies were pushed into negotiations with Alcoa. The abortive March strike and AFL faithlessness burned bright in the collective memory of Local 18356. In the eyes of the New Kensington local, the new round of negotiations represented an opportunity for the AFL to prove both its good faith and commitment to their cause. On 3 August Williams appeared before the local and announced that Alcoa had refused to accept the negotiated agreement.[31]

Alcoa's Roy Hunt made his objections to the agreement clear to the aluminum workers. The checkoff "was not a natural or necessary function of the company." Alcoa would pay "going wage rates" in all localities.[32] A closed shop would violate existing agreements and the NRA codes. Seniority rights, dismissal rules, and grievance procedures were a matter of company policy and were not subject to negotiations with a union. David Williams explained to his hostile audience that if William Green sanctioned a strike, all aluminum workers would walk out at one time.[33]

A strike call was issued on 10 August, but it is clear that Green did not wish to accept responsibility for it. Boris Shiskin was dispatched by Green to New Kensington to serve as consultant to the Aluminum Workers. The presence of Williams and Shiskin insulated Green from the field of action. The strike call itself was issued by telephone through intermediaries Williams and Shiskin. As pickets stood six-hour shifts in drizzling rain, the local press reported that William Green had endorsed the strike. The press reported that he had done so to forestall wildcats by individual locals. The probability of unauthorized strikes had been reported to Green by A. R. Buller, president of the Aluminum Workers Council. Local 18356 President Paul Howlett later claimed that the AFL had no connection with the strike call. Dave Williams countered that the Aluminum Workers Council had called the strike, and it was subsequently sanctioned by the AFL.[34]

The strike, an orphan from the beginning, lasted five weeks. On 6 September an agreement was announced. It was in fact a capitulation. Alcoa recognized the collective bargaining principles embodied in Section 7(a) National Recovery Act. There would be no checkoff, closed shop, or changes in wages. Howlett lamely explained to his shrinking membership that the local had supported the agreement in order not to break ranks with other locals in Massena, New York, and East Saint Louis, Missouri. Nick Zonarich opined that the union would accomplish nothing so long as it was affiliated with the AFL.[35]

For the small band that remained active in the local during the fall of 1934, anti-AFL sentiment took on a renewed vitality. Howlett openly extolled the virtues of an industrial union. Zonarich proclaimed that a union had to be "a fighting organization." Engineers and machinists, already members of AFL internationals, were invited to 18356 meetings. The local also entered the political arena. Howlett wrote to Jim Farley requesting that he help the local defeat the reelection of anti–New Deal senator David Reed. Only the Democratic National Committee was capable of dispensing enough aid to defeat politicians backed by the "predatory wealth of the Mellons."[36] It is clear that Local 18356 had embarked on a political course later taken by the CIO long before John L. Lewis's fist found Bill Hutcheson's jaw.

Howlett's militant anti-Mellon rhetoric belied the fact that the focus of his local's antipathy had shifted from Alcoa to the AFL. In the two years following the August strike, the militant activists who sustained the local fought to disassociate it from Green's domination. Local 18356 continued to call for an international charter. Green responded by calling a convention for the purpose of reorganizing the Aluminum Workers Council. Those antithetical positions made David Williams's chore impossible. Zonarich and his fellow dissidents declared him persona non grata in New Kensington. Obstinate to the bitter end, Williams replied with venom. "The job has been given to me to form the foundation of an International Union and I am going to make that foundation upon a growing membership, and not a bunch of damn Communists." Those who advocated an independent union were not "progressives" but Communists "working undercover." The attempt by Local 18356 "to set itself up bigger than the AFL" was due to "a combination of booze, detective agencies, and Communists."When pressed to appear and prefer charges, Williams refused. He demanded instead that all officers of the local resign and that all radicals be identified and eliminated.[37]

Green's ineptitude and Williams's inflammatory denunciations opened wounds that Local 18356 dissidents were not inclined to let heal. "Save Our Union" fliers financed by penny bingo were circulated among workers disillusioned by AFL failure. Machinist Mark Robb joined Haser and Zonarich in a call for an industrial union at Local 18356 meetings. Machinists' union business agent J. V. Pessamato appeared before Local 18356 and warned of the consequences of "jurisdictional trespass." A. O. Wharton, president of the International Association of Machinists, informed Local 18356 that it must observe the "jurisdictional rights" of his union or face the loss of its charter. David Williams also warned the local that if it did not rescind the membership of the machinists, the matter would be taken to Green. Revocation of its charter would be the probable result. The local responded on 21 March 1935 that the machinists had been disassociated. The local explained that they had been admitted only to prevent them from joining Alcoa's company union. Machinist Robb continued to attend and speak at Local 18356 meetings as late as 7 June. When Green learned of this he dashed off a directive to Local 18356 to disassociate the machinists by 1 July or face expulsion from the AFL. On 28 June Local 18356 complied.[38] That was the last time the AFL was able to intimidate the aluminum workers of New Kensington.

In 1935 the National Recovery Act was struck down by the Supreme Court, the Wagner Act was passed by Congress, and the CIO was born. David Williams continued to direct the Aluminum Workers Council. He negotiated an agreement with Alcoa in October 1935. Management again agreed to accept the principles of collective bargaining, but signed no union contract. Local 18356 praised Williams's "capable and skillful leadership" to government agencies, but the bickering between Williams and the local continued unabated. Williams continued to blame the Aluminum Workers Council for the failure of the August strike, and the local blamed the AFL. In the view of Local 18356, the greatest obstacle to the unionization of New Kensington's aluminum workers was the AFL, not Alcoa. At meetings, complaints were voiced about the federation's "pathetic indifference" to the problems of workers in the aluminum industry. The object of the AFL was apparently to keep aluminum workers "subdued and quiescent." In April 1936 the Allegheny Valley Central Labor Union was forced to surrender its charter to the AFL. That body had voted a public expression of sympathy for the CIO. Local 18356 lost no time in dashing off a letter to William Green demanding the restoration of the charter. Green's refusal was proof positive of his hostile intentions.[39]

The emergence of the CIO offered both an alternative to the AFL and renewed hope to thousands of disenchanted aluminum workers in New Kensington. Thousands who had deserted the union in 1934 returned to the fold in the spring and summer of 1936. The local invited CIO organizer John Brophy to speak to its membership. The *People's Press*, an organ of industrial unionism, was adopted as its official publication. Local 18356 made no attempt to hide its fraternization with the CIO. Other Aluminum Worker locals were invited to attend functions at which Brophy, Pat Fagan, and Glenn McCabe were scheduled to speak. John Haser and Nick Zonarich believed that fraternization with the CIO was nothing less than a prelude to industrial unionism and secession from the AFL. Moderates in the local had not yet given up on the AFL, and hoped that the presence of the CIO in New Kensington would force Green to issue the long-awaited international charter.[40]

William Green continued to stall on the charter question even when faced with the loss of Local 18356 to a rival organization. In order to prevent the creation of a "wild industrial organization" in New Kensington, David Williams announced that his office would monitor the local's finances. Williams was well aware of the successful recruiting drive that was underway and hoped to maintain a measure of control by collecting the per capita tax that locals were required to pay to the AFL. By such an action he hoped to prevent the heretofore bankrupt local from transferring those fresh funds to CIO coffers. Williams remained as tactless as ever. He demanded that the local conduct an audit, implying that its officers had submitted false per capita tax reports. The local promptly refused the audit request. Exasperated, Williams told the local that he was going to get control of its books because Local 18356 was "merely a dues collecting agency for the AFL."[41]

Green's inactivity and Williams's recklessness destroyed both AFL credibility and any hope of reconciliation. It is clear that by January 1937 the CIO faction had become the majority in New Kensington. Perceiving an imminent break with the AFL, members of the executive board moved decisively. Mary Peli withdrew the local's funds from an Arnold bank in February 1937. Nearly $20,000 was stored under her bed pending disposition by the local. Thus having secured the local's financial assets, the executive board convened a special Sunday meeting on 5 March 1937. The executive board announced that the clandestine withdrawal of union funds had been necessitated by the presence of AFL "stool-pigeons" in the local. The establishment of a new CIO account and audit were approved by the membership. An end to the payment of per capita taxes to the AFL was also approved. After grievances against the AFL were aired, the membership agreed to convene an Aluminum Workers convention in New Kensington for the purpose of founding an industrial union under the auspices of the CIO. A call was sent out to all Aluminum Workers locals inviting them to participate.[42]

Members of the executive board were so sure of local anti-AFL sentiment that they issued invitations to the convention to John L. Lewis and William Green ten days prior to the 5 March meeting. Green declined, and Lewis sent surrogate John Brophy. The invitations to the scattered Aluminum Workers locals produced mixed results. Local 19338, Louisville, Kentucky, opposed the break with the AFL, as did Local 18780, East Saint Louis. Williams had visited them and attributed the secession sentiment to a "clique of reds." The Massena, New York, local even refused to receive emissaries sent by Local 18356 for the purpose of promoting the convention. As Local 18356 made preparations for the convention, Williams continued to attribute the rupture to "communists and disrupters." Although Green suspended it on 12 March, Local 18356 refused to return its charter or turn over its treasury to the AFL. On 17 March the AFL filed suit against Local 18356 in federal court in Pittsburgh. The litigation would not be finally settled until 1942, five long years after Local 18356 had jumped to the CIO.[43]

On 12 April 1937, the constitutional convention of the Aluminum Workers of America convened in the Elks Hall in New Kensington. John Brophy and Len DeCaux, editor of the *Union News Service*, were in attendance. Twenty-one delegates, representing only four Aluminum Workers locals, founded the Aluminum Workers of America, CIO. Fourteen of the delegates represented the New Kensington area. Local 20257, Eau Claire, Wisconsin, supported the CIO but did not send delegates. The only non-Pennsylvania locals represented were Fairmont, West Virginia, and Alcoa, Tennessee.[44]

The New Kensington delegation took the lead. Their plant housed six thousand workers employed in thirty-seven different crafts. Traditional craft unions were simply too divided and therefore too weak. The AFL had proven its faithlessness on at least two occasions and had done nothing to unionize the fifty thousand aluminum workers who were as yet unorganized in the aluminum industry.[45]

Following a vote for affiliation with the CIO, a number of resolutions were introduced and passed by the delegates. The convention endorsed a resolution offered by John Haser condemning the AFL. Louis Petrigni demanded and the delegates supported an organizing campaign for all aluminum plants. If that were not done, work might be sent to nonunion sites. Haser and Petrigni also introduced resolutions condemning European fascism and its American offspring, the Black Legion.[46]

The CIO granted the Aluminum Workers of America a charter on 15 June 1937. AFL Local 18356 became Local 2, AWA. Nick Zonarich was elected international president and John Haser became business agent for Local 2. Local 2 became the center of a nationwide organizing drive launched by the CIO. Louis Petrigni and his wife, Mary Peli Petrigni, were dispatched to Alcoa's Cleveland plant. Charles Pauli was sent to Fayette, Indiana, and John Haser to Edgewater, New Jersey.[47] Although the AWA organizing campaign enjoyed widespread success, the goal of a single industrial union representing all aluminum workers was never achieved.[48] A nationwide CIO Aluminum Workers contract with Alcoa was finally signed in 1939.

The newfound power of Local 2 was felt immediately in the Allegheny Valley. Not only did the Aluminum Workers present a united front to Alcoa, but they plunged into politics as well.[49] The local had debated the endorsement of Democratic candidates in local elections while still an AFL affiliate. In 1936 Local 18356 had supported John Dent, president of the Jeannette, Pennsylvania, Rubber Workers local, and Fred Broad for election to the state assembly. But in 1937 four aluminum workers stood for election in New Kensington and Arnold, and candidates representing CIO affiliates dominated the Democratic slate. In New Kensington and Arnold the Aluminum Workers could deliver in excess of ten thousand votes. That power was dramatically reflected by the appearance of persons friendly to labor on school boards, city councils, county commissions, as mayors and burgesses, and in the offices of district attorney and sheriff. Fred Broad, elected Westmoreland County sheriff in 1939 with AWA and UMWA support, polled more votes than any other candidate for office in the election.[50]

Local 2 used a variety of methods to transmit its point of view to its members and the community. Its recording secretary wrote a column in the *New Kensington Daily Dispatch* entitled "Valley Labor News." The local also sponsored the Aluminum Workers Forum, a weekly public affairs program. The CIO message was further disseminated by the *People's Press* and the *Aluminum Workers Journal*. A well organized women's auxiliary insured that the AWA was identified with local civic and philanthropic activities. The local also cultivated good relations with the New Kensington and Arnold police.[51]

On 12 July 1938, Local 2 informed John L. Lewis that the Allegheny Valley, once known as a Black Valley for unionism, had become a CIO Valley. The local claimed that "the spirit of Industrial Unionism" had been "injected into the hearts of every man, woman and child." The new order of things was reflected in the union's dealings with the Aluminum Company of America. The union struck Alcoa in 1937, 1938, and 1939 on the way to the conclusion of a comprehensive union contract signed on 11 November 1939. However, there was generally an absence of rancor and violence in those disputes. Violence had led to tragedy in Alcoa, Tennessee, in July 1937. A union picket was slain by Alcoa guards.[52] But that sort of thing did not occur in New Kensington.

The relatively amicable state of affairs that existed in the Allegheny Valley was discussed at a meeting in Cincinnati on 5 November 1938. The first general conference of the affiliated locals of the Aluminum Workers of America was informed that Local 2 had a rational working relationship with Alcoa. Delegate Edward Troutman explained that the company was "not too arbitrary" and that many problems were settled by "mutual understanding." That amity existed in spite of substantial layoffs in Local 2 and summer-long picket lines in New Kensington. Bert Gravatt, past president of the local, told the gathering that the normalization of relations with Alcoa was due to the aggressive policies adopted by Local 18356. "We didn't believe in sitting tight," Gravatt told his fellow delegates. The organization is "mighty potent" in politics, "municipal, county and state." A coherent publicity campaign carefully orchestrated by the local also brought the union cause favorably into public view. George Hobaugh, past treasurer of Local 2, explained that the "troubles" that an otherwise exemplary New Kensington local was having were attributable not to Alcoa, but to Communists "boring from within."[53]

AWA President Nick Zonarich was a Socialist and an outspoken anti-Communist. But Zonarich balked at a motion to conduct an investigation to ferret out all persons in the AWA with Communist or fascist leanings. Zonarich proposed that the problem be handled diplomatically, so that the radicals might be quietly controlled. An internecine fight would only weaken the union's united front against business. Zonarich was certain that the Communists controlled no locals, and that none were present on the AWA executive board. Bert Gravatt agreed that the Communists constituted a small bloc in New Kensington and that a purge would only drive them underground. The union's most formidable enemy was the "reactionary force." A red-baiting campaign would only give ammunition to the Dies Committee, an enemy of unionism. The motion was defeated by a vote of sixteen to one, and the issue of Communism was quietly buried.[54]

In 1940 Local 2 prospered. War production ended layoffs in an expanding aluminum industry. John Haser reported that the membership of Local 2 had grown to 7,075. The local seemed preoccupied with the draft, leaves of absence for military service, and fingerprinting of Alcoa employees. The local's secretary reported that "working conditions improved to the extent that we seldom find anything wrong with the place in which we work."[55]

On 21 November 1940, the apparent serenity in New Kensington was shattered by a wildcat strike. According to accounts in the press, Thomas Davis, a comitteeman of Local 2, had attempted to collect delinquent dues from an aluminum worker. The worker allegedly responded by brandishing a knife. When word of the altercation reached the members of the work force, they walked off the job and demanded that the worker be disciplined. Management responded that the problem was an internal union dispute. Local 2 agreed that the affair was a matter for the union, but insisted that the walkout was not due to Communists or radicals in the union.[56]

The wildcat strike lasted for eight days. Philip Murray negotiated a solution with Alcoa, and 7,500 aluminum workers returned to their jobs. The recalcitrant worker was ostracized and sent to a lonely boiler room in the Logans Ferry Plant. The furor died down, but only briefly. The issue of radicalism in the local had again been raised, this time publicly. The penetration of "leftist elements" into American unions, particularly those involved in defense industries, had become a matter of nationwide discussion in 1940. Communism would become the consuming issue in the election of officers for Local 2, scheduled for 15 December.

On the eve of the election Nick Zonarich charged that Communists were behind the slate of candidates headed by incumbent president Al Daughenbaugh. Zonarich's volte-face on Communism appears at least in part to have been politically motivated. His presidency depended upon the support of Local 2, which constituted the largest voting bloc in the AWA. The decision to make Communism an issue in the election was denounced by Daughenbaugh as a ploy by Zonarich to arrest the erosion of his support in the local. Daughenbaugh also charged that Zonarich's preelection revelations were designed to cover up the fact that Socialists had dominated the union for several years.[57]

Zonarich was an admitted disciple of Norman Thomas and had a reputation for taking care of his friends in the union. His left-wing connections no doubt caused him some discomfort, for the CIO had begun to identify and banish its radical elements in 1940.[58] The AWA president was clearly vulnerable to Daughenbaugh's charges and to whatever anti-radical pressures the conservative leadership of the CIO might choose to exert on him. The Reverend Charles Owen Rice, chaplain of the Association of Catholic Trade Unionists, joined Zonarich in denouncing the Daughenbaugh slate and its "more pay, less speed up" campaign. Father Rice believed that the election of a slate sprinkled with "Communist stooges" would be a "black day for the AWA and the CIO." Rice acknowledged that Zonarich had been a Socialist in his youth, but gave assurances that Zonarich was now a "foe of Communism" and "a supporter of true American Unionism."[59]

No fewer than four members of the Daughenbaugh slate were thought to have an affinity for Communism. However, the center of conflict was the contest for business agent. Incumbent John Haser, Zonarich's personal choice, was challenged by Louis Petrigni, a man Zonarich claimed had "played real closely with the Communists."[60] The choice for business agent was of critical importance to Zonarich, for that person conducted the day-by-day affairs of the local. If Petrigni were elected, Zonarich would have had great difficulty in controlling a local that was vital to his interests. Haser was a trusted Zonarich ally. Petrigni seemed considerably to the left of Zonarich, and authored many resolutions condemning international fascism at union meetings. It was also clear that Petrigni was an independent type who would not simply follow Zonarich's lead.

The election produced such mixed results that it is impossible to assess the precise impact that the Communism issue had upon the union electorate. Haser defeated Petrigni, thus assuring a measure of control for Zonarich. Daughenbaugh won by a majority of three to one. Two alleged Communist sympathizers were also elected. The storm over the election passed quickly, and union operations resumed their normal course. The major casualty of the conflict was Louis Petrigni. Mary Peli Petrigni reported from Cleveland that her husband had been fired from his job as organizer by Zonarich because he had opposed the Haser-Zonarich faction in the election.[61]

The factional conflict that rocked the AWA in 1940 was not the sole problem plaguing the organization. Although war would bring prosperity to aluminum workers, the financial condition of the AWA remained tenuous. The AWA controlled sixteen of thirty Alcoa plants in 1944. The lion's share of the international's budget was derived from Local 2. That budget supported the international officers' salaries and an organizing staff of five. Nick Zonarich had always favored one large industrial union for all workers in the metals industry. John Haser anticipated a major struggle between the AWA and Alcoa after the war. The AWA could not hope to win such a struggle with its meager resources. Haser and Zonarich therefore quietly promoted the amalgamation of Aluminum Workers with the United Steel Workers of America.[62]

During the war the activities and attitudes of the AWA were shrouded in mystery. In 1944 complaints were raised that Local 2 had not received reports from the international for two years. The international was in fact in debt to the Garment Workers and Steel Workers from whom Zonarich had borrowed funds. John Haser, not Zonarich, sold the amalgamation idea to Local 2. The USWA had 800,000 members; the AWA fewer than 20,000. The USWA had assets of $4 million; the AWA was destitute. The USWA had four hundred organizers; the AWA had five. Local 2 appointed delegates to attend the AWA convention in Hot Springs, Arkansas, on 5 June 1944. The delegates were instructed to support amalgamation if Philip Murray would make a commitment to organize all aluminum workers, and allow local unions to retain autonomy and their assets.[63]

On 13 June 1944, John Haser reported that the AWA delegates had adopted a resolution for amalgamation. Delegate Alan Hill explained that the organization's new name would be the United Steel and Aluminum Workers of America. Hill also announced that John Haser would soon begin a campaign to organize all white-collar workers at Alcoa. On 9 July William Hart and Michael Petrak of the Steel Workers appeared at Local 2 to explain the white-collar organizing campaign. Events were moving far too quickly for some members. President Joseph Carey complained that amalgamation had been pushed on his local without time for analysis. His objections were politely deflected, and the local turned in its old charter. Local 2 became Local 302, United Steel Workers of America.[64]

Amalgamation was accomplished without the benefit of debate by the membership. Some members believed that even though amalgamation had been railroaded through the local by Haser and Zonarich, it was nevertheless warranted. But questions about the new partnership arose quickly. John Haser and Nick Zonarich had been elevated to staff positions in the USWA. The local wanted to know if it would continue to be served by a full-time business agent. Some members feared that a part-time business agent would serve the local from the district USWA office. On 5 September President Carey reported the results of an executive board meeting conducted with Nick Zonarich in attendance. A "full time" business agent would also serve Steel Workers locals in spite of protests. Carey announced that the treasury of Local 302 had been transferred to the USWA. He attributed the failure of the USWA to change its name to the Steel and Aluminum Workers to an oversight by Philip Murray.[65]

On 26 September a special meeting was convened at Local 302 to discuss amalgamation. For the first time, the eighteen-point program for amalgamation adopted at the June convention was read and explained to the membership. Under the terms of the merger Aluminum Workers were governed by the USWA constitution. The union name would be changed to reflect the presence of Aluminum Workers in the USWA.[66] Full-time AWA personnel were transferred to the USWA and would serve the Aluminum Workers whenever practical. William Hart, USWA staff representative, explained that John Haser had become a member of his staff but would continue to serve the aluminum workers. If the local desired a full-time business agent, it would have to bear the expense. AWA assets and collective bargaining contracts were to be assumed by the USWA. Nick Zonarich announced that amalgamation had been "perfected," and could not be changed.[67] The independent Aluminum Workers Union had indeed ceased to exist.

The marriage of the AWA and USWA was not entirely tranquil. The quiet work of Haser and Zonarich on behalf of amalgamation had enabled them to present Local 2 with a fait accompli. But their efforts did not eliminate the insurgent tradition in the local. Sporadic grumbling continued well after Local 2 had received its USWA charter. The Steelworkers had not only reneged on the union name change; some aluminum workers also complained that local autonomy meant little more than neglect by the USWA. Local 302 remained John Haser's responsibility, but the payment of per capita fees was not buying the quality of service to which some members of the local had become accustomed. On 8 July 1946, Local 302 seated officers who were apparently hostile to Haser and the USWA. A flood of recriminations followed. On 20 January 1948, the USWA suspended all local officers and placed Local 302 in trusteeship.

The local officers were charged with misappropriation of funds, illegal court actions, libeling and slandering international officers, impeding the international, and violating the USWA constitution. As the conflict warmed up, allegations of Communism and subversion were added; the officers were accused of consorting with a known Communist organizer. The accused responded that the entire affair was simply a smear campaign inspired by Haser, Hart, and the losing slate in the 1946 election. The object, they asserted, was the usurpation of power in the local. Suspended President Frank Hill claimed that the conflict had begun because Haser and Hart were too busy to take care of the local's business. Vice-president Sam Anthony accused the staff of District 19 of conducting a purge of President Hill and his executive board because of their outspoken criticism of the inadequate services rendered by the USWA.[68]

The suspended officers continued to hold rump sessions long after the trustees had assumed control of the local. Bert Gravatt, past president of the local and a founder of the Aluminum Workers Union, was named chief administrator of the trusteeship by the USWA. Gravatt was immediately assailed as a dictator and a pawn of District 19. The ousted officers attempted to institute countercharges against Gravatt and Haser, but that effort was quashed by the courts. The ousted officers continued to publish their version of the *Aluminum Workers Journal*, official organ of the local.[69] They also had access to the local press. On 2 February Father Casimir Orlemanski, now the pastor at Saint Mary's Roman Catholic Church, defended the suspended officers in the *New Kensington Daily Dispatch*. Orlemanski suggested the restoration of the ousted executive board and the suspension of William Hart for not attending to his job. If the USWA insisted on trying the suspended officers, Orlemanski suggested that the trial be conducted by the rank and file. The priest's implied distrust of District 19 officialdom was clarified in an open appeal written by Sam Chine, suspended recording secretary of Local 302. Chine charged that he had been told by the New Kensington Democratic chairman that Hart and Haser were planning to get rid of Frank Hill and his executive board. Chine also stated that Father Orlemanski had been solicited by Haser and Hart to support their plot to remove Hill and his board. Chine also emphatically denied the existence of a Communist conspiracy in the local.[70]

By March, Communism had replaced official malfeasance as the chief issue in the conflict. The supporters of District 19 alleged that the suspended officers, dubbed "Club 11," were a dangerous political clique backed by Communists. They accused the dissidents of hiring left-wing lawyer Morris J. Kaplan to defend them. Kaplan, they alleged, was identified with Communist unions in New York. The *Daily Worker* countered that the ousted local officers were fighting both the Mellons and their union stooges. The *Daily worker* accused William Hart of forcing an Alcoa inspired "speed-up" on the aluminum workers. The *Daily Worker* also pointed out that Hart was president of the Association of Catholic Trade Unionists and hoped to use the incident to silence opponents of that movement.[71]

It is unclear whether the conflict of 1948 emanated from internal union politics, Communist subversion, or both. The merits of the charges and countercharges remain muddled. It is clear, however, that the USWA chose to use a show trial to resolve the conflict. On 15 July a trial committee convened hearings in New Kensington that would drag on until 16 September. Defendants denounced the trial as a mockery that served the interests of "rotten politics." Others not directly connected with the proceedings questioned the objectivity of the hearing officers and the wisdom of the trial. Some believed that problems connected with elected officials of Local 302 could have been best remedied by the rank and file in the next election.[72]

Trial transcripts reflect a preoccupation with Communist subversion rather than official malfeasance. Six executive board members were found to have engaged in subversive activities. Three were cited for conspiracy to break away from the USWA. Two were found guilty of misappropriation of union funds and records. The trial committee recommended expulsion of President Frank Hill and five others. Probation was recommended for four men, and one man was not sentenced. On 5 November the fate of the eleven men was placed before the electorate of Local 302. The report, findings, and recommendations of the trial committee were rejected by secret ballot, 968 to 615.[73]

The rapid rise and decline of the Aluminum Workers Union was in many ways emblematic of the fate of industrial unionism throughout western Pennsylvania. In New Kensington, what began as a traditional exercise in trade unionism developed into a movement with broad social and political implications. The view of the aluminum workers was not narrow. They apparently believed that their well-being was tied to that of the community at large. The AWU adopted and applied a philosophy of unionism not unlike that espoused by Westinghouse workers in Turtle Creek twenty-five years before. Activity in local government, on school boards, in public affairs programs, and in the media reflected a new spirit of community activism. The AWU seemed to understand that its future was tied to much more than the shop floor and bargaining table. But the AWU, like the rest of the CIO unions, withdrew from the public arena almost as quickly as it had entered. No doubt the war proved to be a great distraction, but the Daughenbaugh controversy, and Lewis's withdrawal from the CIO, suggest that the AWU and industrial unionism had changed course long before Pearl Harbor.

Participatory union democracy and local autonomy proved to be equally ephemeral. AWU rank and file are hard pressed to explain how their union was absorbed by the steelworkers. Most shrug their shoulders, and attribute the demise of local autonomy to John Haser and Nick Zonarich. Most admit that the move was not achieved democratically, but support it because it brought the AWU financial security provided by the USWA treasury. The fact that steelworkers would make decisions for aluminum workers did not seem to matter very much. The furor over the Daughenbaugh slate and the show trial also drove a good many AWU members to the periphery of their union. To oppose Zonarich, Haser, or

USWA domination was to risk being labeled a Communist. Many simply paid their dues and withdrew to the sidelines.[74] Local 302, an appendage of the USWA, robbed of much of its native vitality, would not be prepared to deal effectively with the corporate decisions that brought profound changes to the aluminum industry.

Epilogue

THE RISE AND DECLINE OF INDUSTRIAL UNIONISM IN WESTERN PENNSYL-
vania must in large measure be evaluated in terms of the economic
health of the region. Ironically, industrial unionism came of age decades
after the industrial economy of western Pennsylvania had reached
maturity. According to a study made by economist Glenn McLaughlin,
the Pittsburgh region ended its stage of rapid growth in population and
industrial activity in 1910. McLaughlin predicted continued growth at a
decelerating rate for some industries and a continuing decline in others.
He acknowledged that Alcoa was installing an increasing proportion of
its new operations outside western Pennsylvania, but he believed that
there was "no apparent reason why the making of aluminum products
should leave the area." Steel would continue to stagnate, for national
demand was languid and a prime customer—the railroads—had grown
old. Coal faced southern competition and leveling off in the steel industry. Glass flourished, but the industry faced a continuing "westward
movement." Only a vibrant electrical-equipment manufacturing industry, situated largely in the Turtle Creek Valley, promised dynamic
growth. According to McLaughlin, it alone buoyed an otherwise medi-
ocre industrial growth performance during the 1920s and 1930s[1]
McLaughlin's predictions of economic malaise appear, if anything, to be
understated. Labor had succeeded in organizing an eroding regional
economy, and industrial unionism was, from its very beginnings, vulnerable.

If the health of western Pennsylvania's industrial economy was mar-
ginal that weakness did not often soften the demands of labor. Decades
of growth and profits, accompanied by corporate obstinacy and repression, made caution unlikely. John L. Lewis clearly recognized that coal
was a sick industry, and yet No Backward Step became the battle cry of
the UMWA. Even when such companies as Apollo Steel opened its books
to public scrutiny, militant workers relented only reluctantly in their
demands. The region's industrial workers deserved their reputation for
militance, but that hard line was not rooted in radicalism. The IWW
discovered early that western Pennsylvania's workers were ideologically

conservative. The failure of the Wobblies, Communists, and Socialists to win converts suggests that doctrines of class conflict were not held in much favor. Furthermore, both the Wobblies and their chief rivals, the AFL, acknowledged that industrial workers also resisted union efforts to recruit them. Apparently, the militant but conservative industrial workers of the region possessed no inherent affinity for unionization.

Labor historians have long been intrigued by the connection among labor, unions, and ideology. However, the fascination that ideology has held for scholars was not shared by labor's rank and file. Neither radicals nor scholars have been able to unearth and isolate the specific sources of the region's proletarian conservatism. It is, nevertheless, clear that private property, profits, and economic inequality were in no particular danger in western Pennsylvania. The region produced few radical movements of its own. The Progressive Bloc, born in Pittsburgh, never prospered. The Socialist party functioned in isolated pockets, like Turtle Creek. Imported radicalism, such as the IWW and Communist party, enjoyed meager success. Even more interesting is labor's languid commitment to union democracy.

The proletarian manifesto produced in Turtle Creek in 1914, proclaimed principles of participatory democracy. The UMWA constitution and local charters are laden with references to a union for and by working miners. Likewise, the CIO embraced social and political egalitarianism as well as union democracy. But did the Westinghouse manifesto reflect the will of industrial workers or was it the work of a Socialist coterie led by Fred Merrick? Did not the UMWA miners cast aside union democracy for a Lewis dictatorship? Was not the dissolution of an independent Aluminum Workers Union, for all intents and purposes, carried out in a closet? Proletarian ideology was a by-product rather than a primary source of industrial conflict in western Pennsylvania. The regions's workers were moved to action first and foremost by crisis, not by a body of ideas. Inflation and Taylorism threatened Westinghouse workers. Coal entered a depression a full decade before all other industries. UMWA miners, sensing the chaotic state of their industry and the tradition of schism in their union, knowingly sacrificed democracy for order and direction. A democratic Aluminum Workers Union was born of an unprecedented Depression crisis, but when prosperity returned, union democracy and autonomy dissolved. The commitment of western Pennsylvania's industrial rank and file to ideas and principles, even to those as fundamental as union democracy, was fragile indeed. In that context, the charge that is so often heard—that union leadership is out of touch with its rank and file—is a cliché that misses the mark.

Alleged rank-and-file dissatisfaction with the organization and structure of AFL craft unionism is similarly misstated. The Turtle Creek manifesto and the rapid rise of the CIO certainly suggest a significant loss of support for the AFL in an industrial setting. Some historians have argued that craft unionism was inherently incompatible with the industrial workplace, dominated as it was by unskilled, mass-production labor. Having perceived this, so the argument goes, workers rejected the old regime for a new and more responsive one. No doubt some industrial workers perceived the defects of craft unionism and moved to remedy them. But oral interviews and a review of local union minutes and records reveal that just as many abandoned the AFL, often very reluctantly, for other reasons. Frequently it was a failure to act, to do something, and not structural defects that motivated workers to fight and ultimately abandon Green and Tighe. UMWA miners had been affiliated with the AFL for decades, and had few complaints about the structure of craft unions. But the miners were in an aggressive mood during the early years of the New Deal, and eagerly supported Lewis's break with Green. Dissident steelworkers in Apollo cared little about the nature of their union's hierarchy. What they wanted was recognition and they were more than willing to strike in order to get it. Tighe's refusal to lead aggressively cost him their support. Of all the region's industrial laborers, the aluminum workers seemed to have perceived most clearly the deficiencies of craft unionism. However, it was the conscious policy decisions of Green and not the position of aluminum in a craft structure that induced many to cross the line. All of these workers eventually joined industrial unions, which were larger and less exclusive than the old AFL affiliates. Race, gender, and ethnic origins were no longer absolute obstacles to membership. But the behavior of the bureaucracies remained very much the same. Those entrenched in official posts stopped at nothing to defend of their place and power. Red-baiting, the dispensation of patronage, and the delivery of lucrative contracts pleasing to the rank and file occupied most their time. Much was lost, including industrial labor's sources of authority in the community.

On the eve of World War II, the CIO controlled the shop floor in western Pennsylvania. Nevertheless, labor's authority in the community had already begun to diminish. Support and sympathy for industrial labor's cause had always been tenuous and uneven. There were union towns and company towns, labor priests and company priests, "redneck" squires and company judges. A region renowned for its repressive environment was just as likely to produce Michael Musmanno as it was Judge Langham. Herbert Gutman's arguments that industrial labor did not face monolithic opposition is applicable to western Pennsylvania. Labor enjoyed considerable support, particularly at the local level, but eventually squandered much of it. The aluminum workers are a case in point. When the CIO swept into the Allegheny Valley, the enduring dreams of labor's visionary left seemed possible. Labor marched from the union hall to city hall, to the school board, and to the county sheriff's office. Missionary zeal characterized the activity of aluminum workers. Election to local office, public affairs programs, and newspaper columns stressed labor's commitment to civic duty; the aluminum workers enjoyed moral authority in their community as never before. The AWU seemed prepared to go beyond traditional business unionism. The education of public opinion and the formulation and direction of public policy suggested that CIO industrial unions had struck off in an exciting new direction. However, the absorption of the AWU by the Steelworkers and the rapid bureaucratization of their union cost the aluminum workers much of their identity and influence in their city.

Aluminum workers achieved a measure of financial security by joining the USWA. However, that security exacted a price. Aluminum workers quickly discovered that their interests were not identical to those of their brethren in steel. The USWA bureaucracy showed little interest in the programs built by the aluminum workers before the war, and they disappeared. The New Kensington Central Labor Union, of which the AWU had been a vital part, withered on the vine. Aluminum workers, like their contemporaries in coal and glass, became increasingly isolated from one another and from the community at large. That growing isolation was punctuated by the factional fighting and the show trial that occurred in 1948. In that year, New Kensington was given a ringside seat to an internal power struggle replete with charges of Communist subversion, mismanagement, and corruption. The shoddy character of the proceedings did little to enhance labor's declining public image.

Industrial labor's authority in the community may have recently reached its nadir in western Pennsylvania. The appearance of the Network to Save the Monongehela/Ohio Valley has cast much opprobrium upon an already beleaguered labor movement. Ironically, the new militants cannot be identified with established industrial unions. Disillusioned by decades of plant closings and give-backs, the militants challenge not only corporate power but the leadership and direction of the USWA as well. Much of the network's leadership is provided by dissident USWA local presidents as well as disaffected rank and file. Most advocate direct action: picketing of corporate headquarters and churches where management worships, stuffing of bank safe-deposit boxes with rotten fish, and selective boycotts. The Denominational Ministry Strategy, or DMS, supports unemployed labor from the pulpit and in the streets. Radical clergy have demonstrated, fed the deprived, and in doing so have split their congregations. Today's labor priests have evoked very little sympathy for their cause, and several have run afoul of

their church's ruling bodies. For many, the disruption of religious services and attacks on local banks seem both wanton and unjustified. The
dissidents have been no more successful than the established unions in
making their case in the court of public opinion. In fact, the radicals—
both secular and clerical—seem totally alone. Beyond the establishment
of local food banks to feed the destitute, public sympathy for industrial
labor, and for those who claim to be its advocates, is meager in western
Pennsylvania. Decades of isolation from the community, much of it self-
imposed, have reduced industrial labor to a state of powerlessness not
seen since the eve of the New Deal.

The liberation and regeneration of industrial communities was a common goal shared by Wobblies, Socialists, and the CIO. The industrial
unionists argued that the extension of industrial democracy beyond the
work place and craft offered mill and factory towns an important alternative to the AFL and its narrow business unionism. Western Pennsylvanians were promised a new society, employed by industry yet free from
corporate domination. For all its enlightened rhetoric, industrial labor
rarely used its power to achieve stated community goals. The CIO
courted and cultivated the community, but only briefly. By 1940 the new
unions practiced traditional unionism on an industrial scale. As the CIO
looked inward, its energies were devoted largely to recognition, control
of the shop floor, contracts, and job security. Organized labor once again
had proven to be one-dimensional. The passage of Pennsylvania's so-
called Little New Deal, abolition of industrial police, and the creation of
the State Labor Relations Board could not have been accomplished
without broad community support. After 1940 the quest for local community strength was largely abandoned for professional lobbyists, political action committees, and an alliance with the Democratic party.

How well the CIO-Democratic alliance served the interests of industrial labor remains the subject of lively debate. Critics argued that organized labor became just another interest group attempting to work its
will through the political process. There is much substance in that
allegation. The alliance existed largely to defend the gains made by labor
during the New Deal. Defense of the status quo made labor less than a
dynamic force in the political arena. Partisanship generated other problems as well. After World War II, the appearance of Wallacite Progressives prompted squabbling aluminum workers and steelworkers to
ask who among them were "proper" Democrats and who were "Reds."
For all their partisan maneuvering, western Pennsylvania labor did not
address the local issue most critical to its interests. Industrial malaise was
easy to miss. War and the postwar boom had brought full production,
employment, and prosperity; nevertheless, the signs of decay were everywhere, and corporate Pittsburgh did not fail to notice them. Pitts-

burgh was an old industrial community with serious environmental problems. According to historian Roy Lubove, the decision to revive rather than abandon the city was made by the Mellon banking family. The Pittsburgh Renaissance, a regenerative strategy, was conceived and implemented by a corporate elite in cooperation with Democratic Mayor David Lawrence. The renaissance was not simply an exercise in urban face-lifting. It was designed to maintain the city as a corporate headquarters. Corporate Pittsburgh had moved to prepare its community for the postindustrial future.[2]

Pittsburgh was not only a corporate headquarters, but a major union outpost as well. The city was the economic capital of western Pennsylvania, and its new direction promised to influence the future of labor as much as that of business. Nevertheless, organized labor played no direct role in the city's renaissance. According to Lubove, labor's influence was confined to public complaints by UMWA district president John Busarello that smoke abatement plans were a conspiracy against coal and were therefore inimical to the interests of miners.[3] Busarello's fears were no doubt justified, but his vision and that of labor generally was rather limited. (Beyond the regeneration of the Golden Triangle and programs for pollution control, the renaissance did not include a corporate blueprint for the modernization of plants and equipment.) The Pittsburgh Renaissance was a clear signal that the city's corporate giants were no longer singularly committed to traditional smokestack industries. Alcoa, a firm synonymous with corporate Pittsburgh, was among the first to move in a new direction.

New Kensington had been Alcoa's center of production for more than half a century, and many believed it always would be. After the war, declining production and reductions in the labor force indicated otherwise. In 1966 the membership of Aluminum Workers Local 302, USWA, fell to 2,200. Shop closings threatened 500 more jobs. After arduous negotiations, the USWA signed a save-the-plant agreement with Alcoa that included concessions on seniority, retirement, and incentive provisions of the union's contract. On 1 July 1970, Alcoa announced the termination of its manufactured-products division and the closing of the New Kensington Works. By 31 March 1971, the closings had been accomplished. What remained was a small facility at Logans Ferry and a formidable research center situated five miles east of New Kensington. The latter is a monument to high technology, the direction in which Alcoa and so many former industrial giants seem to be heading. The Aluminum Workers Union and the Aluminum City in which it flourished are now but fading memories.

Aluminum was not an isolated case. After the war, glass all but deserted the Allegheny Valley; steel mills were lost in Apollo, and even in

Vandergrift, where more than 9,000 men had once been employed. Organized labor reacted slowly to industrial malaise. Labor did not appear to recognize the depth of the problem until steel plants in the region's economic heartland—the Monongahela-Ohio Valley—began to close. The strike and picket line, which had long been the primary weapons in industrial labor's arsenal, appeared to be essentially useless against the new threat. Industrial labor's apparent impotence has encouraged concessions, give-backs, and even union busting, and few in the community seem to care.

The region's labor force faces problems that go well beyond the bargaining table. Glenn McLaughlin found that overspecialization in heavy industries reduced the flexibility of labor. A large group of unskilled and semiskilled workers employed in those industries dominated the labor market. In the opinion of McLaughlin, the existence of such a specialized labor force facilitated the expansion of primary industries and their extension into related manufacturing fields. However, the specialization of local industry had the "handicap of restricting employment mainly to a single type of labor. Basic steel put primary emphasis on one kind of labor, that supplied by physically strong, semiskilled and unskilled men." Knowledge of local mechanical processes were passed from father to son, and entire families and communities were locked into employment in those industrial occupations. McLaughlin implied that since the labor force in the Pittsburgh district lacked flexibility, it was vulnerable.[4]

Postwar analysts, such as Peter Drucker, are even less sanguine regarding the future of industrial employment and unions. McLaughlin's findings did not reflect the impact of World War II, the resurgence of European and Third World economies, and the recent revolutions in high technology. Drucker argues that the United States is now part of a "transnational" economy in which the economic sovereignty of the nation has become little more than a "delusion." Drucker predicts the virtual disappearance of traditional assembly lines by the 1990s, continued "production sharing" arrangements with underdeveloped nations, and the continuing exportation of industrial jobs to foreign labor markets.[5] The implications of such a postindustrial environment for the workers of western Pennsylvania are staggering. If Drucker is correct, both the efficacy and survival of industrial unions are in question.

Although the modern industrial union in western Pennsylvania appears impotent in the face of postindustrial challenges, any decision to write its obituary would be premature. The career of organized labor has always been cyclical, and the movement has proven to be quite resilient. However, the problems facing contemporary industrial labor go far beyond the shop floor, managerial intransigence, and political hostility.

Recent plant closings by U.S. Steel and Westinghouse involved the dismissal of management personnel in large numbers, suggesting that the crisis has not been manufactured simply to get unions. Traditional industrial warfare seems to be no remedy for the evaporation of a regional industrial base. That may be why labor solidarity does not exist, and why hard times have not produced a fighting spirit, which in the past has drawn diverse groups of workers together. The new militants, such as DMS, are community activists and are not part of the great industrial unions. The unions are rarely visible in the community, and their activity is largely limited to warnings about foreign imports. Industrial unions appear content to deliver labor's message by lobbying state and federal legislatures. Survival through the erection of trade barriers seems to be their chief priority, but protectionism appears to have little appeal for consumers or their legislators. The Tri-State Conference on Steel has roots in both the community and organized labor. It advocates convening industrial summits, and long-term regional economic planning. Tri-State also recommends legislative activity, but seems to sense that success on that front is only possible if labor recaptures the comunity authority that it forfeited long ago.

The industrial union movement that seemed to come of age in western Pennsylvania during the Depression established little more than a tenuous foothold in the area. Labor solidarity proved ephemeral, and disunity the rule. Industrial labor, even in its most vigorous form—the CIO—was hardly a monolithic presence. Despite much initial promise, industrial unions never became a cohesive, united, integral part of the regions' decision-making process. Corporate influence remained dominant in determining what would or would not be done in Pittsburgh and its industrial environs. Business remained, despite the laws that protected labor, essentially free to shape the life of western Pennsylvania. Industrial unions abandoned their proclaimed mission of social and economic justice and practiced business unionism on an industrial scale. They became guardians of the work place and contract provisions, but paid scant attention to the problems of regional economic decline. Divided and apparently without direction, contemporary industrial labor seems unprepared to deal with challenges associated with global economics and technological change.

Notes

Chapter 1.   Industrial Unionism in the Turtle Creek Valley

1. David Montgomery, *Workers' Control in America.*

2. *Justice,* 30 June 1914. The organization was first known as the Allegheny Congenial Industrial Union. According to Merrick, *Justice* was not an official organ of the Socialist party. Views expressed therein were attributable not to the Socialist party, but rather to individual Socialists on the newspaper's editorial board.

3. *Justice,* 24, 30 June 1914, 31 January 1914, 7 February 1914.

4. Melvyn Dubofsky, *We Shall Be All,* pp. 202–5; John W. Ingham, "A Strike in the Progressive Era: McKees Rocks, 1909," *Pennsylvania Magazine of History and Biography,* Vol. 90 (July 1966): 353–77.

5. *Pittsburgh Press,* 5, 6 June 1914; *Pittsburgh Sun,* 6 June 1914.

6. *Pittsburgh Press,* 6, 7 June 1914; *Pittsburgh Sun,* 6 June 1914; Dubofsky, *We Shall Be All,* pp. 108, 139, 202; *Industrial Union News,* 13 November 1913; *Solidarity,* 29 January 1910, 10 September 1910, 22 June 1912, 10, 31 August 1912, 12 September 1912.

7. *Solidarity,* 4 January 1913, 1 March 1913.

8. *Solidarity,* 22 June 1912, 1 March 1913, 13 September 1913, 25 October 1913, 18 April 1914 13, 18 June 1914; *Industrial Union News,* July 1914; *Pittsburgh Press,* 17 June 1914.

9. *Industrial Union News,* March, April, May, June, July, August, 1914.

10. *Industrial Union News,* March, 1914.

11. *Solidarity,* 18 April 1914, 13, 14 June 1914, July 1914, 14 November 1914.

12. *National Labor Journal,* 16 November 1917, 20 September 1918; *Iron City Trades Journal,* 14 January 1910, 1 January 1914.

13. *Iron City Trades Journal,* 6 February 1914, 5 May 1916; *Industrial Union News,* 14 April 1914; *Solidarity,* 13 July 1912, 4 January 1913, 13 June 1913, 18 April 1914.

14. *Pittsburgh Press,* 9, 15 June 1914; *Pittsburgh Sun,* 10, 13, 18 June 1914.

15. Charles Mills to W. B. Wilson, 25, 29 June 1914, U.S. Department of Labor, Federal Mediation and Conciliation Service, Case File 33–37: *Documents for the Strike of 1914 at Westinghouse Electric Company.*

16. Westinghouse Foundry Company, Union Switch and Signal, Westinghouse Airbrake.

17. *Pittsburgh Press,* 12, 13, 14 June 1914; *Pittsburgh Sun,* 11, 12, 14 June 1914; *Pittsburgh Daily Dispatch,* 11, 15 June 1914.

18. *Pittsburgh Sun,* June 11, 1914; *Pittsburgh Daily Dispatch,* June 15, 1914.

19. Ralph Easley to W. B. Wilson, 7 July 1914, *Documents for the Strike of 1914; Pittsburgh Sun,* 24 June 1914.

20. *Pittsburgh Press,* 13 June 1914.

21. *Pittsburgh Sun,* 10, 15 June 1914; *Pittsburgh Press,* 10 June 1914; David Brody, *Workers in Industrial America,* pp. 108–10.

22. *Pittsburgh Press,* 15, 20 June 1914; *Pittsburgh Sun,* 17, 20 June 1914.

23. *Pittsburgh Sun,* 19, 20, 22, 23 June 1914.

24. H. L. Kerwin to John Price Jackson, 17 June 1914; W. B. Wilson to J. P. Jackson, 18 June 1914; W. B. Wilson to Westinghouse Electric and Manufacturing Company, 19 June 1914; J. P. Jackson to W. B. Wilson, 25 June 1914, *Documents for the Strike of 1914; Pittsburgh Post-Dispatch,* 20 June 1914.

25. *Pittsburgh Sun,* 27 June 1914; Mills to Wilson, 28 June 1914, *Documents for the Strike of 1914.*

26. *Survey,* 1 August 1914; Mills to Wilson, 29 June 1914, *Documents for the Strike of 1914; Pittsburgh Sun,* 29, 30 June 1914; *Pittsburgh Press,* 29 June 1914.

27. Captain Lynn G. Adams to Superintendent, Department of State Police, 30 June 1914, U.S. Congress, *Final Report and Testimony Submitted by the Commission on Industrial Relations* (1916), 2 : 10982–83; Mills to Wilson, 29 June 1914, *Documents for the Strike of 1914.*

28. Herr to Mills, 29 June 1914; Mills to Herr, 29 June 1914, *Documents for the Strike of 1914.*

29. Ralph Easley to W. B. Wilson, 3 July 1914; Mills to Wilson, 30 June 1914, 1, 5 July 1914, *Documents for the Strike of 1914; Pittsburgh Sun,* 1 July 1914; *Pittsburgh Daily Dispatch,* 1 July 1914; Mills to Wilson, 6 July 1914, *Documents for the Strike of 1914; Pittsburgh Sun,* 7, 8 July 1914.

30. Easley to Wilson, 7 July 1914, *Documents for the Strike of 1914.*

31. Wilson to Easley, 10 July 1914; Mills to Wilson, 10 July 1914; Wilson to Jackson, 21 July 1914; Strike Committee to Herr, 8 July 1914, *Documents for the Strike of 1914.*

32. *Pittsburgh Press,* 11 July 1914; *Pittsburgh Sun,* 10, 13 July 1914.

33. Florence Patterson, *Strikes in the United States, 1880–1936,* pp. 24, 35, 37; Commonwealth of Pennsylvania, *Annual Report of the Department of Labor and Industry* (1916), pp. 1069–71.

34. The IAM had engaged in sporadic attempts to organize Westinghouse since 1903.

35. Clifton Reeves to William B. Wilson, 8 May 1916, 15 August 1916, U.S. Department of Labor, Federal Mediation and Conciliation Service, Case File 33-202: *Documents for the Strike of 1916 at Westinghouse Electric Company.*

36. The leadership of the 1914 strike included Michael J. Barrett, Q. L. Leay, C. Edwards, H. F. Weaver, G. L. Rose, Fred Niles, R. J. Hughes, W. J. Loon, J. H. Eaton, Frank Low, George F. Whiteford, Frank Miller, Leon Bowen, Hazel O'Brien, H. T. Kennedy, Michael McNeill, James Liversing, Charles Paul, and William Graham. Socialists included Bridget Kenny, Fred Merrick, George Bradley, John O'Keefe, William Thomas, and George Harshorn. The leadership of the 1916 strike included John Hall, Edgar Donaldson, Thomas Michael, John Genoss (Genosa), Anna K. Bell, Joseph Bean, Joseph MacIntosh, and A. P. Tomasco. Socialists included George Bradley, Bridget Kenny, Fred Merrick, Anna Goldenberg, Sarah Jane Tate, Rudolf Bloom, Karl Jursek, John Lucox, John Benton, Hughey McMillan, William Leger, Ira Huey, Gilbert Munges, J. Kursich, P. Flori, R. Hood, F. Brote, H. McKissick, Thomas Hampton, William Cowen, W. Graham, B. J. Grant, Nicholas Goedit, J. V. Velan, and Pat March.

37. Clifton Reeves to W. B. Wilson, 15 August 1916, *Documents for the Strike 1916; Pittsburgh Sun,* 22 April 1916; *Pittsburgh Press,* 22 April 1916; *Pittsburgh Post,* 22 April 1916.

38. *Pittsburgh Post,* 3 June 1916; *Pittsburgh Sun,* 29 May 1916, 2 June 1916; *Pittsburgh Press,* 1 June 1916.

39. The accounts of the Merrick speech were provided by John Hall, Edgar Donaldson, and Merrick during their trial for inciting to riot.

40. *Pittsburgh Post,* 25 April 1916; Bureau of Social Research, Federation of Social Agencies of Pittsburgh and Allegheny County, *Social Facts concerning East Pittsburgh, Turtle Creek, Wilmerding, North Braddock.* Race was not a visible issue in the 1914 and 1916 strikes. With the exception of in North Braddock, the black population of the aforementioned communities was less than one percent.

41. *Evening Telegram,* 6 May 1916; *Valley Daily News,* 25 April 1916; *Pittsburgh Press,* 24, 25, 29, 30 April 1916; *Pittsburgh Sun,* 26, 27 April 1916; *Pittsburgh Post,* 27, 30 April 1916.

42. *Pittsburgh Press,* April 25, 30, 1916.

43. *Pittsburgh Press,* 24 April 1916.

44. *Pittsburgh Sun,* 24, 28, 29 April 1916, 1 May 1916; *Pittsburgh Post,* 26, 28, 29 April 1916; Diane Kanitra, "The Westinghouse Strike of 1916" (seminar paper, University of Pittsburgh, 1971), p. 10.

45. Kanitra, "Westinghouse Strike of 1916," p. 12; *Pittsburgh Sun,* 2 May 1916; *Evening Telegram,* 2 May 1916; *Pittsburgh Press,* 2 May 1916.

46. *Pittsburgh Post,* 3 May 1916; *Pittsburgh Press,* 3 May 1916; *Valley Daily News,* 3 May 1916.

47. Dante Barton, "The Pittsburgh Strikes," *International Socialist Review* 16 (June 1916): 712–16.

48. Clifton Reeves, memo to William B. Wilson, 13 May 1916; Reeves to Wilson, 15 August 1916, *Documents for the Strike of 1916.*

49. *Pittsburgh Sun,* 4, 6, 7, 9 May 1916; *Pittsburgh Post,* 6, 9 May 1916; Reeves to Herr, 8 May 1916; Herr to Reeves, 9 May 1916, *Documents for the Strike of 1916;* Kanitra, "Westinghouse Strike of 1916," p. 111.

50. *Pittsburgh Post,* 10, 15, 17 May 1916; Reeves to Wilson, 15 August 1916, *Documents for the Strike of 1916.*

51. *Pittsburgh Sun,* 4, 5, 10 May 1916.

52. *Pittsburgh Post,* 6, 8, 23 May 1916; *Pittsburgh Press,* 8 May 1916; Dante Barton, vice-chairman of the U.S. Commission on Industrial Relations, supported the charges of the Trades Council.

53. *Pittsburgh Press,* 23 May 1916; *Pittsburgh Sun,* 23, 29 May 1916; *Pittsburgh Post,* 24 May 1916.

54. *Pittsburgh Post,* 3 June 1916; *Pittsburgh Press,* 1 June 1916; Kanitra, "Westinghouse Strike of 1916," pp. 33–34.

Chapter 2.   Black Valley

1. The Allegheny-Kiskiminetas Valley is known as the Alle-Kiski locally.

2. William Z. Foster, *The Great Steel Strike and Its Lessons,* pp. 146–47; *Amalgamated Journal,* 18 December 1919; John Owens, ed., *First Seventy-five Years: A History of Vandergrift; New Kensington Dispatch,* 25 July 1901; Selig Perlman and Philip Taft, *History of Labor in the United States,* 4:141; *Evening Telegram,* 29 January 1904, 5 May 1905, 1, 15 June 1906, 17 August 1906, 26 October 1906, 10 February 1910.

3. *New Kensington Dispatch,* 28 November 1901.

4. Poleslan Stemplinski interview, 15 December 1978; Robert Szymczak, "East Vandergrift—Across the Atlantic to Morning Sun: An Informal History of East Vandergrift," in *First Seventy-five Years;* Guiseppi Steri interview, 18 May 1978.

5. *New Kensington Dispatch,* 16 September 1893, 19 June 1906, 1 September 1899.

6. *New Kensington Dispatch,* 28 January 1904; *Evening Telegram,* 29 January 1904; *Valley Daily News,* 5 May 1905.

7. Report by Van Bittner, president of District 5, United Mine Workers, *United Mine Workers Journal,* 21 September 1916.

8. *Evening Telegram,* 2, 4, 5, 6, 18 May 1916; *Valley Daily News,* 2, 3, 4, 6, 8, 19 May 1916; *Evening Telegram,* 22 October 1915, 23 November 1915, 30 November 1915, 3 December 1915, 3 January 1916, 24 February 1916, 14 March 1916.

9. John Brophy, *A Miner's Life: An Autobiography,* pp. 132–36; Pat Fagan interview transcript, 24 September 1968, Oral History Collection, Labor Archives, Pennsylvania State University.

10. Melvyn Dubofsky and Warren Van Tine, *John L. Lewis: A Biography,* pp. 31–36; Brophy, *Miner's Life,* 133; report by Philip Murray, president of District 5, United Mine Workers, *United Mine Workers Journal,* 26 March 1917, 20 July 1916, 24 August 1916.

11. *United Mine Workers Journal,* 24 August 1916; Brophy, *Miner's Life,* pp. 135–36.

12. *Evening Telegram,* 31 March 1916; *United Mine Workers Journal,* 29 June 1916.

13. Sam Mendicino interview, 27 December 1977; John Grill interview, 20 January 1978; Steri interview, *Evening Telegram,* 19 October 1914, 22 February 1915, 6 April 1916, 19 July 1916, 5 August 1916, 23 October 1916, 6 December 1916, 19 January 1917, 30 March 1917; *Apollo News-Record,* 9 September 1916; *United Mine Workers Journal,* 19 October 1916. Federkiewicz was driven from the UMWA.

14. *United Mine Workers Journal,* 21 September 1916, 15 February 1917; *Evening Telegram,* 9 March 1916; *Apollo News-Record,* 8 September 1916, 8 December 1916, *Apollo Sentinel,* 21 April 1916; Frank Buccardo interview, 6 June 1978; Steri interview.

15. Mary Harris ("Mother") Jones was an itinerant labor activist in the United States for more than fifty years. Known as the "Miners' Angel," she participated in labor conflicts in West Virginia, Colorado, and Pennsylvania. In 1905 she helped to found the Industrial

Workers of the World, a radical labor organization. See Dale Fetherling, *Mother Jones: The Miners' Angel.*

16. In the *Pittsburgh Post*, 10 May 1916, Sellins was identified as a delegate to a labor conference representing Local 67, a West Virginia Garment Workers local.

17. *Valley Daily News*, 4 March 1916, 11 April 1916, 4, 6 May 1916. UMWA records for District 5 do not exist for the years prior to 1933, and it is therefore not possible to document Sellins's precise arrival date in the Alle-Kiski. In the *United Mine Workers Journal*, March 1976, an article entitled "UMWA Women" includes but a scant three paragraphs about Sellins. *United Mine Workers Journal*, 15 September 1919; *Evening Telegram*, 3 March 1917; *Valley Daily News*, 27 August 1919; *Iron City Trades Journal*, 23 January 1914.

18. *United Mine Workers Journal*, 19 October 1916; *Evening Telegram*, 23 October 1916, 31 January 1917, 3 March 1917.

19. *Apollo Sentinel*, 2 March 1917; *Evening Telegram*, 24 February 1917, 2 April 1917; *United Mine Workers Journal*, 15 March 1917, 2 April 1917.

20. In 1917 the rights to strike and bargain collectively were not established as legal principles.

21. Dubofsky and Van Tine, *John L. Lewis*, pp. 31, 523; Brophy, *Miner's Life*, pp. 132–33; *United Mine Workers Journal*, 1 January 1919; 15 February 1919, 1 April 1919, 1 September 1919; Steri interview; John Schrecengost interview, 1 March 1978.

22. David Brody, *Steel Workers in America*, pp. 214–27; Foster, *Great Steel Strike*, pp. 9, 24, 25, 33–35, 65, 66, 100, 191.

23. It was common practice in Pennsylvania for deputy sheriffs to be hired and paid by private companies. *Valley Daily News*, 23 August 1919; Michael Petrak interview, 9 August 1977.

24. Oscar Morrison and Jim Kerr interview, 1 December 1977; *United Mine Workers Journal*, 6 July 1919; *Amalgamated Journal*, 15, 20 November 1919.

25. *Valley Daily News*, 21, 28 July 1919.

26. *Amalgamated Journal*, 7 August 1919, 4 September 1919.

27. Foster, *Great Steel Strike*, pp. 146–49.

28. *United Mine Workers Journal*, 15 September 1919; *Amalgamated Journal*, 4 September 1919; *Valley Daily News*, 27, 28, 29 August 1919; *New Kensington Dispatch*, 29 August 1919; Foster, *Great Steel Strike*, pp. 146–49; *National Labor Journal*, 8 June 1923.

29. Stanley Czarnowski and Stanley Rafalko interview, 29 September 1979. Stanley Rafalko was seven years old at the time he witnessed Fannie Sellins's death. His recollections of the incident are extraordinarily clear. Information regarding the role and observations of Joseph Czarnowski were supplied by his son, Stanley Czarnowski.

30. Czarnowski and Rafalko interview.

31. Allegheny County, Pennsylvania, Coroner's Records, 133:629, 29 September 1919; *Valley Daily News*, 27 August 1919.

32. Sellins's name was misspelled on the death certificate.

33. Allegheny Coroner's Records, 133:629.

34. Ibid.

35. *Valley Daily News*, 29 September 1919.

36. *Valley Daily News*, 17 October 1919. Sheriff Haddock claimed that a hole had been bored in the back of Sellins's skull. Such an entry would have supported the charge that she had been shot from behind. Sellins was buried in New Kensington, Westmoreland County, which was not in Haddock's jurisdiction. Surveys of local historical sources have not yielded evidence that corroborates the sheriff's allegations.

37. *Valley Daily News*, 25 September 1919; Petrak interview.

38. Foster, *Great Steel Strike*, p. 100; *Amalgamated Journal*, 2, 15 May 1919, 25 September 1919; *Valley Daily News*, 27 September 1919; Everett Beck interview, 15 June 1978; Interchurch World Movement, Commission of Inquiry, *Report on the Steel Strike of 1919*, p. 209.

39. Interview with the former burgess of East Vandergrift, 15 December 1977 (name withheld by request); Stemplinski interview; Petrak interview; *Report on the Steel Strike*, pp. 15, 139–41. Black steelworkers remained outside of the union, but due to their scant numbers, they had little impact upon the strike in the Alle-Kiski.

40. *Amalgamated Journal*, 1, 15 May 1919, 225 September 1919; *Valley Daily News*, 27 September 1919.

41. *Vandergrift News*, 20 March 1919; *Apollo-News Record*, 14 March 1919, 27 June 1919.

42. *Valley Daily News*, 12 September 1919, 15 October 1919, 11, 20 November 1919; *New Kensington Dispatch*, 3, 18 November 1919, 19 December 1919.

43. Schrecengost interview; Steri interview.

44. *New Kensington Dispatch*, 15 November 1919; *Valley Daily News* 22 September 1919.

45. *Leechburg Advance*, 28 February 1919, 25 April 1919, 2 May 1919.

46. *New Kensington Dispatch*, 3, 14, 17, 24, 29 September 1919.

47. *Valley Daily News*, 3 September 1919.

48. *Amalgamated Journal*, 15 January 1920; *New Kensington Daily Dispatch*, 27 February 1920.

49. Morton S. Baratz, *The Union and the Coal Industry*, pp. 60, 32–33, 41, 47.

50. *Evening Telegram*, 9 September 1921; *New Kensington Daily Dispatch*, 11 December 1921, 3 May 1922; *United Mine Workers Journal*, 1 January 1923.

51. *Natrona Daily Press*, 16 July 1923; *Vandergrift News*, 26 January 1922; *Leechburg Advance*, 27 January 1922; *Apollo News-Record*, 16 June 1922.

52. *Valley Daily News*, 31 March 1922, 1 April 22; *New Kensington Daily Dispatch*, 1 March 1922; *Dubofsky and Van Tine, John L. Lewis*, pp. 81–82.

53. Heber Blankenhorn, *The Strike for Union*, p. 96; *Valley Daily News*, 4, 10, 11, 15 April 1925; *New Kensington Daily Dispatch*, 11, 19, 25 1922; *Vandergrift News*, 1, 4 May 1922; *Leechburg Advance*, 5 May 1922; *Apollo News-Record*, 5 May 1922.

54. *New Kensington Daily Dispatch*, 19 July 1922, 14 August 1922; *Valley Daily News*, 21 July 1922, 15 August 1922; A. R. Pollock of Ford Collieries resigned as president of the Freeport Thick Vein Association when it refused to attend the Cleveland Conference.

55. *New Kensington Daily Dispatch*, 17, 19, 21, 23, August 1922; *Valley Daily News*, 19, 22 August 1922.

56. *National Labor Tribune*, 24 August 1922; *New Kensington Daily Dispatch*, 30 January 1923.

57. *United Mine Workers Journal*, 1 January 1923.

58. *Pittsburgh Press*, 31 May 1923, 3 June 1923; *Pittsburgh Post*, 3, 4 June 1923, *United Mine Workers Journal*, 1 July 1923.

59. *New Kensington Daily Dispatch*, 15 February 1922, 5, 7, 8 June 1923; *Evening Telegram*, 2 June 1923; *Natrona Daily Press*, 5, 6, 7, 8, 9 June 1923; *Pittsburgh Press*, 5, 7, 9 June 1923; *Pittsburgh Post*, 6, 8, 9 June 1923; Allegheny Coroner's Records, 133:629.

60. *Pittsburg Press*, 5, 7, 9, June 1923; *Pittsburgh Post*, 6, 8, 9, June 1923.

61. Young Stanley Rafalko was not permitted to testify.

Chapter 3. The Great Coal Strike

1. Dubofsky and Van Tine, *John L. Lewis*, pp. 133–46; Federal Council of Churches of Christ in America, *The Coal Strike in Western Pennsylvania*, pp. 20, 23, 61; Anna Rochester, *Labor and Coal*, pp. 178–238; Baratz, *Union and Coal Industry*, pp. 31–35, 41.

2. *National Labor Tribune*, 4, 11 September 1924; *Coal Strike in Western Pennsylvania*, p. 4.

3. The "continuously competitive" scale was adopted by most western Pennsylvania operators in 1927.

4. Dubofsky and Van Tine, *John L. Lewis*, p. 143; Rochester, *Labor and Coal*, p. 205.

5. *Pittsburgh Press*, 1, 31 January 1928, 12 March 1928; U.S. Congress, Senate Committee on Interstate Commerce, *Conditions in the Coal Fields of Pennsylvania, West Virginia and Ohio: Report of the Subcommittee on Interstate Commerce persuant to Senate Resolution 105*, 70th Congress, 1st session (1928), pp. 893–907.

6. *Conditions in the Coal Fields*, 893–907.

7. *Conditions in the Coal Fields*, pp. 573–77, 1281, 1347; *Pittsburgh Press*, 31 January 1928.

8. *New Kensington Daily Dispatch*, 27, 28 October 1926, 2 November 1926, 2 November 1923, 20 January 1927; *Vandergrift Citizen*, 28 October 1926; *Daily Leader-Times*, 4 April 1927; Mendecino interview.

9. *New Kensington Daily Dispatch*, 11 December 1921; Gerald E. Allen, "The Negro Coal Miner in the Pittsburgh District," Master's thesis, University of Pittsburgh, 1927.

10. *Conditions in the Coal Fields,* pp. 1280–81.

11. O. R. Check, Superintendent of Police, to T. R. Johns, General Manager, Bethlehem Mines, 1 January 1927, in Bethlehem Mines Corporation, *Annual Police Reports,* Archives of the Industrial Society, University of Pittsburgh Library; *Pittsburgh Press,* 30 April 1927.

12. *Indiana Evening Gazette,* 28 May 1927; *Pittsburgh Press,* 31 January 1928.

13. *Pittsburgh Press,* 30 April 1927; *Valley Daily News,* 5, 20, 23 May 1927; *New Kensington Daily Dispatch,* 20, 23 May 1927; *National Labor Tribune,* 26 May 1927; *Valley Daily News,* 14 July 1927, 2, 3, 5 August 1927; *Indiana Evening Gazette,* 2 July 1927.

14. O. R. Check to T. R. Johns, 1 January 1928, in Bethlehem Mines, *Police Reports,* pp. 15–16; *Pittsburgh Press,* 1, 27 January 1928.

15. Philip Murray to the Council of Churches of Christ in Pittsburgh, 23 March 1927, in Allen, "Negro Coal Miner," p. 78; *Pittsburgh Press,* 22 June, 1927; Paul Nyden, *Black Coal Miners in the United States; New Kensington Daily Dispatch,* 20, 22 April 1927.

16. *National Labor Tribune,* 9, 30 December 1926; Sterling D. Spero and Abram L. Harris, *The Black Worker: The Negro and the Labor Movement,* pp. 375, 235–43; Allen, "Negro Coal Miner," pp. 36–39, 16–18; *Conditions in the Coal Fields,* pp. 892–93, 294.

17. *Conditions in the Coal Fields,* pp. 1021, 58, 84; Spero and Harris, *Black Worker,* p. 231; Allen, "Negro Coal Miner," p. 31.

18. Upper Burrell Township, *The First One Hundred Years, 1879–1979,* pp. 14–15; *Conditions in the Coal Fields,* pp. 146–51.

19. *New Kensington Daily Dispatch,* 4, 6, 7, 8, 29 June 1927, 1 July 1927; *Valley Daily News,* 4, 7 June 1927; *Vandergrift Economist,* 15 June 1927; *Pittsburgh Press,* 7 June 1927; *Apollo News-Record,* 10 June 1927; *Conditions in the Coal Fields,* p. 146.

20. *Pittsburgh Press,* 9 March 1927, 11 August 1927; *Conditions in the Coal Fields,* pp. 70–98.

21. *Pittsburgh Courier,* 13, 20, 27 November 1926, 4 December 1926, 5 March 1927, 7, 9 April 1927, 26 October 1929.

22. *Pittsburgh Courier,* 13, 20, 27 November 1926, 5 December 1926, 5 March 1927, 7, 9 April 1927, 26 October 1929.

23. *Pittsburgh Courier,* 5 March 1927; *United Mine Workers Journal,* 15 May 1926; *Pittsburgh Press,* 28 January 1928.

24. *New Kensington Daily Dispatch,* 6 August 1927; *Pittsburgh Press,* 7 August 1927, 11 October 1927; *Conditions in the Coal Fields,* pp. 3327–29.

25. *Pittsburgh Press,* 11 February 1927; *Conditions in the Coal Fields,* pp. 935–40, 960.

26. *Pittsburgh Sun,* 26 January 1928; *Conditions in the Coal Fields,* p. 981; *Pittsburgh Press,* 4 January 1927, 17 December 1927; *New Kensington Daily Dispatch,* 26 February 1928; Thomas Coode and John Bauman, *People, Poverty and Politics in Pennsylvania during the Great Depression,* pp. 40, 134; George A. Parker, "A Doctor Looks at the Coal Camps," *Survey* 61 (October 1928): 85–86.

27. *Pittsburgh Press,* 1, 7 May 1927; *Conditions in the Coal Fields,* p. 1359.

28. *Conditions in the Coal Fields,* pp. 2858–59, 893.

29. *Conditions in the Coal Fields,* pp. 17, 3293–94; *Pittsburgh Press,* 15 April 1927, 7 May 1927; *New Kensington Daily Dispatch,* 4 May 1927, 19, 20, 22 September 1927, 22 October 1927, 13, 15 December 1927; *Valley Daily News,* 10 June 1927, 27 September 1927, 11, 17 October 1927, 28 November 1927, 3, 12, 15, 16, 17 December 1927; *Vandergrift News,* 22 November 1927; *Pittsburgh Press,* 26 November 1927, 17 December 1927.

30. *Pittsburgh Press,* 20, 21 August 1927, 30 September 1927, 11 October 1927, 26 November 1927; *New Kensington Daily Dispatch,* 1, 9, 30 September 1927; *Valley Daily News,* 11, 17, 22, 29 October 1927.

31. *Pittsburgh Press,* 20 November 1927; Indiana County, Pennsylvania, Court of Common Pleas, Old Equity Docket Book No. 6, 8 November 1927; *Conditions in the Coal Fields,* pp. 279–80.

32. Frank J. Basile, *Rossiter, Pennsylvania: Her People Past and Present,* pp. 36–37, 74–76, 50–68.

33. Ibid.

34. *Indiana Evening Gazette,* 24, 27 February 1928; *Conditions in the Coal Fields,* pp. 324–25; Basile, *Rossiter,* p. 76; *Pittsburgh Press,* 17, 20 November 1927.

35. According to Frank Basile, the population of Rossiter was one-third Italian, one-third Slavic and Hungarian and one-third English, German, and Welsh (*Rossiter,* pp. 50–51).

36. *Conditions in the Coal Fields,* p. 973.

37. Ibid., pp. 293, 511, 509, 523, 283.

38. Indiana County Court of Common Pleas, Old Equity Docket Book No. 6, pp. 9, 12–13, 130–32, 391; *Valley Daily News,* 28 February 1928; *Conditions in the Coal Fields,* pp. 511, 270–77.

39. *Indiana Evening Gazette,* 28, 29 February 1928; *Conditions in the Coal Fields,* pp. 263–70. A hearing was finally held in Judge Langham's court, on 23 May and the injunction was made permanent (*Pittsburgh Press,* 15, 26, 27 May 1927).

40. *Pittsburgh Press,* 6 April 1927, 17, 18 December 1927; *National Labor Tribune,* 9 February 1928.

41. *Conditions in the Coal Fields,* p. 500; William A. Cornell, "The Political Career of John S. Fisher," Master's thesis, University of Pittsburgh, 1949; *Valley Daily News,* 29, 30 November 1927; *Pittsburgh Press,* 30 November 1927; *New Kensington Daily Dispatch,* 30 November 1927, 1 December 1927.

42. *Conditions in the Coal Fields,* p. 1063; *Pittsburgh Press,* 12 February 1928; *New Kensington Daily Dispatch,* 2, 6, 8 February 1928.

43. *Pittsburgh Press,* 19 February 1928; *New Kensington Daily Dispatch,* 6 February 1928.

44. *Indiana Evening Gazette,* 9 February 1928; John Fisher to J. N. Langham, 2 March 1928; Langham to Fisher, 6 March 1928; Fisher to Senator David Reed, 8 March 1928, John Fisher Papers, boxes 18, 24, Pennsylvania Historical and Museum Commission Archives, Harrisburg.

45. Fisher to Reed, 8 March 1928, Fisher Papers.

46. *Indiana Evening Gazette,* 17 March 1928; *Valley Daily News,* 17 March 1928; *Pittsburgh Press,* 19, 20, 22 March 1928, 1, 5, 8, 9, 10 April 1928; *New Kensington Daily Dispatch,* 9 April 1928; *Pittsburgh Post-Gazette,* 2 May 1928; Langham to Fisher, 25 March 1928, box 18, Fisher Papers.

47. *Pittsburgh Press,* 7 May 1928; Edward N. Clopper, "Pittsburgh Unites for Relief," *Survey* 60 (April 1928): 85–86; Helen M. Harris, "Miners in the Mud," *Survey* 60 (August 1928): 502–3.

48. *Conditions in the Coal Fields,* p. 912; *Vandergrift News,* 1 February 1928; *Valley Daily News,* 23 November 1927; *Pittsburgh Press,* 19 December 1927; *New Kensington Daily Dispatch,* 17 June 1927, 6 November 1927.

49. *Pittsburgh Press,* 21 March 1927; *National Labor Tribune,* 18 August 1927; *New Kensington Daily Dispatch,* 17 June 1927, 23 January 1927, 24 March 1927; George Medrick Diary, pp. 1, 16, 29–30, 47–48, 94, George Medrick Papers, Labor Archives, Pennsylvania State University.

Chapter 4. Save the Union

1. *Pittsburgh Press,* 23 August 1927; *Labor Unity,* 1 August 1927. Powers Hapgood was arrested and committed to a Massachusetts mental hospital following his participation in a Sacco and Vanzetti demonstration.

2. *Pittsburgh Press,* 29 February 1928; *New Kensington Daily Dispatch,* 4 February 1927, 22, 23 August 1927; *Pittsburgh Post-Gazette,* 23 August 1927; *Labor Unity,* 15 October 1927.

3. *Daily Worker,* 3 June 1927; *Labor Unity,* 1 January 1927; Medrick Diary, p. 43.

4. Bethlehem Mines, *Police Reports,* 1 January 1927, p. 14, 1 January 1928, p. 14, 23 January 1919, p. 12; *Valley Daily News,* 7, 10, 20 March 1928; *Pittsburgh Press,* 22, 23, 24 March 1928; *New Kensington Daily Dispatch,* 10, 14 March 1928, 29 June 1928.

5. *Conditions in the Coal Fields,* pp. 141, 912, 1006, 1021.

6. *Pittsburgh Press,* 30 January 1928, 29 February 1928; *Conditions in the Coal fields,* pp. 1323, 206, 1021, 142.

7. Grill interview; Mendecino interview.

8. Minutes of the Progressive International Conference of the United Mine Workers of America, Powers Hapgood Papers, Lilly Library, University of Indiana. The executive

board of the Progressive Bloc included William Guiler, Charleroi; Thomas Ray, McDonald; Tom Myerscough, Pittsburgh; Tony Leone, Iselin; Sylvesteer Calabre, Russellton; and John Snyder, Uniontown.

9. Brophy, *Miner's Life*, p. 205.

10. John L. Lewis to John Brophy, 9, 11 July 1923; Powers Hapgood to "Dearest Mother and Father," 20 July 1923, Hapgood Papers; *United Mine Workers Journal*, 1 July 1923.

11. Brophy, *Miner's Life*, p. 191; Brophy to Hapgood, 10 March 1926, Hapgood Papers; *National Labor Tribune*, 8 January 1925; Hapgood to "Dearest Mother," 20 April 1926, Hapgood Papers.

12. Hapgood to "Dearest Mother," 20 June 1926, Hapgood Papers; Dubofsky and Van Tine, *John L. Lewis*, p. 128. The Communists claimed the "Save the Union" slogan as their own (see William Z. Foster, *Pages from a Worker's Life*, pp. 177–179); Hapgood to "Dearest Mother and Father," 5, 21, 26 July 1926, Hapgood Papers.

13. Hapgood to "Dearest Mother and Father," 12 August 1926, Hapgood Papers; news releases by John Brophy, 6 August 1926, 15 October 1926, 24 September 1926, John Brophy Papers, Catholic University of America; Hapgood to "Dearest Mother and Father," 1 December 1926, Hapgood Papers; *United Mine Workers Journal*, 1 December 1926; Hapgood to "Mother and Father," 1 May 1927, Hapgood Papers; Brophy appeal to the International Executive Board, 28 May 1927, Brophy Papers; *Daily Worker*, 28, 31 May 1927. UMWA District 5 records do not exist for the years prior to 1933. It is therefore impossible to substantiate charges of election fraud.

14. Hapgood to "Dearest Mother," 9 January 1927, Hapgood Papers; *Pittsburgh Press*, 27 January 1927.

15. Hapgood to Evelyn, 2 May 1927; Hapgood to "Dearest Mother and Father," 8 December 1927, Hapgood Papers; *Daily Worker*, 3 August 1927, 28 May 1927; Brophy to P. P. Patrick, recording secretary, Local 1386, Nanty-Glo (no date), box 8, Brophy Papers; Brophy diary, Brophy Papers.

16. Brophy, *Miner's Life*, p. 229; *Pittsburgh Post-Gazette*, 7 January 1928; *Daily Worker*, 7 January 1928.

17. "Coal Digger" to Senate Committee, 24 February 1928, *Conditions in the Coal Fields*, pp. 222–23; *Pittsburgh Press*, 3 March 1928; *Daily Worker*, 3, 24 February 1928; *Coal Digger*, 15 February 1928; A. Wagenknecht to Hapgood, 20 January 1928, Hapgood Papers.

18. *Party Organizer* (January–February 1928): 19; *Daily Worker*, 12 January 1928, 24 February 1928, 16, 24 April 1928; *Pittsburgh Courier*, 7 April 1928, 12 May 1928.

19. *Daily Worker*, 24 February 1928; *Pittsburgh Courier*, 7 April 1928.

20. Brophy diary, 12 January 1928, 4, 6 March 1928; Brophy to Burton K. Wheeler, 9 July 1928, box 8, Brophy Papers; *Pittsburgh Post-Gazette*, 2 May 1928; *Daily Worker*, 3 May 1928; *Pittsburgh Post*, 8 June 1923. Alexander Howat was a UMWA district president in Iowa who challenged John L. Lewis for the UMWA presidency. He was charged with sodomy, a charge dismissed by the court (Allegheny County, Pennsylvania, Court of Common Pleas, Docket No. 50, September 1923).

21. Brophy Diary, 6 March 1928; Andy Evanoff to Hapgood, 7 December 1926, Hapgood Papers; Brophy, *Miner's Life*, p. 229; *New Kensington Daily Dispatch*, 7 March 1928; *Pittsburgh Press*, 7 March 1928.

22. *Valley Daily News*, 6 April 1928; *New Kensington Daily Dispatch*, 20 March 1928.

23. *Minutes*, Save the Union Conference, 1–2 April 1928, Hapgood Papers; *Pittsburgh Courier*, 7 April 1928; *New Kensington Daily Dispatch*, 2 April 1928; *Daily Worker*, 6 April 1928.

24. *Party Organizer*, (March–April 1928): 3–6; *New Kensington Daily Dispatch*, 16 April 1928; *Pittsburgh Post-Gazette*, 16, 17 April 1928; *Daily worker*, 16 April 1928; Bethlehem Mines, *Annual Police Reports*, 23 January 1929.

25. *Vandergrift News*, 16 March 1928, 17, 20, 21, 25 April 1928; *Leechburg Advance*, 20 April 1928; *Valley Daily News*, 19, 20 April 1928; *New Kensington Daily Dispatch*, 21 April 1928; *Pittsburgh Post-Gazette*, 21 April 1928; *Daily Worker*, 23, 24 April 1928.

26. *Valley Daily News*, 20 April 1928; *Vandergrift News*, 2, 10 May 1928; *Leechburg Advance*, 4 May 1928.

27. *Pittsburg Press*, 21 April 1928; *Indiana Evening Gazette*, 21 April 1928; *New Kensington Daily Dispatch*, 18, 23 May 1928.

28. Brophy to Hapgood, 20 June 1928; Hapgood to "Dear Tony," 22 June 1928; Tony Minerich to Hapgood, 16 July 1928, Hapgood Papers.

29. *Daily Worker*, 29 May 1928; *Party Organizer* (May–June, 1928): 4–5.

30. *Pittsburgh Post-Gazette*, 19 December 1928; *New Kensington Daily Dispatch*, 19 December 1928; Brophy to Hapgood, 8 July 1928, Hapgood Papers.

31. *Pittsburgh Post-Gazette*, 13 September 1928; Ella Reeve Bloor to Hapgood, 13 September 1928; Hapgood to Bloor, 26 September 1928, Hapgood Papers; Brophy to Oscar Ameringer, 25 October 1919, box 8, Brophy Papers.

Chapter 5.   The National Miners Union

1. Ella Reeve Bloor, *We Are Many*, p. 220; *Pittsburgh Post-Gazette*, 10, 11 September 1928; *Daily Worker*, 10, 11, 14, 19 September 1928; *Pittsburgh Courier*, 15 September 1928.

2. Bethlehem Mines, *Annual Police Reports*, 23 January 1929; Hapgood to "Mary Darling," 9, 11 September 1928, Hapgood Papers.

3. *National Labor Tribune*, 7 June 1928, 13 September 1928; Hapgood to "Dearest Mary," 8, 9, 11 September 1928, Hapgood Papers; *Pittsburgh Post-Gazette*, 10 September 1928; *Daily Worker*, 10, 11, 14 September 1928. Although the NMU was active at Bethlehem Mines' Bentleyville pits, the confidential industrial police records of that company indicate no collaboration between its police and the NMU. NMU spokesman claimed that John Buzzarelli directed UMWA street violence.

4. Bert Cochran, *Labor and Communism*, pp. 6, 52; David J. Saposs, *Left Wing Unionism*, pp. 48–55; Theodore Draper, "Communists and Miners, 1928–1933," *Dissent* (Spring 1972), pp. 371–92; Linda Nyden, "Black Miners in Western Pennsylvania, 1925–1931: The National Miners Union and the United Mine Workers of America," *Science and Society* 41 (Spring 1977): 69–101.

5. Neil Betten, *Catholic Activism and the Industrial Worker*, pp. 77–78, 113–15; *Daily Worker*, 14 September 1928; Brophy to John Watt, 18 March 1929, Hapgood Papers.

6. Brophy to Watt, 18 March 1929, Hapgood Papers; Grill interview; Mendecino interview. Reliable data concerning the number of miners actually enrolled by the NMU apparently do not exist. NMU news releases invariably spoke of strikers and picketers, which included women, children, and party functionaries as well as miners. The number of miners in the NMU in all probability never exceeded 5,000 in western Pennsylvania.

7. Draper, "Communists and Miners," p. 375; *Party Organizer* (January–February, March–April, May–June, 1928).

8. Pat Toohey to Powers Hapgood, 3 October 1928; *Daily Worker*, 22, 23, 27 March 1929; *Valley Daily News*, 23, 25 March 1927; *United Mine Workers Journal*, 1 April 1920, 1 June 1929.

9. Valley Daily News, 5 January 1931; Frank Borich, "How the Present Miners' Strike Was Prepared," *Party Organizer* (August 1931); *Daily Worker*, 25 May 1931.

10. *Daily Worker*, 16 January 1931, 18 February 1931, 7 March 1931, 27, 28 April 1931, 6, 28 May 1931; *Party Organizer* (August 1931); *Labor Unity*, 6 June 1931.

11. *Labor Unity*, 6 June 1931; *Daily Worker*, 28 May 1931.

12. *Party Organizer* (May 1931); *Valley Daily News*, 1, 4, 6 June 1931; *Daily Leader-Times*, 3 June 1931; *Indiana Evening Gazette*, 4 June 1931.

13. *Valley Daily News*, 1, 5, 6, 10 June 1931; *Daily Worker*, 8 June 1931.

14. *Valley Daily News*, 4, 9, 11 June 1931.

15. *Valley Daily News*, 12, 13, 15, 16, 18 June 1931; *Daily Worker*, 15 June 1931.

16. *Valley Daily News*, 16 June 1931.

17. Ibid.

18. *United Mine Workers Journal*, 1 July 1931.

19. *Labor Unity*, 18 July 1981; *Vandergrift News*, 16 June 1931; *Valley Daily News*, 13, 17, 19 June 1931; *Daily Leader-Times*, 13 June 1931.

20. *Daily Leader Times*, 17, 18, 19, 23, 25, 30 June 1931; *Vandergrift News*, 18 June 1931; *Daily Worker*, 19 June 1931.

21. *Daily Leader-Times*, 25 June 1931, 1, 3 June 1931; *Indiana Evening Gazette*, 13 July 1931.

22. *Daily Leader-Times,* 8, 14, 23, 26, 28, 30, 31 July 1931; *Indiana Evening Gazette,* 8, 9, 10, 17, 21 July 1931; open letter by B. M. Clark to Gifford Pinchot, 31 July 1931, *Daily Leader-Times,* 31 July 1931.

23. *Daily Leader-Times,* 23, 24, 28 July 1931; 6 August 1931; *Daily Worker,* 28 July 1931; *Vandergrift News,* 24, 27, 29 July 1931.

24. *Labor Unity,* 13, 20 June 1931; *Daily Worker,* 13, 26 June 1931; *Valley Daily News,* 16 June 1931.

25. *Valley Daily News,* 22, 23, 24 June 1931, 7, 8 July 1931.

26. *Valley Daily News,* 22, 23, 24 June 1931, 7, 8 July 1931.

27. *Daily Worker,* 24 June 1931; *Valley Daily News,* 7, 9 July 1931, 23 June 1931; *United Mine Workers Journal,* 15 August 1931. Thomas Myerscough was sentenced to two-years' imprisonment at the Allegheny County Workhouse in Blawnox for manslaughter.

28. *Valley Daily News,* 23, 24 June 1931, 7 July 1931.

29. *Labor Unity,* 27 June 1931; *Daily Worker,* 22, 25, 26 June 1931; *Valley Daily News,* 25, 29 June 1931; *Indiana Evening Gazette,* 26 June 1931.

30. *United Mine Workers Journal,* 1 August 1931; *Daily Worker,* 13 June 1931.

31. *United Mine Workers Journal,* 1 August 1931; Lauren Gilfillan, *I Went to Pit College.*

32. Gilfillan, *Pit College,* p. 222.

33. *Valley Daily News,* 27 July 1931; *United Mine Workers Journal,* 1 August 1931; Dubofsky and Van Tine, *John L. Lewis,* pp. 515, 525–29.

34. *Labor Unity,* 25 July 1931, 1, 15, 29 August 1931, 12 September 1931; *Daily Worker,* 4, 21 August 1931, 7, 16 September 1931, 5, 21 October 1931, 12 November 1931.

35. Gilfillan, *Pit College,* pp. 25, 27, 29, 30, 31.

36. Ibid., pp. 255, 275.

37. Jack Johnstone, "Organizing Strike Committees," *Party Organizer* (July 1931).

38. A. Markoff, "Building a Party in Mine Strike Area," *Party Organizer* (August 1931); Johnstone, "Strike Committee."

39. *Labor Unity,* 25 July 1931; *Party Organizer,* (August 1931).

40. Nyden, "Black Miners," pp. 69, 101; *Party Organizer* (August 1931); *Labor Unity,* 19 September 1931; Gilfillan, *Pit College,* p. 19.

41. Nyden, "Black Miners," pp. 100–101.

42. *Valley Daily News,* 12 June 1931; *Daily Worker,* 10, 13, 14 June 1931. The Herrin "massacre" involved a mass killing of non-union miners by UMWA strikers near Herrin Illinois, in 1922.

43. Draper, "Communists and Miners," p. 370; Bethlehem Mines, *Annual Police Reports,* January 1934.

44. *Daily Worker,* 19, 21 March 1932, 4 June 1932.

45. *Daily Worker,* 4 June 1932, 27 September 1932; Memo, Tom Myerscough to all AFL local unions, 18 November 1932, box 47, Brophy Papers; *Daily Worker,* 7 February 1933, 15 March 1933; Bethlehem Mines, *Annual Police Reports,* January 1934.

46. *Daily Worker,* 15, 24 March 1933, 5 April 1933.

47. James P. Johnson, "Reorganizing the United Mine Workers in America in Pennsylvania during the New Deal," *Pennsylvania History* 37 (April 1970): 117–31; Brophy, *Miner's Life,* p. 236; Mendecino interview; Grill interview; Dubofsky and Van Tine, *John L. Lewis,* pp. 190–91.

48. John Ghizzoni to John L. Lewis, 12 June 1933, box 47, Brophy Papers; Mendecino interview; Preston Busch interview, 9 June 1982; *Vandergrift News,* 3, 5, 6, 9, 10, 22 June 1933, 13, 18, 19 July 1933; *Apollo Sentinel,* 9 June 1933; *Valley Daily News,* 5, 6, 10 June 1933, 20 July 1933.

49. *New Kensington Daily Dispatch,* 28 June 1933; *Valley Daily News,* 29 May 1933, 19, 21 July 1933.

50. Dubofsky and Van Tine, *John L. Lewis,* p. 186; Johnson, "Reorganizing during the New Deal," pp. 123–26; *Vandergrift News,* 23, 24 June 1933, 13 July 1933; *Valley Daily News,* 29 May 1933, 2 June 1933.

51. Johnson, "Reorganizing during the New Deal," pp. 126–30; Bethlehem Mines, *Annual Police Reports,* 1 January 1934.

52. Johnson, "Reorganizing during the New Deal," p. 127; *Valley Daily News,* 4, 5 August

1933, 15, 16, 25 26 September 1933; *Vandergrift News*, 26, 27 September 1933, 4, 5, 7 October 1933.

53. *Valley Daily News*, 7, 16 October 1933; Johnson, "Reorganizing during the New Deal," pp. 127–31.

54. *Daily Worker*, 30 September 1933, 28 October 1933.

55. *Daily Worker*, 5 June 1933, 28 July 1933, 10, 26 August 1933, 9 September 1933; Foster, *Worker's Life*, p. 182; Bloor, *We Are Many*, p. 221.

Chapter 6.   The Arbiters

1. Jeremiah P. Shalloo, *Private Police; with a Special Reference to Pennsylvania*, p. 112; News Release No. 35, Pennsylvania-Ohio Relief Committee, Hapgood Papers; *Pittsburgh Press*, 11 February 1928; *Conditions in the Coal Fields*, pp. 90–91.

2. *Pittsburgh Press*, 11 February 1928; *Conditions in the Coal Fields*, p. 1006; *Valley Daily News*, 11 June 1931.

3. *Valley Daily News*, 8, 10, 11 June 1931.

4. *Conditions in the Coal Fields*, p. 151; *New Kensington Daily Dispatch*, 8, 25 February 1928.

5. *Valley Daily News*, 10 June 1931.

6. *Valley Daily News*, 22, 23 June 1931, 7, 9 July 1931.

7. Shalloo, *Private Police*, pp. 129, 89–90; Blankenhorn, *Strike for Union*, p. 96; *Conditions in the Coal Fields*, pp. 3074, 975. Records regarding the employment of deputy sheriffs in Armstrong, Allegheny, and Westmoreland counties apparently do not exist. *Report to Governor Pinchot by Commission on Special Policing in Industry*, Special Bulletin No. 38 (Harrisburg, 1934), pp. 8–9).

8. Shalloo, *Private Police*, pp. 58–61, 64, 107; *Conditions in the Coal Fields*, pp. 1063–65, 2775–80, 539–45; *Pittsburg Post-Gazette*, 2 May 1928; *National Labor Tribune*, 25 August 1927.

9. *Conditions in the Coal Fields*, pp. 2893–99, 950, 130–33; *Pittsburgh Post*, 2 June 1927; *United Mine Workers Journal*, 1 October 1927, 15 January 1928.

10. Bethlehem Mines, *Annual Police Reports*, 1 January 1927, 1 January 1928.

11. *Conditions in the Coal Fields*, pp. 2894–95, 2643–45; Shalloo, *Private Police*, p. 129.

12. Shalloo, *Private Police*, p. 108.

13. Bethlehem Mines, *Annual Police Reports*, 1 January 1927, 1 January 1928, 1 January 1929. According to the *Daily Worker*, 10 November 1927, Bethlehem had machine guns mounted everywhere. That was no doubt an exaggeration, since the company listed only two Thompson submachine guns in its inventory (*Conditions in the Coal Fields*, p. 970).

14. Bethlehem Mines, *Annual Police Reports*, 1 January 1927; *Conditions in the Coal Fields*, pp. 2893–95, 2643–45; Shalloo, *Private Police*, p. 126.

15. American Civil Liberties Union, *Report No. 7*, (December, 1928): 6–7; Shalloo, *Private Police*, p. 86; Philip Conti, *The Pennsylvania State Police*, pp. 31–40.

16. *Final Report on Industrial Relations*, 2:10929–11065; James Maurer, *The American Cossack*, pp. 6–17, 30–31, 75–77; Conti, *State Police*, p. 210; E. E. Greenwalt, president of the Pennsylvania AFL, also opposed the constabulary because it fostered "military despotism." *Iron City Trades Journal*, 12 February 1909, 17 December 1909.

17. Maurer, *American Cossack*; Conti, *State Police*, pp. 103–7; *Final Report on Industrial Relations*, 2:10929–11065.

18. John C. Groome, *A Reply to the American Cossack*, p. 11; Maurer, *American Cossack*, pp. 75–77; *Vandergrift News*, 10 October 1933; Conti, *State Police*, pp. 103–7.

19. *Final Report on Industrial Relations*, 1:97–98.

20. American Civil Liberties Union, *Report No. 7*, p. 6; *Daily Worker*, 10, 13 October 1927; *Conditions in the Coal Fields*, p. 3122.

21. *Valley Daily News*, 31 January 1928; *Pittsburgh Press*, 1, 8 February 1928.

22. Cornell, "John S. Fisher," pp. 81–88; *United Mine Workers Journal*, 1 April 1929; *Vandergrift News*, 12, 14, 15 February 1929.

23. Shalloo, *Private Police*, pp. 67–68; Cornell, "John S. Fisher," pp. 82–83; *Pittsburgh Press*, 18 April 1929; *Pittsburgh Sun*, 20 April 1929.

24. *Vandergrift News,* 20, 26 April 1929, 28, 30 September 1929; *Pittsburgh Courier,* 26 October 1929; *United Mine Workers Journal,* 15 February 1930.

25. J. N. Langham to Fisher, 20 April 1929; Fisher to Langham, 23 April 1929, box 18, Fisher Papers; Lynn G. Adams to Fisher, Fisher to Adams, 9 May 1929, box 23, Fisher Papers.

26. Fisher to Adams 9 May 1929, box 23, Fisher papers.

27. George Lumb to Fisher, 4 October 1929, 6 January 1930, box 5, Fisher Papers.

28. *Vandergrift News,* 24 March 1931, 25 May 1931; Shalloo, *Private Police,* pp. 72–80; *United Mine Workers Journal,* 1 April 1931, 1 June 1931; *Indiana Evening Gazette,* 30 June 1931.

29. Conti, *State Police,* p. 210; M. Nelson McGeary, *Gifford Pinchot, Forester—Politician,* p. 378.

30. McGeary, *Gifford Pinchot,* pp. 378–81; *Report to Governor Pinchot,* pp. 8–9.

Chapter 7.   Last Chance

1. Brophy, *Miner's Life,* p. 248; Robert R. Brooks, *As Steel Goes . . .* pp. 4, 67.

2. *Valley Daily News,* 15, 29, 30 August 1919, 18–25 September 1919.

3. *New Kensington Daily Dispatch,* 24, 25 1919; *Valley Daily News,* 25 September 1919, 4, 5, 6, 7 October 1919.

4. Herbert Gutman, "The Worker's Search for Power: Labor in the Gilded Age," in *The Gilded Age,* by H. Wayne Morgan, pp. 38–68.

5. *First Seventy-five Years;* Ida M. Tarbell, *New Ideals in Business,* pp. 147–55, 172–73, 118–19; Eugene Buffington, "Making Cities for Workmen," *Harper's Weekly,* 53 (May 1909): 15–17.

6. *New Kensington Daily Dispatch,* 25 July 1901; Tarbell, *New Ideals* pp. 151–52.

7. Tarbell, *New Ideals* pp. 22–23, 118–19, 146, 171–73, 149–51.

8. *Vandergrift News,* 12 August 1915; *Evening Telegram,* 7 August 1915.

9. *Vandergrift News,* 9 April 1930; *Amalgamated Journal,* 15 July 1909; *Iron City Trades Journal,* 17 December 1909.

10. *Apollo Sentinel,* 30 July 1909; *Apollo News-Record,* 30 July 1909, 13, 26 August 1909; *Amalgamated Journal,* 26 August 1909.

11. *Amalgamated Journal,* 5, 12, 31 August 1909, 9 September 1909; *Iron City Trades Journal,* 17 December 1909; *Apollo News-Record,* 6 August 1909.

12. T. J. Henry, *History of Apollo, 1816–1916,* p. 57; *Vandergrift News,* 9 October 1919.

13. *Amalgamated Journal,* 11 December 1919.

14. *Vandergrift News,* 25 September 1919, 2, 9, 16, 23 October 1919.

15. *Vandergrift News,* 20 November 1919; *Amalgamated Journal,* 20 November 1919, 7, 11, 18 December 1919.

16. *Vandergrift Citizen,* 22 March 1917; *Weekly Advance,* 18 March 1927; *New Kensington Daily Dispatch,* 19 March 1927; *Apollo Sentinel,* 25 March 1927; Giacomo Bruno interview, 11 November 1978; Beck interview; Kerr and Morrison interview; Roy and Harvey Bruner interview, 20 May 1978. The Steelworkers Relief Association distributed death benefits to families of workers killed in accidents. The workers contributed to the fund.

17. *Vandergrift News,* 8, 12 February 1936, 1 March 1936, 7, 9, 10, 12, 14 April 1936; *Apollo Sentinel,* 11 April 1930. Preston Busch interview, 9 June 1982.

18. *Apollo Sentinel,* 11, 18 April 1930; *Vandergrift News,* 9, 10, 12 April 1930.

19. *National Labor Tribune,* 3 January 1929; Harry Reese interview, 15 June 1981. Harry Reese possesses a check drawn on the account of Apollo Steel Company, dated 30 April 1933, in the amount of $.01. That amount represents payment for one day's labor.

20. *Amalgamated Journal,* 29 June 1933; *Vandergrift News,* 17, 20, 21, 22, 28 July 1933; *Apollo Sentinel,* 21, 28 July 1933.

21. *Amalgamated Journal,* 27 July 1933, 25 September 1933; *Vandergrift News,* 29 July 1933.

22. Busch interview; Reese interview.

23. *Apollo Sentinel,* 21 July 1933, 4 August 1933; *Vandergrift News,* 19 June 1933, 15, 27 July 1933, 19 August 1933, 1, 18 September 1933; *Valley Daily News,* 23 September 1933.

24. *Amalgamated Journal*, 5 October 1933; *Vandergrift News*, 20 October 1933, 8, 14 November 1933; *Valley Daily News*, 1, 14 September 1933; 16, 20 October 1933.

25. Busch interview; Reese interview; *Vandergrift News*, 6, 9, 10 October 1933; *Valley Daily News*, 10 October 1933.

26. *Vandergrift News*, 10, 11 October 1933, 27 February 1934.

27. *Vandergrift News*, 17 July 1933; *Valley Daily News*, 23, 24 November 1933. Turner's denunciations were given top billing on the front pages of the *Vandergrift News*.

28. *Vandergrift News*, 7, 10, 12 October 1933; *Valley Daily News*, 10 October 1933; Busch interview; Reese interview.

29. *Vandergrift News*, 10, 12 October 1933; *Apollo Sentinel*, 13 October 1933.

30. *Vandergrift News*, 10, 12 October 1933; *Apollo Sentinel*, 13 October 1933.

31. *Amalgamated Journal*, 23, 30 November 1933; *Valley Daily News*, 23 November 1933.

32. *Vandergrift News*, 4, 10 May 1934.

33. Horace C. Cayton and George S. Mitchell, *Black Workers and the New Unions*, pp. 125–26; *Valley Daily News*, 8, 15 August 1933, 18 December 1933; *Amalgamated Journal*, 23 November 1933, 5 February 1934; Busch interview; Reese interview.

34. *Vandergrift News*, 27, 28 February 1933, 7 June 1933, 30 August 1933, 18 September 1933; *Amalgamated Journal*, 13, 20, 27 November 1933.

35. *Amalgamated Journal*, 10, 22, 29 March 1934, 26 April 1934; *Vandergrift News*, 26 March 1934; *Apollo Sentinel*, 6 October 1933, 20 April 1934, 11 May 1934; *Vandergrift News*, 19, 30 April 1934.

36. Busch interview; Reese interview; *Amalgamated Journal*, 26 April 1934, 31 May 1934; Brooks, *As Steel Goes*, pp. 4, 67; *Vandergrift News*, 19 May 1934.

37. *Vandergrift News*, 2, 12 June 1934; *Amalgamated Journal*, 14 June 1934; Cayton and Mitchell, *Black Workers*, pp. 148–54; Busch interview.

38. Cayton and Mitchell, *Black Workers*, pp. 148–54; Brooks, *As Steel Goes*, p. 67; Busch interview.

39. Busch interview; Reese interview; Cayton and Mitchell, *Black Workers*, p. 148; *Vandergrift News*, 19 February 1934, 28 July 1934, 11, 14, 15 August 1934; *Apollo Sentinel*, 17 August 1934.

40. *Amalgamated Journal*, 30 July 1934, 2, 18 August 1934; *Vandergrift News*, 11, 14, 15, 18, 20, 25 August 1934; Cayton and Mitchell, *Black Workers*, p. 148.

41. Cayton and Mitchell, *Black Workers*, p. 148; *Amalgamated Journal*, 18 August 1934; *Vandergrift News*, 18 August 1934.

42. *Vandergrift News*, 20, 22, 25 August 1934, 1 September 1934.

43. *Vandergrift News*, 25 August 1934, 21 September 1934; *Amalgamated Journal*, 27 September 1934.

44. *Amalgamated Journal*, 31 January 1935.

45. *Amalgamated Journal*, 7, 14 February 1935; *Vandergrift News*, 7, 8, 21 February 1935.

46. *Vandergrift News*, 21 February 1935; *Amalgamated Journal*, 14 February 1935.

47. *Vandergrift News*, 20, 22, 23 February 1935, 11, 18, 23, 29 April 1935.

48. Fagan interview; *Vandergrift News*, 21, 28 December 1936, 7, 15, 22 January 1937.

49. *Vandergrift News*, 22, 23 January 1937, 16, 18, 22 February 1937, 1, 3 March 1937.

50. Busch interview; Bruno interview; *Vandergrift News*, 6, 8, 11, 15, 19 March 1937.

51. *Vandergrift News*, 8 March 1937.

52. *Vandergrift News*, 15, 31 March 1937, 12 April 1937; Busch interview.

53. Busch interview; Reese interview; Bruno interview.

Chapter 8. CIO Victory

1. *New Kensington Dispatch*, 30 March 1900, 6 April 1900.

2. *New Kensington Dispatch*, 30 March 1900, 6 April 1900.

3. *New Kensington Dispatch*, 23 December 1898, 14 September 1900, 12 December 1900, 25 July 1901, 22 August 1901, 19 September 1901.

4. In 1907 the Pittsburgh Reduction Company assumed the name Aluminum Company of America.

5. *New Kensington Dispatch*, 23 January 1908, 13 February 1908.

6. Charles Martin Hall to Julia Hall, 10 May 1891, Junias Edwards, *The Immortal Woodshed*, p. 150.

7. *New Kensington Dispatch*, 28 November 1901.

8. *New Kensington Dispatch*, 4 April 1912, 6 February 1913.

9. *New Kensington Dispatch*, 21 September 1911, 7 August 1913, 17 September 1914.

10. The Industrial Workers of the World was a radical labor organization. Its activities in the Allegheny Valley are difficult to document, but its representatives did distribute literature in local coalfields.

11. *New Kensington Dispatch*, 27 March 1913.

12. *New Kensington Dispatch*, 2, 5, 9, 12, 16 May 1916.

13. *New Kensington Dispatch*, 22 November 1919.

14. *New Kensington Daily Dispatch*, 28 June 1933, 20 July 1933, 1 March 1934.

15. Fred Broad was the son-in-law of Fannie Sellins, a UMWA organizer slain by Allegheny Steel Company deputies in West Natrona, Pennsylvania, on 26 August 1919.

16. All records of Aluminum Workers Union Local 18356, AFL; Aluminum Workers Union Local 2, CIO; and Local 302, USWA are held by the Pennsylvania Labor Archives, Pennsylvania State University. (The collection has not yet been cataloged or assigned box numbers.) *New Kensington Daily Dispatch*, 26 August 1933; Richard Kearns to John A. Phillip, 1 October 1934, Aluminum Workers Papers.

17. Nick Zonarich and John Haser interview transcripts, September 1966, Oral History Collection, Labor Archives, Pennsylvania State University. Nick Zonarich was president of Aluminum Workers International Union, CIO. John Haser served as business agent of the New Kensington local for eight years.

18. Mary Peli Petrigni interview, 8 January 1980.

19. Charles Pauli and Jack Garbinski interview, 12 July 1979.

20. Petrigni interview.

21. Ibid.; Pauli and Garbinski interview; Haser interview; *Minutes*, Local 18356, 14 June 1935; Petrigni interview.

22. Roy A. Hunt to Executive Committee, Aluminum Workers Union Local 18356, 9 December 1933; *Minutes*, Local 18356, 10 August 1933, 23 February 1934, Aluminum Workers Papers.

23. National Recovery Administration, *A Basic Code of Fair Competition for the Fabricated Metal Products Manufacturing Industry*, pp. 4–5. Under these codes, a Southern wage differential was also established. Southern aluminum workers received a rate of thirty-five cents per hour for males, thirty cents for females.

24. *New Kensington Daily Dispatch*, 2 January 1934; Paul Howlett to Boris Shiskin, 13 May 1934, 19 June 1934; Richard Kearns to Hugh Johnson, 10 July 1934, Aluminum Workers Papers.

25. Letter of resignation by Karl Burke Guiney, 1 March 1934, Aluminum Workers Papers; Haser interview.

26. *New Kensington Daily Dispatch*, 1, 2, 9 March 1934. There is no record of a strike vote in the Aluminum Workers *Minutes*. I. W. Wilson to Local 18356, 2, 7 March 1934, Aluminum Workers Papers.

27. Haser interview; resolution by Extrusion Department, 3 March 1934, Aluminum Workers Papers.

28. Haser interview; Zonarich interview.

29. Ray Giordano to William Green, 16 May 1934; Paul Howlett to Green, 24 May 1934; William Green to (R.) Giordano, 22 May 1934, Aluminum Workers Papers.

30. Anthony Giordano to A. R. Buller, 19 June 1934; H. G. Flaugh to A. Giordano, 5 June 1934; A. Giordano to Mark Robb, 19 June 1934; *Minutes*, Local 18356, 22 June 1934, Aluminum Workers papers.

31. *Minutes*, Local 18356, 3 August 1934, Aluminum Workers Papers.

32. Roy Hunt to Fred A. Wetmore, 3 August 1934, Aluminum Workers Papers.

33. *Minutes*, Local 18356, 3 August 1934, Aluminum Workers Papers.

34. *New Kensington Daily Dispatch*, 11, 12 August 1934; *Minutes*, Local 18356, 21 September 1934, Aluminum Workers Papers.

35. *New Kensington Daily Dispatch*, 6 September 1934; *Minutes*, Local 18356, 21 September 1934, Aluminum Worker Papers.

36. *Minutes,* Local 18356, 5 October 1934; Richard Kearns to T. Swartz, Mark Robb, 20 October 1934; Paul Howlett to Jim Farley, 22 October 1934, Aluminum Workers Papers.

37. Richard Kearns to Green, 28 November 1934; Green to Howlett, 14 January 1935; David Williams to Raymond Giordano, 30 December 1934, 19 March 1935; Williams to Bert Gravatt, 11, 24, 28 June 1935; Gravatt to Williams, 24 June 1935, Aluminum Workers Papers.

38. Haser interview; *Minutes,* Local 18356, 3, 5, 15, 18, 21, 28, 31 March 1934; A. O. Wharton to R. Giordano, 28 March 1935; D. Williams to Local 18356, 18 March 1935; P. Howlett to D. Williams, 21 March 1935; (R.) Giordano to W. Green, 22 March 1935; *Minutes,* Local 18356, 31 May 1935, 7 June 1935; William Green to B. Gravatt, 25 June 1935; Gravatt to Green, 28 June 1935, Aluminum Workers Papers.

39. B. Gravatt to George Berry, 6 November 1935; *Minutes,* Local 18356, 22 November 1935; Gravatt to William J. Kelly, 5 December 1935; *Minutes,* Local 18356, 26 May 1936, 7 April 1936; B. Gravatt to W. Green, 22 May 1936; Green to Gravatt, 3 June 1936, Aluminum Workers Papers.

40. John Brophy to B. Gravatt, 22 June 1936; *Minutes,* Local 18356, 23, 30 June 1936, 7 July 1936, 1 December 1936; Howlett to Local 19104, 7 July 1936, Aluminum Workers Papers; Haser, Zonarich, Petrigni, Garbinski-Pauli interviews.

41. W. Green to B. Gravatt, 28 July 1936; D. Williams to P. Howlett, 4 March 1936; *Minutes,* Local 18356, 19 July 1936; D. Williams to Gravatt, 30 September 1936; *Minutes,* special meeting, Local 18356, 5 March 1937, Aluminum Workers Papers.

42. Petrigni interview; *Minutes,* Local 18356, 5 March 1937, Aluminum Workers Papers.

43. W. Pasnick to J. L. Lewis, 25 February 1937; Pasnick to William Green, 25 February 1937; Thomas R. Jarrell to B. Gravatt, 7 March 1937; Local 18780 to W. Pasnick, 6 March 1937; L. H. Fallon to Keith Sward, 1 March 1937; L. H. Fallon to Walter Pasnick, 1 March 1937; Williams to Local 18356, 6 March 1937; John Haser to W. Green, 16 March 1937; *AFL* v. *Aluminum Workers Local 18356,* U.S. District Court, Pittsburgh, 17 March 1937, Aluminum Workers Papers.

44. *Constitutional Convention of the Aluminum Workers of America,* New Kensington, Pennsylvania, 12–15 April 1937; B. Gravatt to Leonard Break, 26 March 1937, Aluminum Workers papers.

45. *Constitutional Convention of the Aluminum Workers of America,* New Kensington, Pennsylvania, 12–15 April 1937.

46. Ibid.

47. John Haser to Local 2, 15 May 1939; Mary Peli Petrigni to Local 2, 9 February 1938, Aluminum Workers papers.

48. John Haser reported in 1944 that the AWA controlled sixteen Alcoa plants; the Steelworkers, two; the Die-Casters, three; the Auto Workers, three; and the AFL, six. John Haser to George Hobaugh, 24 May 1944, Aluminum Workers Papers.

49. Local 2 reported the presence of a "rump movement" sponsored by AFL "stooges" in 1939. No one seemed to take the AFL drive seriously, and it did in fact fail. John Haser to Louis and Mary Petrigni, 3 February 1939; William Hanka to George Hobaugh, 31 January 1939; Hanka to Wesley Crampton, 3 February 1939, Aluminum Workers Papers.

50. *Minutes,* Local 18356, 11 October 1935; John Dent to Bert Gravatt, 24 March 1936; Fred Broad to Bert Gravatt, 18 November 1936; Fred Broad to William Hanka, 2 December 1939, Aluminum Workers Papers.

51. The Arnold chief of police was a guest speaker at the constitutional convention on 12 April 1937. The local took pains to thank the police publicly following every strike. Local law enforcement agencies were never an adversary during Aluminum Workers strikes.

52. Frank Carson to John L. Lewis, 12 July 1938; Nick Zonarich to George Hobaugh, 28 December 1939; Fred Wetmore to John Haser, 9 July 1937, Aluminum Workers Papers.

53. *The First General Conference of the Affiliated Locals of the Aluminum Workers of America,* Cincinnati, 5, 6 November 1938.

54. Ibid.; Zonarich interview.

55. John Haser to all shop committees, 16 October 1940; R. M. Ferry to Local 2, 16 October 1940, 11 November 1940; John Haser to Committeemen, 29 March 1940; William J. Hanka to O. B. Lackey, 8 February 1940, Aluminum Workers Papers.

56. *New Kensington Daily Dispatch,* 23, 27, 29 November 1940.

57. *New Kensington Daily Dispatch,* 13, 14, 15 December 1940; *Valley Daily News,* 13, 14, 16 December 1940.

58. *People's Press,* edited by Keith Sward, was replaced as the official organ of the AWA because of its editor's alleged pro-Communist leanings. The nature of Nick Zonarich's ideological commitments to Socialism are not clear. The contents of his Labor Archives interview indicate that he became a pragmatic union bureaucrat. Zonarich confirmed the presence of Communist "noise makers" in Local 2, but claimed that they never achieved domination. John Haser also claimed in his interview that New Kensington had its share of Communists, like all mill towns. Haser believed these people were not anti-American and dropped their affiliation upon learning that the party was controlled from outside the United States.

59. *Pittsburgh Press,* 13, 15, 16 December 1940; *New Kensington Daily Dispatch,* 13, 14, 16 December 1940.

60. Zonarich interview.

61. *New Kensington Daily Dispatch,* 16, 17 December 1940; *New Kensington Dispatch* undated clipping, Aluminum Workers Papers.

62. Zonarich, Haser interviews; Haser to George Hobaugh, 24 May 1944, Aluminum Workers Papers.

63. *Minutes,* Local 2, 4 April 1944; Louis Saulle interview, 20 June 1980; John Haser to Theodore Beal, 24 May 1944; Haser to Hosbaugh, 24 May 1944; *Minutes,* Local 2, 14 May 1944, Aluminum Workers Papers.

64. *Minutes,* Local 2, 14 June 1944, 9 July 1944, 10 August 1944, Aluminum Workers Papers.

65. Garbinski-Pauli interview; Saulle interview; *Minutes,* executive board, Local 302, 10 August 1944; *Minutes,* Local 302, 22 August 1944; 5 September 1944, Aluminum Workers Papers.

66. The name of the union was never changed.

67. *Minutes,* special meeting, Local 302, 26 September 1944, Aluminum Workers Papers.

68. *New Kensington Daily Dispatch,* 6 April 1948, 2 February 1948. The minutes for the local are not reliable for this period.

69. *Aluminum Workers Journal,* 26 February 1948. On 10 March 1948, two different editions of the *Aluminum Workers Journal* appeared in New Kensington. The editorial staffs and opinions reflected the contending factions in the local.

70. *New Kensington Daily Dispatch,* 2 February 1948, 24 March 1948.

71. *Aluminum Workers Journal,* 10 March 1948; *Daily Worker* (Penn. ed.,) 29 February 1948; *Daily Worker,* 2, 7 April 1948.

72. Transcript of testimony before the Trial Committee, Local 302, United Steel Workers of America, CIO, 15 July 1948, 16 September 1948; *New Kensington Daily Dispatch,* 28 July 1948; Garbinski-Pauli interview; Saulle interview.

73. Transcript of testimony; Bert Gravatt to Sam Chine, 6 November 1948, Aluminum Workers Papers.

74. Garbinski interview.

Epilogue

1. Glenn E. McLaughlin, *Growth of American Manufacturing Areas: A Comparative Analysis with Special Emphasis on Trends in the Pittsburgh District,* pp. 303, 314, 318, 331–40.

2. Roy Lubove, *Twentieth-Century Pittsburgh,* pp. 5–6.

3. Ibid.

4. McLaughlin, *Growth of American Manufacturing Areas,* pp. 331–40.

5. Peter Drucker, *Managing in Turbulent Times,* pp. 95–96, 102–3, 109–10, 146–47, 169, 199–200.

Bibliography

Manuscript Sources

Aluminum Workers Papers. Labor Archives, Pennsylvania State University.

Bethlehem Mines Corporation. *Annual Police Reports,* 1926–33. Archives of the Industrial Society, University of Pittsburgh Library.

Brophy, John. Papers. Catholic University of America.

Fisher, John. Papers. Pennsylvania Historical and Museum Commission Archives, Harrisburg.

Hapgood, Powers. Papers. Lilly Library, University of Indiana.

Lewis, John L. Papers (microfilm). State Historical Society of Wisconsin, Madison.

Medrick, George. Papers. Labor Archives, Pennsylvania State University.

Murray, Philip. Papers. Catholic University of America.

Pinchot, Gifford. Diaries. Library of Congress (microfilm).

Government Documents and Records

Allegheny County, Pennsylvania. Coroner's Records, 133: 629, 29 September 1919.

Allegheny County, Pennsylvania. Court of Common Pleas. Docket no. 50, September 1923.

Bureau of Social Research, Federation of Social Agencies of Pittsburgh and Allegheny Country. *Social Facts concerning East Pittsburgh, Turtle Creek, Wilmerding, North Braddock.* Pittsburgh, 1940.

Commonwealth of Pennsylvania. *Second Annual Report of the Commission on Labor and Industry.* Harrisburg, 1914.

Commonwealth of Pennsylvania. *Annual Report of the Department of Labor and Industry.* Harrisburg, 1916.

Indiana County, Pennsylvania. Court of Common Pleas. Old Equity Docket Book no. 6, 1927–28.

Report to Governor Pinchot by Commission on Special Policing in Industry. Harrisburg, 1934.

U.S. Congress. *Final Report and Testimony Submitted by the Commission on Industrial Relations.* 1916.

U.S. Congress. Senate. Reports of the Immigration Commission. Immigrants in Industries. 27 vols. 61st Cong., 2d. sess., S. Doc. 633.1911.

U.S. Congress. Senate. Committee on Interstate Commerce. *Conditions in the Coal Fields of Pennsylvania, West Virginia and Ohio: Report of the Subcommittee on Interstate Commerce pursuant to Senate Resolution 105.* 70th cong., 1st sess., 1928.

U.S. Department of Labor. Federal Mediation and Conciliation Service. Case File 33–37: *Documents for the Strike of 1914 at Westinghouse Electric Company.* n.d.

U.S. Department of Labor. Federal Mediation and Conciliation Service. Case File 33-202: *Documents for the Strike of 1916 at Westinghouse Electric Company.* n.d.

Labor and Trade Journals

Aluminum Workers Journal
Amalgamated Journal
CIO News
Coal Age
Coal Digger
Coal Trade Bulletin
The Communist
Industrial Union News
Iron City Trades Journal
Justice
Labor Unity
Labor World
National Labor Journal
National Labor Tribune
Party Organizer
People's Press
Solidarity
United Mine Workers Journal

Interviews

Everett Beck, steelworker, Apollo, 15 June 1978.

Giacomo Bruno, steelworker, Vandergrift, 11 November 1978.

Roy and Harvey Bruner, Apollo, 20 May 1978.

Frank Buccardo, coal miner, Foster, 6 June 1978.

Preston Busch, steelworker, Kiskiminetas Township, 9 June 1982.

Stanley Czarnowski, steelworker, West Natrona, 29 September 1979.

Harold Doutt, steelworker, Vandergrift, 8 December 1977.

Pat Fagan, interview transcript, Oral History Collection, Labor Archives, Pennsylvania State University.

Jack Garbinski, aluminum worker, Arnold, 12 July 1979.

John Grill, coal miner, Russellton, 20 January 1978.

John Haser, interview transcript, September 1966, Oral History Collection, Labor Archives, Pennsylvania State University.

James Kerr, steelworker, Apollo, 1 December 1977.

Sam Mendecino, coal miner, Vandergrift, 27 December 1977.

Oscar Morrison, steelworker, Apollo, 1 December 1977.

W. E. Pavitt, steelmill foreman, Tarentum, 5 June 1978.

Charles Pauli, aluminum worker, New Kensington, 12 July 1979.

Michael Petrak, steelworker, Braeburn Heights, 9 August 1977.

Mary Peli Petrigni, aluminum worker, Upper Burrell, 8 January 1980.

Stanley Rafalko, steelworker, Natrona Heights, 29 September 1979.

Harry Reese, steelworker, Apollo, 15 June 1981.

Louis Saulle, aluminum worker, Arnold, 20 June 1980.

John Schrecengost, coal miner, Kiskiminetas Township, 1 March 1978.

Poleslan Stemplinski, steelworker, East Vandergrift, 15 December 1978.

Guiseppi Steri, coal miner, Apollo, 18 May 1978.

Nick Zonarich, interview transcript, September 1966, Oral History Collection, Labor Archives, Pennsylvania State University.

Newspapers

Apollo News-Record
Apollo Sentinel
Daily Leader-Times
Evening Telegram
Indiana Evening Gazette
Leechburg Advance
Natrona Daily Press
New Kensington Daily Dispatch
Pittsburgh Courier
Pittsburgh Daily Dispatch
Pittsburgh Gazette-Times
Pittsburgh Leader
Pittsburgh Post
Pittsburgh Post-Gazette
Pittsburgh Press
Pittsburgh Sun
Valley Daily News
Vandergrift Citizen
Vandergrift Economist
Vandergrift News

Articles

Asher, Robert. "Painful Memories." *Pennsylvania History* 45 (January 1978): 61–88.

Barton, Dante. "The Pittsburgh Strikes." *International Socialist Review* 16 (June 1916): 712–16.

Brown, Don. "So This Is America." *New Republic* (12 October 1927).

Buffington, Eugene. "Making Cities for Workmen." *Harper's Weekly*, 53 (9 May 1909).

Butler, Frank. "Pennsylvania's Bloody Mine War." *Nation* (July 1931).

Clopper, Edward N. "Pittsburgh Unites for Relief." *Survey* 60 (April 1928): 85–86.

Draper, Theodore. "Communists and Miners, 1928–1933." *Dissent* (Spring 1972): 371–92.

Filippelli, Ronald. "Diary of a Strike: George Medrick and the Coal Strike of 1927 in Western Pennsylvania." *Pennsylvania History* 43 (July 1976): 253–66.

Harris, Helen M. "Miners in the Mud." *Survey* 60 (15 August 1928): 502–3.

Ingham, John W. "A Strike in the Progressive Era: McKees Rocks, 1909." *Pennsylvania Magazine of History and Biography* 90 (July 1966); 353–77.

Johnson, James P. "Reorganizing the United Mine Workers of America in Pennsylvania during the New Deal." *Pennsylvania History* 37 (April 1970): 117–32.

Michaelis, George V. S. "The Westinghouse Strike." *Survey* 32 (August 1914): 463–65.

Nyden, Linda. "Black Miners in Western Pennsylvania, 1925–1931: The National Miners Union and the United Mine Workers of America." *Science and Society* (Spring 1977): 69–101.

Parker, George A. "A Doctor Looks at the Coal Camps." *Survey* 61 (October 1928): 85–86.

Warne, Colston. "The United Mine Workers in Defeat." *Survey* 61 (November 1928): 223–24.

Wilson, Edmund. "Frank Keeney's Coal Diggers." *New Republic* (July 1931).

Books, Pamphlets, Reports

Allen, Gerald E. "The Negro Coal Miner in the Pittsburgh District." Master's thesis, University of Pittsburgh, 1927.

American Civil Liberties Union, *Report No. 7*. New York: American Civil Liberties Union, 1928.

Baratz, Morton S. *The Union and the Coal Industry*. Port Washington, N.Y.: Kennikat Press, 1955.

Basile, Frank J. *Rossiter, Pennsylvania: Her People Past and Present*. Greensburg, Pa.: Charles M. Henry Publishing Co., 1979.

Bernstein, Irving. *The Lean Years: A History of the American Worker, 1920–1932*. Boston: Houghton Mifflin, 1966.

Betten, Neil. *Catholic Activism and the Industrial Worker*. Gainesville: University Presses of Florida, 1976.

Blankenhorn, Heber. *The Strike for Union*. New York: H. W. Wilson, 1924.

Bloor, Ella Reeve. *We Are Many*. New York: International Publishers, 1940.

Brody, David. *Steel Workers in America: The Non-Union Era*. New York: Harper and Row, 1960.

———. *Workers in Industrial America*. New York: Oxford University Press, 1980.

Brooks, Robert R. *As Steel Goes. . . .* New Haven: Yale University Press, 1940.

Brophy, John. *A Miner's Life: An Autobiography* Madison: University of Wisconsin Press, 1964.

Buni, Andrew. *Robert L. Vann of the "Pittsburgh Courier."* Pittsburgh: University of Pittsburgh Press, 1974.

Carr, Charles C. *Alcoa: An American Enterprise.* New York: Rinehart, 1952.

Cayton, Horace C., and George S. Mitchell. *Black Workers and the New Unions.* Chapel Hill: University of North Carolina Press, 1931.

Cochran, Bert. *Labor and Communism.* Princeton: Princeton University Press, 1977.

Coleman, McAlister. *Men and Coal.* New York: Farrar and Rinehart, 1943.

Conti, Philip M. *The Pennsylvania State Police.* Harrisburg, Pa.: Stackpole Books, 1977.

Coode, Thomas, and John Bauman. *People, Poverty and Politics in Pennsylvania during the Great Depression.* Lewisburg: Pa.: Bucknell University Press, 1981.

Cornell, William A. "The Political Career of John S. Fisher." Master's thesis, University of Pittsburgh, 1949.

Drucker, Peter F. *The New Society,* New York: Harper and Row, 1962.

———. *The Future of Industrial Man.* New York: New American Library, 1965.

———. *Managing in Turbulent Times.* New York: Harper and Row, 1980.

Dubofsky, Melvyn. *We Shall Be All.* New York: Quadrangle Books and the New York Times, 1969.

Dubofsky, Melvyn, and Warren Van Tine. *John L. Lewis: A Biography.* New York: N.Y.: Quadrangle Books and the New York Times, 1977.

Edwards, Junias. *The Immortal Woodshed.* New York: Dodd, Mead, 1955.

Federal Council of Churches of Christ in America. *The Coal Strike in Western Pennsylvania.* New York: Department of Research and Education, Federal Council of Churches of Christ, 1928.

Fetherling, Dale. *Mother Jones: The Miners Angel.* Carbondale: Southern Illinois University Press,1974.

Fitch, John. *The Steel Workers.* New York: Russell Sage Foundation, 1911.

Foner, Philip. *Women and the Labor Movement.* New York: Free Press, 1979.

Foster, William Z. *Pages from a Workers Life.* New York: International Publishers, 1939.

———. *American Trade Unionism.* New York: International Publishers, 1947.

———. *The Great Steel Strike and Its Lessons.* New York: Arno Press and the New York Times, 1969.

Gilfillan, Lauren. *I Went to Pit College.* New York: Viking Press, 1934.

Groome, John C. *A Reply to the American Cossack.* Harrisburg: Commonwealth of Pennsylvania, 1915.

Henry, T. J. *History of Apollo, 1816–1916.* Apollo, Pa.: News-Record Publishing Co., 1916.

Interchurch World Movement, Commission of Inquiry. *Report on the Steel Strike of 1919.* New York: Harcourt, Brace and Howe, 1920.

Johnson, James P. *The Politics of Soft Coal.* Urbana: University of Illinois Press, 1979.

Kanitra, Diane. "The Westinghouse Strike of 1916." Seminar paper, University of Pittsburgh, 1971.

Laslett, John. *Labor and the Left.* New York: Basic Books, 1970.

Lubove, Roy. *Twentieth-Century Pittsburgh.* New York: John Wiley and Sons, 1969.

McGeary, M. Nelson. *Gifford Pinchot: Forester-Politician.* Princeton: Princeton University Press, 1960.

McLaughlin, Glenn E. *Growth of American Manufacturing Areas: A Comparative Analysis with Special Emphasis on Trends in the Pittsburgh District.* Pittsburgh: University of Pittsburgh Press, 1938.

Maurer, James. *The American Cossack.* New York: Arno Press and the New York Times, 1971.

Montgomery, David. *Workers' Control in America.* New York: Cambridge University Press, 1979.

Morgan, H. Wayne. *The Gilded Age.* Syracuse N.Y.: Syracuse University Press, 1963.

Morris, Homer L. *The Plight of the Bituminous Coal Miner.* Philadelphia: University of Pennsylvania Press, 1934.

Nash, Michael. *Conflict and Accommodation: Coal Miners, Steel Workers and Socialism, 1890–1920.* Westport, Conn.: Greenwood Press, 1982.

Nyden, Paul. *Black Coal Miners in the United States.* New York: American Institute for Marxist Studies, 1974.

Owens, John, ed. *First Seventy-five Years: A History of Vandergrift.* Vandergrift, Pa.: Vandergrift News-Citizen, 1972.

Patterson, Florence. *Strikes in the United States, 1880–1936.* Bulletin no. 651, U.S. Department of Labor, Bureau of Labor Statistics. Washington: Government Printing Office, 1938.

Perlman, Selig, and Philip Taft. *History of Labor in the United States, 1896–1932.* Vol. 4 of *History of Labor in the United States,* edited by J. R. Commons et al. 4 vols. New York: A. M. Kelley, 1966.

Preston, William. *Aliens and Dissenters: Federal Suppression of Radicals, 1903–1933.* Cambridge: Harvard University Press, 1963.

Reid, Ira D. *Negro Membership in American Labor Unions.* New York: National Urban League. 1930.

Ringer, Strawder A. "A History of the United Mine Workers." Master's thesis, University of Pittsburgh, 1929.

Rochester, Anna. *Labor and Coal.* New York: International Publishers, 1931.

Saposs, David J. *Left Wing Unionism.* New York: International Publishers, 1926.

Schatz, Ronald W. *The Electrical Workers: A History of Labor at General Electric and Westinghouse.* Urbana: University of Illinois Press, 1983.

Shalloo, Jeremiah P. *Private Police; with a Special Reference to Pennsylvania.* Philadelphia: American Academy of Political and Social Science, 1933.

Shergold, Peter. *Working-Class Life.* Pittsburgh: University of Pittsburgh Press, 1982.

Spero, Sterling D., and Abram L. Harris. *The Black Worker: The Negro and the Labor Movement.* New York: Columbia University Press, 1931.

Tarbell, Ida M. *New Ideals in Business.* New York: Macmillan, 1916.

Upper Burrell Township. *The First One Hundred Years, 1879–1979.* Upper Burrell, Pa.: Upper Burrell Lions Club, 1979.

Index